In This Arab Time

The Pursuit of Deliverance

Winter 2014 New York

FOUAD AJAMI
(September 18, 1945–June 22, 2014)

HERBERT & JANE DWIGHT WORKING GROUP ON ISLAMISM AND THE INTERNATIONAL ORDER

In This Arab Time

The Pursuit of Deliverance

Fouad Ajami

HOOVER INSTITUTION PRESS

STANFORD UNIVERSITY | STANFORD, CALIFORNIA

The Hoover Institution on War, Revolution and Peace, founded at Stanford University in 1919 by Herbert Hoover, who went on to become the thirty-first president of the United States, is an interdisciplinary research center for advanced study on domestic and international affairs. The views expressed in its publications are entirely those of the authors and do not necessarily reflect the views of the staff, officers, or Board of Overseers of the Hoover Institution.

www.hoover.org

Hoover Institution Press Publication No. 623

Hoover Institution at Leland Stanford Junior University, Stanford, California 94305-6010

The Hoover Institution would like to thank *The New Republic, Foreign Affairs*, and *TriQuarterly* for their cooperation and consent to the republication, in slightly adapted form, of essays and articles that originally appeared in their journals. Source information for any previously published essay can be found in a footnote on the first page of the corresponding chapter.

Frontispiece sketch of Fouad Ajami is by Michelle Ajami.

For permission to reuse material from *In This Arab Time: The Pursuit of Deliverance,* by Fouad Ajami, ISBN 978-0-8179-1494-3, please access www.copyright.com or contact the Copyright Clearance Center, Inc. (CCC), 222 Rosewood Drive, Danvers, MA 01923, 978-750-8400. CCC is a not-for-profit organization that provides licenses and registration for a variety of uses.

First printing 2014
21 20 19 18 17 16 15 14   9 8 7 6 5 4 3 2

Manufactured in the United States of America

The paper used in this publication meets the minimum Requirements of the American National Standard for Information Sciences—Permanence of Paper for Printed Library Materials, ANSI/NISO Z39.48-1992. ∞

Cataloging-in-Publication Data is available from the Library of Congress.
ISBN 978-0-8179-1494-3 (cloth : alk. paper)
ISBN 978-0-8179-1496-7 (e-pub)
ISBN 978-0-8179-1497-4 (mobi)
ISBN 978-0-8179-1498-1 (e-PDF)

*The Hoover Institution gratefully acknowledges
the following individuals and foundations
for their significant support of the*

**HERBERT AND JANE DWIGHT WORKING GROUP
ON ISLAMISM AND THE INTERNATIONAL ORDER:**

Herbert and Jane Dwight

**Donald and Joan Beall
Beall Family Foundation**

S. D. Bechtel, Jr. Foundation

Lynde and Harry Bradley Foundation

Stephen and Susan Brown

Mr. and Mrs. Clayton W. Frye Jr.

Lakeside Foundation

CONTENTS

Part III

Part IV

FOREWORD

Fouad Ajami, who passed away on June 22, 2014, was a gifted scholar, teacher, writer, adviser, and public commentator. He was also a dear friend to me and many colleagues and supporters of the Hoover Institution. It is our distinct pleasure to present this profound collection of essays assembled personally by Fouad just prior to his death. I am confident the insights contained in this book will shed light on our understanding of the Middle East, but more importantly, affirm Fouad's abiding convictions toward peace and freedom for all people. Many of Fouad's lifetime achievements are noted at the end of these collected works.

Further, Fouad led an important working group at the Hoover Institution for several years with Hoover fellow Charles Hill, focusing on Islamism and the International Order and sponsored by Herb and Jane Dwight. The product of this significant effort is summarized later in this treatise.

JOHN RAISIAN
Tad and Dianne Taube Director
Hoover Institution, Stanford University

Our Magus

"Cut these words and they would bleed;
they are vascular and alive; they walk and run"
—RALPH WALDO EMERSON

One dark December day I walked to the Union League on Chapel Street, early for lunch with Fouad Ajami, who was taking the train from Manhattan to New Haven. I settled in to look at a book while I waited for his arrival; bright flames silently flickered in the fireplace; through the high window Yale's gray, stately Vanderbilt Hall loomed across the way. A half-hour passed as other diners arrived to fill the room. Then forty-five minutes. I craned my neck to survey the place. There was Fouad, alone at a table on the far side, happily holding a book; he had been there all along, coming in well ahead of me.

This is not the way we usually thought of Fouad: he was far more likely to be standing at a lectern, or on a television panel, or in seemingly constant travel, or in animated discussions with friends and adversaries alike. Here at the Union League I could see that he was not reading that book, he was thinking. He possessed a perpetual energy of mind; he was, as Emerson hoped for, "man thinking," always in the sense of thinking *as* acting. That is why that scene in the Union League made an impression. Fouad resembled some erudite but intrepid Victorian-era gentleman contentedly at ease in his club chair yet poised to be off in a trice to the hellholes of the earth to accumulate the knowledge that civilization most needs to know.

When we first met, Fouad and I were both college teachers. But Fouad had many more dimensions than I. Every time, and it was often, that we talked about his role in the university and I in mine, it was clear that he felt hemmed in by the four walls of the seminar room. One fall semester he invited me to join him in teaching his class at the Johns Hopkins University School of Advanced International Studies in Washington, D.C. He was a transcendent teacher, vitally exuberant, a challenging, loving mentor, clearly adored by his students. But he always had an audience of larger demographic magnitude on his mind, an American, Middle Eastern, and world population. He would soon give up his professorship to take up full-time his veritable vocation. Which was what? We have no entirely apt label for it. Like Emerson, he invented a career for himself alone. We can say that Fouad Ajami was the foremost example in our time of the lineage of intellectual-moral, thinker-travelers who from ancient times onward have illuminated the human condition and, as great writers and transfixing speakers, drawn lessons from it for us to contemplate and act upon. Yet even knowing this much about him, Fouad's true significance has yet to be understood.

Fouad and his philosophical-historical forebears took on the simplest yet most perplexing challenge: what is going on, and why? The peoples of the world have organized themselves in ways multifarious beyond number. How are these differing systems and their cultures by which they define themselves structured, and why does it matter? Can such diversity ever interact coherently, productively, and peacefully? Is one as good as any other? Or can we be judgmental and conclude that some, or one, is preferable?

Fouad was naturally gifted in this role, and he educated and honed his gifts incessantly: he was both an insider and an outsider wherever he went—except in his home village, but he knew that "You can't go home again." He was an Arab with a family name that conveyed Persian-ness. He was a Shia, a faith constructed on loss, relegation, and righteous victimization; as a believer, he was both reverential and skeptical. In appearance, voice, and demeanor, he seemed the epitome of all things Middle Eastern, yet he was a nonhyphenated American patriot. He was poet, philosopher, statesman, historian, bon vivant, and, to his Jewish following, mensch.

To each of his multiple roles and talents Fouad brought, again in Emersonian terms, perceptions viewed from an original angle to the universe. As historian, he exhausted himself in the collection, organization, and interpretation of facts as numberless as the desert sands, yet he always felt the forces of history within which facts traveled. As anthropologist, he could be at once one of the tribe studied yet a gimlet-eyed analyst of their mores. A natural talent this was: as a reporter, he would be welcomed by dictators into their tents with majestic hospitality; they would see him on his way with their thanks even as they knew full well he would not spare them in his next published essay. He could enter and express the innermost thoughts of the potentates and the impoverished alike.

In sum, no college "discipline," field, or department was big enough to hold Fouad Ajami; he knew that the world does not come at us in the neatly wrapped packages of a time-slotted college syllabus; it comes all at once, in all forms if not formless, and in a blur of time lines.

Fouad was not only an individual genius (the MacArthur Foundation early on certified him as that) but also an organizer, manager, and editor, professional occupations to which he brought what the military would call "command presence" and which foundations could admire as "convening power." Single-handedly he invented a project to study the troubles and possibilities of the Middle East through weaving together an unprecedented network of writers, activists, intellectuals, and former diplomats from across the Middle East: Sunni, Shia, Jewish, Christian, Arab, Persian, Turk, male and female in an amazing parade of ideas and interpretations all made possible by the vast generosity and wise counsel of Herbert and Jane Dwight through their Working Group on Islamism and the International Order centered at the Hoover Institution, Stanford University.

Fouad Ajami's own voluminous corpus of writings, his *oeuvre*, has yet to be fully studied, comprehended, and assessed as a whole. In it will be located, not only as in this present book, his posthumous collection of essays *In This Arab Time: The Pursuit of Deliverance*, the novelists, terrorists, tyrants, states and revolutions, grandeurs and grotesqueries of the globe's Arab-Islamic swath, but also a window on human nature itself. Doctoral dissertations of the future will find philosophical, material, and cultural profundities of lasting consequence in such masterpieces as Ajami's *The Arab Predicament* and *The Dream Palace of the Arabs*.

Fouad's unprecedented prose style, substance-packed, is not just for Arabists, or those concerned with the chaotic course of foreign policy and world affairs. It's also a lasting artistic contribution to understanding the matter, meaning, and direction of world history as a whole. And here is where we can track his lineage:

Like Herodotus, he traveled ceaselessly to gather the stories that peoples tell themselves about themselves, stories that give shape to politics and cultures. Like Herodotus, Fouad's descriptions are brilliantly quirky, as he puts unusual words in unexpected places in order to convey an original perception.

As in Tacitus's annals of Nero's Rome, Fouad understands the power of rumor and gossip in the courts of power (Fouad himself was a delightful and profligate purveyor of gossip about the powerful figures of our time). Like Tacitus, Fouad's style was ironic, a sophisticated way of forging a bond between writer and reader to the exclusion of others who "just don't get it."

With Edward Gibbon's *The Decline and Fall of the Roman Empire*, Fouad recognized that the intelligible field of study may have to be imperial in scale; that the ghosts of Arab empires haunt our own era. And in a Gibbonian way, Fouad's writing shows an awesome ability to organize and master massive amounts of evidence and source materials.

And like Alexis de Tocqueville, Fouad knew in his bones that freedom is the force of history of potentially monumental significance—albeit a force that could be halted or set back by the enemies of freedom. He was, therefore, an instantaneous champion of the original Arab Spring demonstrations, the young people who took their lives in their hands when they ventured into the city squares encircled by the regime's armed forces. He was anguished when this new generation, untainted by the old military, Islamist, or autocratic bosses, were so swiftly muscled aside, many to suffer awful consequences.

As the West has been insightfully designated "Faustian" and the Arab world "Magian," Fouad was the latter's Magus, the modern embodiment of the wise man and seer from the time of the ancient Medes and Persians to today's not so Fertile Crescent. He saw, with unparalleled clarity, that today's Arab-Islamic realm may be a case of what Oswald Spengler called "pseudomorphosis," a set of thin surface-level societies sitting atop not only the lower layer of seventh-century Islam but also on an even deeper stratum of suppressed geological-cultural power that one day, and perhaps that day has just dawned, will erupt in violence to first devastate and subsequently liberate the region to enable it to take a productive role in the history of the world to come.

What is so magical about this our Magus is that such heavy and consequential thinking has been given to us by this charmed and charming, magisterial and merry exemplar of the gracious best in the human spirit, Fouad Ajami.

CHARLES HILL
Distinguished Fellow of the Brady-Johnson Program in Grand Strategy at Yale University;
Research Fellow, Hoover Institution—
Cochairman, Herbert and Jane Dwight Working Group on Islamism and the International Order

July 2014

ACKNOWLEDGMENTS

Fouad would often brush off our efforts to imitate him with a version of Mark Twain's "You only know the words, you don't know the tune." Here, we cannot re-create his music, but we both knew his heart. Gratitude was something he embraced in his soul, and he would have thanked many people here. Hopefully, he will grace our efforts in his stead.

These essays have passed through the hands of many good colleagues and friends. Leon Wieseltier, Jim Hoge, Gideon Rose, and Henry Bienen first brought these essays to life—their trust and their friendship have been treasured for many years. Marshall Blanchard, Jennifer Presley, Jennifer Navarrette, Barbara Arellano, and Ann Wood at Hoover Press have yet again worked their magic, and without them this collection of essays would still be wishful thinking. Jeff Jones gently guided this project, and we thank him for his support and care. We are grateful to Tunku Varadarajan for lending us his keen editor's eye. Our copy editor, Oie Lian Yeh, is an extraordinary woman—her intellect, her patience, and her good humor made the editing process a pleasure.

So much is owed to Herb and Jane Dwight, who had a vision for a humane and intelligent approach to understanding the problems of the modern Middle East and who saw in Fouad someone who embodied that. Their faith in him was a constant source of encouragement. Their financial support made everything possible.

Fouad's great partner at Hoover, his sidekick, was the incomparable Charlie Hill. More than anything, they complemented each other and inspired each other. For Fouad, that was the essence of intellectual life—the essence of life.

And that life at Hoover he so cherished was the gift of John Raisian—"our beloved leader" was the only way Fouad would describe him. For John, he would have crossed the mountains of the moon.

MICHELLE AJAMI
MEGAN RING
July 2014

Megan Ring worked with Fouad for nearly twenty years. She was not only an assistant on many ventures but also a trusted friend. He loved her for her wit and sharp intelligence, her loyalty and belief in him, and her bigness of heart. They were a great team. This book is theirs.—M.A.

Fouad dedicated this book to Michelle, and in so many ways that tells us all we need to know. She was his inspiration.—M.R.

For Michelle,
the journey that
started together
ended together.

A World Foreshadowed

An astute student of the Arab world reviewing my most recent book, *The Syrian Rebellion*, wrote that after years of "judgmental aloofness toward the Arab world," I had "finally managed to get into, rather than under, the skin" of my protagonists. The reviewer was John Waterbury, he had spent years in Egypt, he had presided over the American University of Beirut. He had a long trail in Arab studies, he had come to the Arab world through immersion in Moroccan affairs. He learned and mastered the language, and in a field filled with acrimonies of all kinds, he had managed to stay above the fray and the feuds. His work was always cool and cerebral, he was the sympathetic outsider.

I could claim no such legacy. I was born in Lebanon, grew up in Beirut in the 1950s and early 1960s. I had left for the United States in my late teens, the Arab world was no disinterested field of study for me. In truth, I had never intended to write about Arab affairs. When I quit Lebanon, I knew I would never return. We had a legend in our small country: all those who packed up and gave up on the place swore that their sojourn abroad would be brief. The academic degrees completed in

America, or the fortune scraped together in West Africa, the traveler would return. A house of stone would be built in the ancestral village, a parliamentary seat would be secured, the right bride from the proper family would be found. The time away, the foreign interlude, would be forgotten. Our country— suffocatingly small, its people filled with dreams and ambitions the country could not sustain—insisted on the myth of its completeness. Our elders and ancestors beheld the foreign world with condescension and indifference. My grandfather, Shaykh Mohamed Ajami, a tobacco grower, a man of our ancestral village in Southern Lebanon, had once known adventure. He had gone to South America, he had lived in Montevideo, and fathered a daughter there. It must have been in the years of the Great War. He had come back, married the woman who would be my parental grandmother, said very little about his time in South America. We didn't know where Montevideo was, that kind of curiosity was not part of the world of our elders.

In quitting Lebanon, I was eager to be released from its hold. I was not alone in that, my peers, my older brother, scrambling for an "I 20" form, a student visa from the American embassy, had come into greater awareness of things. The embassy was approached with awe. Its officers with crew cuts, narrow ties, and white short sleeve shirts were the emissaries of a distant, glamorous power. These men held the key to a magical world. I can't imagine what they thought of us—eager petitioners in pursuit of an escape from our country. We knew that our country was small, a gossipy place where people eyed and circled one another. In that passage to America I never thought I would become a chronicler of Arab woes. I became an academic, and bigger subjects, I insisted, would beckon me. I needed the distance from the Arab world, and I found it in a field that sounded reassuringly antiseptic and large: international relations. I found shelter in the material, and the distance from the Arab world was healing. Air travel was different then, more forbidding. It was a dozen years after my departure that I would return for a summer in Lebanon. I had missed so much of my family's life, there had been marriages, new children and deaths aplenty. My beloved grandfather had died two or three years earlier. He had been my solace and protector when so much around me had given way. He had been a man stoical, unperturbed by the tumult of our family. In his younger years, perhaps after his South American interlude, he had gone to the Shia holy city of Najaf, in Iraq. His mother, a strong-willed widow who had married a Persian who had come into that hill country from the city of Tabriz, had wanted him to become a religious scholar. He had indulged her, but the life of the seminaries was not for him. The students, the *talabeh*, were wretchedly poor, and the arid curriculum could not hold him. His mother had accompanied him to Najaf, he had lived a privileged life when compared to that of the other seminarians: the Persian father had left money and land for his widow and son. My grandfather had deep reservoirs of religious skepticism in him. He honored the traditional world—he built a small mosque in his village, and a *Husseiniyya*, a place of religious observance, named after Imam Hussein, the iconic figure of Shi'ism. But he knew that the old world was giving way.

With my grandfather's death, I had no mooring in the old country. It could make no claims on me. Yet there came a time, in the late 1970s, when the Arab world began to tug at me. Its material became my abiding concern. I had escaped the Shia world—its hurts and lamentations—but I would find myself writing of the life of a celebrated Shia cleric, Imam Musa al-Sadr, who had come to Lebanon from his birthplace in Iran, transformed and re-interpreted Lebanese Shi'ism, and disappeared in Libya in the summer of 1978, a victim of foul play by Muammar Qaddafi. The rich life he led, and the mystery of his disappearance hooked me. The book I wrote forced me into a deeper encounter with Shi'ism and its history of grief and disinheritance. Shi'ism had contained and anchored the life of my mother, and I had been nearly neurotic in my determination to wash myself clean of that heritage. That war against the past, though, had failed. In the summer of 2006, my inquiries into Iraq took me to Najaf. I had come to examine and write about the American war in Iraq, but I had that older connection to that holy city. I could feel the presence of my grandfather, I could understand why the place weighed on him and drove him away; he was a restless man who loved his horses and excursions to Acre and Safad, and the Syrian coast. It would be idle to pretend that this Iraqi world, and its seminarians, were purely new to me.

I had written of Arab nationalism. My first book, *The Arab Predicament*, (1981) had defined me. The Arab intellectual class hadn't thought much of that book. The book had the requisite scholarly apparatus—after all, it was my major entry into the academic guild. But Arab nationalism, and the belief in that one Arab nation with an immortal mission—that was the intellectual banner of that movement—was the sacred, unexamined inheritance of two generation of Arabs. I had felt the pull and the call of that idea in the mid-1950s, and had wept in the summer of 1967, after the defeat of the Arab armies in the Six Day War. I can never forget that day, I was in California, anxious to find summer work in the canneries. I sat there, shell-shocked, with a couple of my Arab friends, reading the papers and taking in the magnitude of the defeat that had befallen the Arabs.

A decade earlier, as a young boy, I had defied my elders, and taken a bus to Damascus, to catch a glimpse of the Egyptian leader Gamal Abdel Nasser. A union had been forged between Syria and Egypt, and Nasser had cast his spell over politically conscious Arabs. The Syrians had pleaded for the union, and then had plotted against it. The union had been dissolved. But for one brief shining moment, the dream of Arab unity seemed within reach. We could hardly catch a glimpse of the great man. From a balcony, he greeted the crowds, and the trip from Beirut seemed all worthwhile. A nemesis awaited that dream, and in that catastrophic summer of 1967—a mere nine years after that bus ride—there we were taking in that defeat and its sorrow. The author who wrote *The Arab Predicament* was, in part, writing of the unmaking of a dream he once shared.

So for more than three decades, I would return to old memories and associations and turn them into less personal material. But unlike the Arabists who had honed their craft through academic preparation, I was falling through trapdoors into my own past. The reviewer who wrote that I had been getting under the skin of the Arabs had it right. I had broken with the orthodoxy of Arab nationalism; I had uttered, in public, and in English, truths about the Arab world that were to be kept unnamed and unacknowledged. I no longer shared the fidelities of the Arab intellectual class; I didn't thrill to the passions of that fabled "Arab Street." I did not partake of the Arab obsession with the Palestinian question. The Arab exiles in the diaspora, in Western Europe and North America, were passionate in their attachment to the causes of the Arab world. Exile politics are like that, and unforgiving. In the writings of Joseph Conrad, I found this sublime reflection on home and betrayal: "No charge of faithlessness ought to be lightly uttered . . . It would take too long to explain the intimate alliance of contradictions which makes love itself wear at times the desperate shape of betrayal." Over the past four decades, the world of the Arabs was laid bare, no author could prettify it, or give away its old secrets. Violence had overwhelmed it, no ship of sorrow could take the Arabs to the verities and the world they knew. The authors and their quarrels no longer mattered. The dictators and the strongmen who had been hailed and acclaimed had wrought ruin and grief in their wake. Arabs had been the authors of their own demise.

Today in the Arab world I am (almost) a stranger. If the songs and lyrics are old, I can recognize them. I know the writers and the poets of the 1950s and 1960s, the bearers of a modernity that was our lodestar as my generation came into its own. Beirut was not as brilliant, as worldly, as the obituaries would make it after its fall. But it was our home, and in its modern neighborhoods we could partake of the fragments that the city jumbled together—pieces of America and of France, Arab nationalist doctrines, an easy divide between the Muslim and the Christian neighborhoods. There was movement in our world: we were stepping out of the world of our elders. They were not a forgiving lot, they insisted on obedience, and woe to those, particularly among the young women, who ran afoul of them. The elders had to be humored, and tricked. A flamboyant young girl who would in time go on to become a daring novelist wore her headscarf in front of her parents then stuffed it into her schoolbag when she was safely outside her neighborhood. A new generation of Arab writers, Cairenes for the most part, was opening up our world, defying the old forms of expression and the worn-out pieties.

There are promptings that come an author's way that could, in retrospect, be seen as opening up whole writing endeavors. I had started *The Arab Predicament* with the tale of a Lebanese journalist, Salim al-Lawzi, who had been found dead and mutilated in early March 1980, on the outskirts of Beirut. Lawzi had been an outspoken critic of the Syrian regime of Hafez al-Assad, and his murder foreshadowed much greater cruelties to come. This was still an Arab world easy to shock, and Lawzi's writing hand, disfigured by acid, was all that was needed to tell what this crime was about. My account of the man's death was something of an outline, I did not possess a fuller narrative of Lawzi's life, and the things that led to his murder. I had what I needed then, an entry into the new culture of dictatorship and cruelty.

In retrospect, Lawzi's tale had given me a measure of daring. The Arab political world was coming apart—and how! A civil war that had broken out in Lebanon in 1975 had grown in savagery. It was both a war among the Lebanese, and a war among the Arabs. Beirut was a garden without fences, an astute Palestinian political operative said of the city that had been, in its better days, a center of Arab modernity. And there it was being claimed by religious and sectarian atavisms. The atavisms were unleashed, embarrassed at first, then with abandon. Indeed, the book I would write, meant to be an indictment of a political tradition, was outpaced by the realities descending on the Arabs. I was justified in my sense that Lawzi's murder was the prelude to a new, more unforgiving time, for the Arabs.

It was many years later, thanks, in part, to a book published in Cairo, in 1997, by the author Faiza Saad, entitled *From the Secrets of Journalism and the Intelligence Services*, I would pick up his trail, the drama of his life and times had not dimmed with the years. Lawzi had scaled the heights of Lebanese journalism. He had become a publisher of his own magazine, *Hawadith, Events*. He was a man of substantial means, then based in London, where he had gone to escape the furies of Lebanon and the wrath of the Assad regime. But Lawzi's beginnings were humble, he had risen out of the destitution of Tripoli, Lebanon's second largest city, on its northern coast. He was born in 1922 to a Sunni family, the dominant faith in Tripoli. His father had been a street peddler of confections, and in the journalist's legend the boy had taken to the printed word from reading the newspaper wrappings of his father's sweets. He had been schooled in the old-fashioned way of the Muslim poor, learning to read the Koran at the hands of a religious teacher. He had an ear for Arabic, and a determination to quit Tripoli for the lights and opportunities of Beirut. He enrolled in a vocational school, but was quick to abandon it. He made his way to Jaffa in 1944, as a young man of twenty-two, found work with a radio station. It was a short stint, and Salim then set out for Cairo. He joined a thriving magazine, *Ruz al-Yusuf*.

In Cairo, the method that would serve him and see him through was to emerge: "listen and learn," seek out the mighty. It was his luck that he would befriend an ambitious military conspirator, an army officer by the name of Anwar el-Sadat. The officer was on the run when Lawzi met him, he had been part of an assassination ring that had targeted an ancien regime politician, a friend of the British rulers, Amin Othman. This would have been around 1946–47, a few years before the coup d'état that brought the Officer Corps to power. Sadat was to go through a celebrated trial, he was cashiered out of the army and then reinstated. (It was the fame acquired during the trial that brought him to the attention of a beautiful young woman of British-Egyptian stock, a decade younger, the future Jihan el-Sadat, who would defy her parents to marry a man without prospects, already married, with children and burdens aplenty.) Lawzi had sheltered and helped Sadat, and this would come in handy in the future.

Back in Lebanon, Lawzi had found his niche, "society journalism." He was in awe of the rich, in a city where glitter trumped all else. The "listen and learn" method would serve him well. He managed to make it into the entourage of Henri Pharaon, arguably the country's most influential merchant-aristocrat. Pharaon had a love of horses and horse racing; his stables boasted the best horses in the region. From the poverty of Tripoli's alleyways, Lawzi was a stranger to all this, but he was a sponge, he turned himself into a raconteur in Pharaon's entourage.

The transforming event in Lawzi's life was his acquiring a license for a magazine. Such licenses were difficult to obtain, the press in Lebanon was an affair of the barons of Beirut, and the foreign embassies that sponsored rival publications. This was where that old, blessed connection to Anwar el-Sadat paid off. Both Sadat and his boss, Gamal Abdel Nasser, had a sense of themselves as men of the written word. Sadat had been given an editorship of one of Cairo's major dailies by his colleagues in the junta. Lawzi offered his services to the Cairo regime, the launching of a magazine that would be a mouthpiece of theirs in the press wars of Lebanon; Beirut had emerged as a coveted prize in the "Arab Cold War" that had broken out between Cairo and its rivals in Baghdad and the Arabian Peninsula. The Saudis had their newspapers that they subsidized, Cairo had its own. A seven-story building that belonged to *Hawadith* arose in the city. The Tripoli boy had fulfilled his dreams. The Egyptian embassy was a mighty force in Lebanon, Gamal Abdel Nasser was a darling of the crowd, and Lawzi was on the side of the angels. He plowed through personal tragedy—a young child of his had died in a freak accident, fell out of a restaurant window in Damascus.

The press wars were not always genteel. In 1966, a celebrated journalist, Kamel Mroue, himself a publisher of a noted daily, *Al-Hayat*, was assassinated as he sat down in his office to write his daily column. Mroue was a figure of great talent and controversy. In Lawzi's fashion, but a decade earlier, Mroue was a self-made man. He had emerged out of the poverty of Shia southern Lebanon to the apex of Lebanese journalism. He had led a colorful life, he had the gift of a fluent pen. He had fled Lebanon for Nazi Germany when the Free French and the British had evicted the Vichy forces. His newspaper, *Al-Hayat*, was known to be close to the House of Saud. Mroue had stirred up the wrath of Gamal Abdel Nasser, the man was not a journalist, Nasser said of Mroue, but a political party. A well-known thug from the Sunni street of Beirut had pulled off Mroue's assassination. A dark role was played by Lawzi in this affair. He incited against Mroue, he enlisted a prominent lawyer, an ally of his, to defend the ringleader in the assassination.

Candor visited Lawzi now and then. In 1967, in the aftermath of the Six Day War, he described Gamal Abdel Nasser as the defeated leader of a defeated nation. A Nasserite operative reminded him how the seven-story building of *Hawadith* had been acquired. One of my favorite and most telling anecdotes about Lawzi was a column he wrote in which he bragged about the Mercedes Benz given him by the Emir of Kuwait. This was Beirut, and no shame attached itself to the revelation.

Beirut's world was turned upside down in the 1970s. Cairo had pulled back from Beirut, it had wearied of the inter-Arab wars. Ironically, it was Lawzi's old patron, Anwar el-Sadat, who had altered Egyptian policy. The ground in Lebanon had been cleared for the Syrians. A cunning ruler, Hafez Assad, had used Egypt's retreat to insert his regime, full force into the quarrels of Lebanon. Lawzi's luck had begun to run out. His magazine, so eager to please the Egyptian rulers, was now at odds with Damascus. His Tripoli roots were a factor in this antagonism. His hometown was a conservative, hidebound place. Its people didn't think much of the rest of Lebanon; they had been forced into the state of Greater Lebanon that the French had put together. Their cultural and political allegiance belonged to Syria, now across an international frontier. Tripoli was (and now remains) the setting of a sectarian feud between its Sunni majority and the Alawi minority. The Alawis of Tripoli were now emboldened, they were riding the coattails of the Damascus regime. The Syrian *mukhabarat* had the run of Tripoli and Beirut. The Damascus strongman had made it clear that Lebanon now lay within his sphere of influence, that Egypt, and the Western powers as well, had pulled up stakes in Lebanon. Lawzi was in the crossfire: He ran for cover, left Beirut for London. In London, he took up the craft he knew. He published *Hawadith*, this time in English, *Events*. Arabic journalism was now putting down roots in London and Paris, driven into exile by official terror in Arab lands.

From London, Lawzi grew more strident about the Syrian regime. He spoke openly of a grave matter that the master in Damascus was desperate to finesse: Assad's Alawite identity, and the sectarian basis of his regime. A Sunni insurgency was gathering force in Syria, and the journalist from Tripoli lent this insurgency his support. In Paris, Lawzi was to meet one of the two historic figures of the Baath, Salah al-Din al-Bitar. Bitar, a Sunni, and his partner from the days of the *Quartier Latin* in Paris, the Greek Orthodox Michel Aflaq, had lost out in the deadly struggle for Syria, and its cycle of coups and counter-coups. Bitar, who would be killed by the Syrian *mukhabarat* in Paris, warned Lawzi against the follies of playing with fire. Stay away from evil, and sing to it, Bitar told the publisher, an Arabic maxim that sprang out of the deeper recesses of a culture that knew the force of evil.

Lawzi was undeterred: he wrote his best on the matter of Syria under the new dictatorship. He warned Hafez Assad against the nemesis of arrogance. Syria will be visited by the same sectarian furies that had undone Lebanon, he warned. He was dismissive of the secular claims of the Baath. He wrote that Damascus was a difficult city—that it does not bare its secrets, and is not easily seduced or frightened. Damascus had confused the great Gamal Abdel Nasser, he wrote. "Nasser had entered Damascus as a legend and left it as a tragic figure." The reference here was of course to the short-lived union between Syria and Egypt, 1958–1961. The Syrians had agitated for the union and then began to conspire against it. Hafez Assad had set out to break the spirit of a once-rebellious country, he knew his country more than did the publisher in London. Distance provided no safety from the wrath of the Syrian ruler. In the midst of this vendetta, the Syrian *mukhabarat* struck: they killed Lawzi's younger brother Mustapha in mid-1979. Mustapha was on the beach, in his hometown, in his swimming trunks, he was gunned down in broad daylight. Lawzi's sister-in-law, in her grief, had held the older brother responsible for her husband's death. Salim al-Lawzi knew it to be so, his guilt over his brother's death would stay with him to the end. He threw caution to the wind after that murder, and the anti-Syrian writing grew more embittered.

It would have been the better part of wisdom to heed his brother's fate and put Lebanon behind him. But his mother's death intruded, and he felt the obligation to go back for her funeral. More careful friends warned him about the risks of a return visit. But there was duty to the dead, and a family's honor. He returned on the last day of the rites of farewell for his mother. He was set to leave the next morning, but this was Salim al-Lawzi, he delayed his departure when told that he had been given an appointment with the president of the republic. The appointment did not materialize, he made the best of the day, he visited the campus of the American University of Beirut and the offices of the newspaper *An-Nahar*.

On Sunday (February 25, 1980) he set out for the Beirut airport, his wife was with him and some family and friends in another car. At a checkpoint, he was separated from his wife and could be seen driven in the direction of the southern coastal town of Damur. His wife was blindfolded and let out in a wooded area.

The search for him was a big story. His wife sought out the powers in the country. She tried Yasir Arafat, he had a kingdom of his own in Beirut then. But he was helpless, he said, because of his own "terrible relations" with Hafez Assad. The Lebanese authorities offered no help either. It was all to no avail: on March 4, a shepherd boy reported that his dog had come upon the corpse of a man that the shepherd did not recognize. It had been a gruesome end for Lawzi: the pathology report established that he had been subjected to punishing torture. He had been shot in the jaw with the aim of wounding him but keeping him alive for the torture. More importantly, there was that writing hand, burned and dipped in acid. (The shepherd was murdered a few days later.)

Lawzi had foreseen his own end. His wife said that he had told her that she had to learn to live without him. In London, he had penned the following lines—this was wisdom beyond knowing emirs and Beirut barons: "I came to you, oh world, as a stranger. I lived as a guest, I leave you as an echo."

* * *

Salim al-Lawzi had been part of my luck as an author. In the years that followed, the truths about the sectarianism of the Arab world that had been papered over were laid bare. I had held out scant hope for the Arabs' political condition. The 1980s would make a mockery of what had been said and taught in Arab political writings. "Arabism is love," Michel Aflaq had written. He had said that in an infinitely more hopeful time when he, and his partner Salah-al-Din-al-Bitar, fresh from their years in Paris could still hope that the text and ideas of modernity could overcome the sectarian fault-lines and phobias of that world. Aflaq and Bitar couldn't have imagined that a boy of the Alawi mountains, Hafez Assad, would emerge to sweep aside the ideas they had brought with them from France. By the Syrian political annals, Assad had been born in utter rural destitution, but had come down from his birthplace to the coastal city of Latakia then to the military academy and to Damascus. He was a stranger to the world of the merchants and the landed bureaucrats who ruled his country. Assad had not cared for theory. The political refinements of Aflaq and Bitar were not for him. There was a political tradition of the urban elites and that tradition had contained the life of Damascus, as it did the life of Aleppo and Homs, and our own West Beirut as well. There were urban notables, men of property and social and political standing. They exuded confidence, heirs to a tradition that harked back to the Ottoman world. Assad bore that tradition burning animus. It had been the tradition of a social class that had looked with contempt on the countryside and on the Alawi sect from which Assad hailed. The cunning officer indulged the ideologues all the while as he was plotting the undoing of that older world. A thin veneer of ideas, of modernist pretensions, was being emptied of any truth. The sectarianism could no longer be hidden as it had been when Salim al-Lawzi confronted it.

* * *

There had been violence in the Arab world, assassins had struck down emirs and noted men of politics. Military seizures of power had upended ruling regimes, there had been, in the 1950s and 1960s, the "Military Communiqué Number One" that announced the demise of old rulers and the rise of new masters. One such coup, in 1952, in Egypt, had been a genteel affair. A feeble monarch was sent into exile aboard his yacht, from his palace in Alexandria, and had been given the respect and decorum befitting a monarch. Six years later, in Baghdad, on a summer day, the Hashemite monarchy was swept away without mercy, a boy king, Faisal II, and his family were gunned down, and the body of the Regent had been dismembered and dragged through the streets.

It hadn't been pretty or safe, that Arab political condition. But it was in the 1980s, as some of the essays assembled here intimate, that the world of the Arabs succumbed to greater brutalities. There had been politico-religious movements aplenty—

the Muslim Brotherhood dates back to the late 1920s, and its secret apparatus was no stranger to assassinations and foul play—but a new stridency came into the intersection of faith and politics. From one end of the Arab world to the other, old verities were being undone, old surplus swept out of the way. Some attributed this to the demographic explosion that hit the region—newly urbanized young men jostling for a place in the world, their pride coming up against scarcity, in conflict with older generations who had fallen into things and acquired turfs of their own. The world of the Arabs had closed in on itself. For all our distress in the 1950s and 1960s, my generation of Arabs could still hold onto the idea of progress and advancement. On the whole we had a discreet and proper relation with Islam. It was the faith of our elders, but secular, irreverent ideas held us and guided our lives. We paid the men of religion scant attention, the mullahs who visited my family home inspired no awe in me or in my siblings and cousins. The books they knew, the narrative they told, the incantation—they all seemed to fly in the face of reason. We had Baathists and Communists and Arab nationalists and self-avowed skeptics aplenty. The two generations to come would know no such ease or confidence. The social peace was shattered, the cries of pain were audible to all but those who preferred to bury their heads in the sand.

I had been lucky to escape, the New World had given me the opportunity to write, and the safety. It would be my fate to return to the material of that older world that I had quit—a world that would continue to tug at me in my new surroundings.

Part I

Chapter 1

The Arab Awakening, 2011

The Year of Living Dangerously

"Dear Brother: I write these few lines to let you know we're doing well, on the whole, though it varies from day to day: sometimes the wind changes, it rains lead, life bleeds from every pore," the celebrated Algerian writer Boualem Sansal wrote in an open letter to the Tunisian vendor, Mohamed Bouazizi, who had set himself ablaze and launched this time of Arab tumult and promise. Sansal wrote this in June of 2011, six months after Bouazizi's self-immolation. Sansal is a man unillusioned. He had lived through, and chronicled, the Algerian bloodletting of the 1990s. He had summoned the memory of Bouazizi with both hope and dread. "But let's take the long view for a moment. Does he who does not know where to go find the way? Is driving the dictator out the end? From where you are, Mohamed, next to God, you can tell that not all roads lead to Rome; ousting a tyrant does not lead to freedom. Prisoners like

This essay originally appeared in *Foreign Affairs*, Vol. 91, No. 2, March/April 2012, with the title "The Arab Spring at One: A Year of Living Dangerously"; it is republished here in slightly different form with the cooperation and consent of the original publisher.

trading one prison for another, for a change of scenery and the chance to get a little something along the way."

A rhythmic chant echoed through Arab lands throughout 2011: "The people want to topple the regime." It skipped Arab borders with ease, carried by print and Twitter and Facebook, on the airwaves of Al Jazeera and Al Arabiya. It had the gift of economy. The regime could be Tunisian or Yemeni, Egyptian or Libyan; the popular wrath knew no boundaries. Arab nationalism had been written off—I own up to being one of the writers of its obituary—but there, in full bloom, was what most certainly looked like a pan-Arab awakening. There were aged rulers—the Syrian despot the exception—and young people in search of political freedom and economic opportunity, made weary of waking up to the same tedium day after day. The rulers had closed up the political world; they had become country owners in all but name. There settled upon the Arabs the sense that they were cursed and alone among the nations, doomed to despotism, the tyranny in their DNA. Waves of democracy washed upon the shores of other nations—Latin America shook off the caudillo tradition; East Asia, whose Confucianism was once seen as a barrier to democratic capitalism, was transformed. Now and then, where they could sustain it and when they could keep the tribalism and the anarchy at bay, Africans flirted with democracy. The solitude of the Arabs in the contemporary order of nations, their exceptionalism if you will, had become a huge moral embarrassment to the Arabs themselves. It was as though they had left history and had become spectators to their own destiny. It was a bleak landscape: terrible rulers, sullen populations, and a terrorist fringe that hurled itself in frustration at an order bereft of any legitimacy. This was the despots' dreamland, it seemed. The postcolonial state among the Arabs had hatched a monstrous world. Kleptocracies had taken hold, and the rulers and their families "devoured the green and the dry." It was estimated that "The Family," as the clan of the former Tunisian ruler and his wife was known, controlled a third of the national economy. The heirs of Hafez al-Assad—his children, his nephews—had come to great wealth and monopolized key sectors of the economy. Muammar Qaddafi may have ranted about socialism, but he and his family knew no line between what was theirs and what was public treasure.

Powers beyond had winked at this reality. This was the best the Arabs could do, it was thought. In a sudden burst of Wilsonianism, in the aftermath of the American invasion of Iraq, American power had given the support of liberty a try. The "diplomacy of freedom," a child of the Iraq war, shook up the dominant Arab order. Saddam Hussein was flushed out of a spider hole, the Syrian brigades of terror and extortion were pushed out of Lebanon, and the despotism of Hosni Mubarak, long a pillar of the Pax Americana, appeared to lose its mastery. Dissidents stepped forth to challenge Pharaoh and, for a fleeting moment, Washington signaled its unease with the Egyptian ruler. Iraq held out mixed messages to Arabs beyond its borders: there was blood in the streets and sectarianism, but there were the chaotic ways of a new democracy, the surprising attachment Iraqis displayed to their experiment with democratic practice. The autocracies hunkered down and did their best to thwart this new Iraqi project. They fed the flames of Iraq, and their jihadists and slick media alike were pressed into this big fight. Iraq was set ablaze, and the Arab autocrats could point to it as a cautionary tale of the folly of unseating even the worst of despots. That fight issued in a standoff: the Arabs could not snuff out this Iraqi project, but the Iraqi example did not turn out to be the subversive democratic message that its proponents held it out to be.

Iraq carried a double burden: the bearer of liberty that had upended the Baghdad tyranny was the United States, and the war had empowered the Shia stepchildren of the Arab world. A traumatic change had taken place. Baghdad, the seat of the Abbasid empire, had fallen to the Shia; the American war propelled a hitherto frightened Shia community to power. The last time the Shia had ruled Baghdad was—literally—a millennium ago. And that primacy did not last long, as Sunni internationalism reclaimed it. Now power had come to the Shia courtesy of an American invasion. Baghdad could not carry the torch of Arab freedom. The sectarianism of the Arab world—the dread and contempt for the Shia—blunted the force of this new challenge. In 2003–2005, when this history was unfolding, it was said by Arabs themselves that George W. Bush had unleashed a tsunami on the region. True, but the Arabs were good at waiting out storms, and before long the Americans themselves would lose heart and abandon the quest. An election in 2006 in the Palestinian territories went the way of Hamas, and a new disillusionment with democracy's verdict overtook the Bush administration.

The American war in Iraq had to be rescued, and the "surge" came in the nick of time to turn that war around. The more ambitious vision of "reforming" the Arab world was given up. America could not want freedom for the Arabs more than they wanted it themselves, and the autocracies had survived a brief moment of American assertiveness. A new standard-bearer of American power, Barack Obama, delivered the autocracies a reassuring message. America was done with the diplomacy of change; it would make its peace with the status quo. There were these two rogue regimes, in Damascus and Tehran: the custodians of American power would set out to "engage" them. Iraq had become a big American disappointment. The patina of cosmopolitanism attached to President Obama concealed the unease with the foreign world at the core of his worldview. He was not exactly a declinist, but he had risen to power at a time of American fatigue and economic retrenchment. This was not a man to tilt at windmills in Araby. He would make a stand in Afghanistan—the good war of necessity that he embraced as a rebuke to the war in Iraq—with no illusions about that country. America was to remain on the Kabul hook, even as the president believed that Afghanistan was a hopeless undertaking. The greater Middle East would be left to its furies.

It did not take long for the embattled liberals in the Arab-Islamic world to catch on: when a revolt erupted in Iran against the theocrats in the first summer of his presidency, Obama was caught flat-footed by the turmoil. He was out to conciliate the rulers, and he couldn't even find the language to speak to Iran's rebellion. Meanwhile, the Syrians were in the midst of seller's remorse: they had given up their dominion in Lebanon under duress and were now keen to retrieve it. A stealth campaign of terror and assassinations, the power of Hezbollah on the ground, and the subsidies of Iran all but snuffed out the exquisitely choreographed Cedar Revolution, which had been the pride of the Bush diplomacy.

Realists who assessed the (apparent) balance of forces in this region would have been right to concede the autocrats an eternal dominion. They would have prophesied for the repressive national security states the dynastic succession that had all but transformed the republics of the Arab world into hereditary monarchies. Beholding Bashar al-Assad in Damascus, they would have been forgiven the conclusion that a similar fate awaited Libya, Yemen, Tunisia, and the large Egyptian state that had been the trendsetter in Arab political and cultural life. Beneath this surface stability there was the political misery and sterility of the Arab world. No Arabs with a scant awareness of the world needed "human development reports" to remind them of the desolation of their politics. Consent had drained out of public life, and the glue between ruler and ruled was the pervasive fear and suspicion that poisoned the political realm. The drumbeats of anti-Americanism were steady—this was the release a pent-up population was permitted by its rulers. Modernity, the lodestar of earlier generations of Arabs, had gone into eclipse.

There was no public project to bequeath a generation coming into its own—and this was the youngest population in the world, the "youth bulge" about to sweep away the stagnant order. Bouazizi had taken one way out, and millions of unnamed Bouazizis would take to the streets. The despots, secure in their dominion, deities in all but name, were now on the run. For its part, the United States scurried to catch up with the upheaval. "In too many places, in too many ways, the region's foundations are sinking into the sand," Secretary of State Hillary Clinton proclaimed in mid-January 2011 in Qatar, as the storm had broken out. The Arab landscape lent her remarks ample confirmation; what she omitted was that American diplomacy, too, would be buried in this avalanche.

This was, through and through, an Arab revolt, a settlement of the account between the powers that be and populations determined to be done with the despots. These may have been akin to prison revolts; the protesters had not been given skills at governance, but Arabs were done with quiescence. In the manner of big upheavals, this rebellion that broke out in Tunisia had a scent for the geography of things. It had erupted in a small country on the margins of the Arab political experience—more educated and prosperous than the norm in lands to its east, with a sustained traffic with Europe across the Mediterranean. As the rebellion made its way eastward, it skipped Libya and arrived in Cairo, or *Umm al-Dunya* (the mother of the world), which Egyptians and other Arabs call this great metropolis. In Cairo, this awakening found a stage worthy of its ambitions. This most enigmatic of lands has always played tricks on those who would pronounce on its temperament. This "hydraulic society" often written off as the quintessential land of political submission, on the banks of an orderly and well-mannered river, has known ferocious rebellions. A classic account of this country is found in *The Nile in Egypt* (1937), by Emil Ludwig: "Once the *fellahin* (the peasants) and the workers of Egypt revolted against their masters; once their resentment burst out, a revolution dispossessed the rich men and the priests of Egypt of their power." One such revolution at the end of the Old Kingdom raged intermittently for two centuries (2350 BC–2150 BC). It had been Mubarak's good fortune that the land tolerated him for three decades and that he had been the designated successor of Anwar el-Sadat. His reign had become the third longest since Ramses II. He had been a cautious man, but his reign now sprouted dynastic ambitions. For 18 magical days in Tahrir Square, Egyptians of all walks of life came together to be rid of him. He had come out of the officer corps, and now the senior commanders of the armed forces cast him aside. He joined his fellow despot, the Tunisian Zine el-Abidine Ben Ali, who had made a run for it a month earlier.

From Cairo, this awakening now had the chance to be a pan-Arab affair. It caught fire eastward in Yemen and Bahrain—the latter being the exception, a monarchy in a season where the republics of strongmen were the ones seized with unrest. The monarchies were whole, they had a fit between ruler and ruled; Bahrain stood apart, riven by a fault line between its Sunni rulers and Shia majority. It was in the nature of things that an eruption in Bahrain would turn into a sectarian feud. Yemen was the poorest of the Arab states, secessionist movements raged in its north and south, and its strongman, Ali Abdullah Saleh, was a polarizing figure who had no other skill save the art of political survival. The feuds of Yemen were obscure; they were quarrels of tribes and warlords. The wider Arab tumult had given Yemenis eager to be rid of this ruler the heart to persist in their challenge to him.

Then the revolt doubled back westward to Libya, flanked as that country was by Tunisia and Egypt. This was the kingdom of silence, the realm of the deranged "dean of Arab rulers," Muammar Qaddafi. For four tormenting decades, the Libyans were at the mercy of this warden of a big prison who was part tyrant, part buffoon. Qaddafi had eviscerated his society, the richest country in Africa with an abysmally impoverished population. This brutalized country had been ill-served by history. In the interwar years it had known savage colonial rule under the Italians. It had had a brief respite under an ascetic ruler, King Idris. But a revolutionary fever gripped it in the late 1960s. *Iblis wa la Idris*, "Better the devil than Idris," went the maxim of the time. And this country got what it wanted. Oil sustained the madness, European leaders and American intellectuals alike came courting, the ruler had wealth to dispense and bedouin kitsch. Qaddafi, a barely literate child of desert adversity, had his animal instinct: the ferocity with which he defended the regimes of Mubarak and Ben Ali gave away his panic. He and his entitled children must have prepared for a reckoning of this kind: the underground tunnels were the works of a man who, on some level, intuited his own end. Benghazi, at some remove from his capital, rose against him; history now gave the Libyans a chance.

Qaddafi had erred. When Benghazi defied him, he had warned that his armor was on the way, that he would crush this rebellion house by house, neighborhood by neighborhood, alleyway by alleyway. The League of Arab States, which had never stood up to a tyrant, gave a warrant for a Western intervention against him; he had offended and belittled his fellow rulers, turned his back on the Arab world, and dubbed himself "king of the kings of Africa." He was a man alone when Britain and France took the lead against him, and a reluctant American president, "leading from behind," launched a military intervention that decapitated this tyrannical regime. Barack Obama wanted no shades of Rwanda on his conscience, no mass slaughter in Benghazi staining his record. The Libyans had been lucky. Barack Obama himself would say that the intervention was a close-run affair, a 51–49 proposition, he would tell an interviewer for *Vanity Fair*. NATO functioned as the air force of this rebellion, and without foreign support it is certain that the despot and his mercenaries and his money would have crushed the rebellion.

* * *

The Egyptian rulers had said that their country was not Tunisia; Qaddafi had asserted that his republic differed from that of the Tunisians and the Egyptians. In the same vein, the ruler in

Damascus said that his country differed from Tunisia, Egypt, and Libya. He was young whereas the rulers in those lands had been old men, and there was the myth of being a "confrontation state" against Israel to see his regime through. He spoke too soon: in mid-March, it was Syria's turn. The rebellion had not erupted in Aleppo or Damascus, nor had it flared up in Hama, the city in the central plains whose name evokes the terror of the war between Hafez al-Assad and the Muslim Brotherhood, which ended in terrible slaughter in February of 1982. This rebellion broke out in Deraa, a remote provincial town in the south by the border with Jordan, the kind of place out of which the Baath Party had risen in the early 1960s and had outgrown as it fell for the charms and ease of Damascus. Despotism and sectarianism—the rule of the Alawi minority that dominated the security forces and the army—begot the most fearsome state in the Arab east. This had been the handiwork of Hafez al-Assad, a man of supreme cunning and political skill.

Syria, Damascus in particular, occupied a special place in the memory and reverence of orthodox, mainstream Islam. This had been the province where Islam made its first home, when it outgrew the Arabian Peninsula; this was the original home of the Arab kingdom in the middle years of the seventh century, before Islam slipped out of the hands of the Arabs and came under the control of the Persians and the Turkish soldiers. Yet here was Damascus, under a community of schismatics who had ridden the military and the Baath Party to absolute power. This revolt had a distinct geography, as Fabrice Balanche, a French political geographer who has done extensive field research in Syria, has documented. The rebellion has been based in the territories—and the urban quarters—of the Sunni Arabs. There was Deraa, of course, where it all began, and then it spread to Hama, Homs, Jisr al-Shughour, Rastan, Idlib, Deir al-Zour, etc. The revolt did not take in the Kurdish territories, or in Jebel Druze, or, of course, in the mountain villages and the coastal towns that make up the Alawi strongholds.

There can be no denying the sectarian dimension of this fight: Homs, the third largest city in Syria, bears this out. The violence was most pronounced in Homs because the demography was explosive: Homs is two-thirds Sunni, one-fourth Alawi, one-fifth Christian. The Alawis were newcomers to the city, they had ridden the coattails of the state and the army, and they huddled among their own in their own neighborhoods. If Homs came to conjure up the memory of Sarajevo—the snipers, the warring neighborhoods—the demography goes a long way toward explaining the violence. Sectarianism was not all, of course. Syria has had one of the highest birthrates in the region—when this ruling cabal came to power in 1970, Syria had a rural population of six million; now it is home to twenty-three million people. A young population had known no other rule than that of the Assads; the arteries of the regime had hardened. A military-merchant complex had formed at the apex of political and economic life. There wasn't much patronage left for the state to dispose of; under the banner of privatization, the state had pulled off a disappearing act. The neglected provinces and towns conquered their fear, shook off the memory of the bloodletting of the 1970s and early 1980s, and made a run at the regime. Their revolt fused a sense of economic disinheritance, and the wrath of a Sunni majority determined to rid itself of the rule of a godless lot.

If the Sunni Arabs had lost Baghdad to the Shia, there was suddenly within grasp the prospect of restoring Damascus to its "proper" place, breaking its alliance with the Persian state and

Hezbollah, and seeing it once again under the rule of Sunni Islam. There was no mystery in the exit that Hamas made out of Damascus in December of 2011. That Palestinian movement which had made a home of sorts in Damascus could not risk being left out of the mounting Arab consensus against the Syrian regime. "No Iran, no Hezbollah, we want rulers who fear Allah" was one of the more meaningful chants of the protesters. Alawi rule was an anomaly, and this brutal regime, with its security forces desecrating mosques, firing at worshippers, and ordering hapless captives to proclaim that there is no God but Bashar, had written its own banishment. The Arab sense of outrage was genuine. There was Sunni solidarity at work; but, in all fairness, there was anger at the brutality that the iPhones and the YouTube postings and the television channels transmitted to all corners of the Arab world. Old Man Assad had committed cruelties of his own, but always remained within the fold of the Arab consensus. Bashar was a different creature—he left no room for ambiguity or compromise. It was this recklessness and the steady display of official cruelty that had prompted the Arab world's most influential ruler, the Saudi monarch, to condemn the "killing machine" of the Damascus cabal. And, three months later, the Arab League surprised the Syrians by suspending Damascus's membership in that organization.

* * *

Syria put on cruel display the deformities of the Arab state—state power as *ghanima* (war booty), the isolation of the rulers, the nexus between state power and economic plunder, and the narrow sectarian or clan base of the ruling cabals. The Syrian people no doubt knew they were in for a long fight. In a refugee camp on the outskirts of Antakya, a young lawyer from Jisr al-Shughour told me that he fled his town in the summer months but brought his winter clothing with him. He knew that the entrenched dictatorship would fight for the dominion it had conquered and grown addicted to. The embattled ruler appeared convinced that he can resist the very laws of gravity. There had been substantial defections from the army, but the instruments of repression remained more or less intact. A "Libya envy" came to grip the Syrian protesters, but no foreign rescue mission was on the horizon. Turkey and the Arab states were invested in this bloody fight for the country. With all the uncertainties, this much can be said: the fearsome security state that Hafez al-Assad and the Baath Party and the Alawi soldiers and intelligence barons had built was gone for good. When consent and popular enthusiasm fell away, the state rested on fear, and fear was defeated. The bonds between the holders of power and the population have been broken.

There was, of course, no uniform script for the Arab regimes in play. Tunisia, home of the Jasmine Revolution, in an old state with a defined national identity, settled its affairs with relative ease. It elected a constituent assembly, and Ennahda, an Islamist party, secured the largest number of seats—89 out of 217. There were votes across the entire spectrum—even the Communists secured three seats of their own. The leader of Ennahda, Rachid Ghannouchi, was a shrewd man: years in exile had taught him caution. His party would form a coalition government with two secular parties. In Libya, Qaddafi was pulled out of a drainage pipe, beaten, and murdered—and so was one of his sons. Another son, Khamis, with a brigade named after him, would be killed in October 2012, a year to the day after his father's gruesome end. Men are not angels. These were the hatreds and the wrath that the ruler himself had sown; he had reaped what he had planted.

In Bahrain there hovered over that archipelago kingdom the shadows of Iran and Saudi Arabia, but there is a Bahraini malady, and an international commission of inquiry authorized by the ruler himself gave Bahrain a searching assessment. There is no Syrian-scale terror here, but the political order is not pretty. There is sectarian discrimination and the oddness of a ruling dynasty, the House of Khalifa, which had conquered this place in the late years of the eighteenth century but still retained the mindset of a ruling caste that had not made its peace with the population. Outsiders—from Jordan and Pakistan among others—man the security forces, and the peace between the Shia majority and the regime seems a long way off. As for Yemen, this is the quintessential failed state. For both better and worse, the footprint of the state is light here and the rulers offer no redemption, but there is no draconian terror. The country is running out of water, and jihadists on the run from the Hindu Kush have found a home in Yemen, Afghanistan with a coastline. The men and women who went out into the streets of Sanaa sought the rehabilitation of their country. They wanted for it a politics more dignified than the cynical acrobat at the helm for more than three decades aiding and abetting the forces of terror and backwardness, as he offers his services to outsiders with deep pockets keen to keep the pathologies of Yemen in check. (Yemen is the birthplace of the Nobel Peace Prize laureate Tawakkol Karman, a mother, an activist, and, at 32 years of age, the youngest peace prize recipient.)

We return to *Umm al-Dunya*, Cairo, and the fate of Egypt. The country may have lost the luster of old, and Arabs may no longer be fixated on that city as they had once been, but this

Arab time shall be judged by what comes to pass in Egypt. In the scenarios of catastrophe, this revolution would spawn an Islamic republic: the Coptic minority would take to the road; tourism, a historic source of livelihood, would be lost for good; and Egyptians would yearn for the iron grip of a pharaoh. The results of the parliamentary elections—the strong performance of the Muslim Brotherhood, the surprise of a Salafi party coming in second after the Brotherhood, the disarray and splitting of the vote among the secular liberal parties—seemed to justify the worries about the country's direction.

Memories of a period of a proud liberal history, the interwar years of the past century, play upon Egyptians. Six decades of uninterrupted military rule had robbed them of the very experience of open politics. Egyptians were now without a pharaoh. Say what you will about these elections, they were generally transparent—and clarifying. The broad secular-liberal forces were not ready for the contest. The Brotherhood, with eight decades of political life behind it, had been waiting for this historic moment, and it had made its good fortune. The Salafis had come out of the catacombs, but no sooner had they made their appearance they began to unnerve the population and to pull back from fire-and-brimstone positions on tourism, on women, on the place of the Copts in public life, and on the space for individual liberty.

Tahrir Square had transfixed us all, but as the immensely talented young Egyptian intellectual Samuel Tadros puts it, Tahrir Square was not Cairo and Cairo was not Egypt. By the time the dust settled, three forces were contesting the Egyptian future—the army, the Brotherhood, and a broad liberal and secular coalition of those who want a civil polity, the separation of religion and politics, and the saving graces of a "normal" political life. For the Brotherhood, this is the fulfillment of a dream—and then some, for there is ample evidence that the Brotherhood went beyond the electoral gains it had wanted for itself. There had been a special time in the history of the Brotherhood, a very brief moment in the aftermath of the Free Officers coup d'état in 1952. The Brotherhood had described the coup as a blessed movement. The Brotherhood struck an alliance with the junta, or so it thought. Gamal Abdel Nasser sought political monopoly, and an assassination attempt on him by the Brotherhood in 1954 sealed the group's fate. The would-be assassins were sent to the gallows and thousands were dispatched to prison—the Brotherhood was never the same again.

To this current struggle to reshape Egypt, the Brotherhood brought its time-honored mix of political cunning and its essential commitment to its mission—the imposition of a political order shaped in its image. This was the tradition bequeathed the Brotherhood by its founder, Hassan al-Banna, who was struck down by an assassin in 1949 but still stalks the politics of the Islamic world, from Morocco to Indonesia. Banna, a ceaseless plotter, was the quintessential chameleon, a man possessed. A village boy, he mastered the politics of Cairo. In the unsettled world of Egypt of his time—the Great Depression, the bottomless anger of a country that wanted the British out but could not expel them, the distant thunder of Fascist and collectivist movements, the growing pauperization of the urban middle class—Banna was in his element. He knew worldly politics. He talked of God and His rule, but in the shadows he struck deals with the palace against the dominant political party of his time—the Wafd. He played the political game as he put together a formidable paramilitary force. He sought to penetrate the officer corps, and his inheritors have pined for this coalition ever since. Doubtless, he would look with admiration on the tactical skills of his inheritors, maneuvering between the liberals and the Supreme Council of the Armed Forces, partaking of the tumult of Tahrir Square, but stepping back from the exuberance to underline their commitment to sobriety and public order.

* * *

Tahrir Square gave rise to a second republic, but the square would not dominate this new order. The final round of the presidential election, held a little more than a year after the abdication of Mubarak, pitted a figure of the *feloul* (the remnants of the old regime), a retired military officer, against a functionary of the Muslim Brotherhood. It was a close contest: the candidate of the Brotherhood, Mohamed Morsi, emerged with a slim edge (51.7 percent to 48.3 percent) over Ahmed Shafiq, a Mubarak crony.

There was nothing flamboyant or special about Morsi. He was the ultimate organization man. The Brotherhood had thrust him forward when a more powerful figure within its ranks had been banned from contesting the election on technical grounds. A village boy from the impoverished Delta, born in 1951, he was to go to university, the prestigious college of engineering, courtesy of the populism of the Nasser regime. A government scholarship took him to the University of Southern California, where he obtained a doctorate in 1982. In hindsight, he would claim that he was shaped by America only "scientifically." But he hadn't been eager to leave the United States after completing his degree. He stayed on for three years as a faculty member at California State University at Northridge. Two sons of his were born in the United States and were said to hold American citizenship, and it was in Los Angeles that his very traditional and pious wife was pulled into the orbit of the Muslim Brotherhood. The group may have railed against America and the shadow it cast over Egypt, but leading technocrats from the Brotherhood, Morsi among them, rose to professional success and prominence through American degrees, and their years in America took them beyond the cloistered world from which they hailed.

"I don't think that we consider them an ally, but we don't consider them an enemy," Obama said on September 12 of the tangled relationship with the Muslim Brotherhood government in Cairo. "They're a new government that is trying to find its way, and there would be some rocky times ahead." The day before, crowds had scaled the wall of the American Embassy in Cairo, burning the Stars and Stripes in protest against a video, "The Innocence of Muslims," which had triggered protests in twenty Muslim nations. No diplomats were killed in Egypt, as they were next door in Benghazi, but an American president then obsessed with his own election was reminded of the difficulties sure to make themselves felt in the relationship between the American patrons and the new order in Cairo.

"That depends on your definition of ally," Morsi told *The New York Times* days later, on the eve of a visit to the annual United Nations General Assembly meeting. Morsi had been passionate in his condemnation of that vulgar video—ironically, the work of an Egyptian Copt, a fraudster who made his home in California—but had been slow to condemn the protests. "We took our time," he said, "but in the end acted decisively." He did not step back: "Successive administrations," he added, "essentially purchased with American taxpayer money the dislike, if not the hatred, of the peoples of the region." Mubarak was at times a prickly ally in his own way, but this first civilian ruler of

Egypt since 1952 had served notice that it would not be easy dealing with this new breed of Islamists.

Still, Morsi and the collective leadership of the Muslim Brotherhood were under no illusions about the terms of Egypt's relationship with the United States. They were in need of American patronage—theirs is a country that is the world's top importer of wheat, a burdened economy running a budget deficit of 11 percent of GDP. Governance in Egypt has been tethered to feeding and subsidizing a huge and rebellious population. Rulers have had leeway in that crowded country, but food riots have been the rulers' nightmare. American help was vital, and the Brotherhood knew when purity had to yield to necessity. In the immediate aftermath of Mubarak's demise, the Brotherhood had proudly asserted that it would not turn to the International Monetary Fund for assistance: populism was the rage. The Brotherhood talked of raising a $3.2 billion loan on the domestic market. But this populism was pushed aside, the loan rose to $4.8 billion, and the technocrats of the Brotherhood, negotiating with the IMF, were full of sweet reason.

The Brotherhood had not reinvented this weary land. Egyptian governments had long perfected the art of playing cat and mouse with the IMF and with foreign donors, mixing dependence and defiance, at once needy but proud and brittle. Like riverboat gamblers, Egypt's rulers seem to relish the game, secure in the knowledge that a country of 80 million people at the crossroads of so vital a region, so near to the oil fields of the Arabian Peninsula and the Gulf, a Sunni balance to Iran, will always be bailed out, that it is too big to fail.

The plain truth of it is that Egypt lacks the economic means with which an Islamic order—whatever that means—can be erected. The rule of the jurist in Iran rests on oil, and even the much milder ascendency of Turkey's Prime Minister Recep Tayyip Erdogan, and his party, issues from a prosperity secured by the "devout bourgeoisie" in the Anatolian hill towns. Egypt lies at the crossroads of the world; it lives off tourism, the Suez Canal, infusions of foreign aid by nations invested in its security, and remittances from Egyptians abroad. Virtue has to bow to necessity: the country's foreign reserves have dwindled from $36 billion when the political troubles began to $20 billion a year later. Inflation hammered at the door. Four finance ministers came and went in the course of a single year. A desire for stability had begun to check the heady satisfaction that a despot had been brought down.

The Egypt the Muslim Brotherhood had in mind was anathema to the free spirits in the land. It is perhaps a fragile hope, but this has always been a country of coffeehouses and storytellers, a people given to humor and forgiving of the follies of others. This is not stern Arabia, but a land with a vibrant street and night life, banter between the sexes, an earthiness that looks with suspicion on zealots and the "virtue" they claim to uphold. In a moment of national turmoil, when the Brotherhood-led regime was battling the forces arrayed against it, Morsi in late January 2013 declared a curfew and a state of emergency in the cities of Suez, Port Said, and Ismailia. The inhabitants of these cities defied him, and untold thousands took to the streets at night and sang and danced and played soccer. They were determined to hold onto the world they knew. They needed no instruction in religious devotion. They trusted themselves with their own faith; the enforcers of the Brotherhood could not intimidate them or write them out of their own tradition.

It fell to the country's leading playwright and satirist, Ali Salem, so thoroughly a man of his land and an irreverent free spirit, to offer a biting commentary on the aridity of the Brother-hood's utopia. (Salem, born in 1936, had been doing this for decades. In the mid-1990s he had journeyed to Israel, wrote a book about it, and ignored the taboos of the writers guild.) In a short satire, Salem turns up at the counter of the national carrier, Egypt Air, and asks for an economy booking to Egypt at any-time that is available. Those around him waiting to conduct their own business look at him with wonder, as does the agent at the counter. "What's so strange about my request, what's so odd about a man who loves his country and yearns to return to it?" Salem asks. "But you are in Egypt already, having coffee in Cairo's Talaat Harb Square, in the offices of Egypt Air. Which Egypt do you want to travel to?" the agent inquires. "Misr, Egypt, is my home, I did not say I wanted to go to Egypt, I said I want to return to Egypt," he insists. The agent is not amused, she is ready to help him book passage to any capital in the world. But she can't countenance his stubbornness and frivol-ity; she knew of him. His reputation had spread around the airline offices and the travel agencies. "You folks are now not only preventing Egyptians from returning to Egypt but also preventing Egypt returning to Egyptians," he says.

The police turn up, because the agent had used the time to tip them off about this quarrelsome man. He is hauled off to the police station, and the commissioner on the scene, on the verge of retirement, is keen to finesse the matter. He could, he tells the nettlesome man, commit him to a mental asylum. But he will write in the official report that the man had been misun-derstood, that he had asked for a booking to London and the agent had mistaken his request. He gives in grudgingly, takes his leave, and resists the impulse to go to other airline counters. "I must confess that the Egypt I know no longer exists, that it is impossible to travel there. I must reconcile myself to the Egypt all around me, to the Nile as it is, to these ugly tents [on Tahrir Square]. I must not get angry when I hear that some people now lay siege to the courts and the judges and burn their legal files. I must accept and live with a sorrow so immense that no newspaper anywhere in the world could accommodate."

Salem is heir to a distinguished tradition in Egyptian letters. There is a special roster, a pantheon of luminaries that any country in the world would be proud to claim as its own—the playwright Tawfik al-Hakim, Taha Hussein, the Nobel laureate Naguib Mahfouz, Mohamed Sid-Ahmed, Louis Awad, Yusuf Idris, etc. All have passed away, and Salem is the link to them. He carries their torch. Egyptian modernism may be fragile, and the voters in the countryside may have given the edge to a repressive constitution. Given a choice between a man of the *feloul* (the remnants of the old regime) and a functionary of the Muslim Brotherhood, Egyptian liberalism had proved timid and inadequate, and its leaders quarreled among themselves. But the saving grace of an "Egyptianness" that is merciful and tempered, shaped by two centuries of striving for things and ways modern, was not resigned to going gently into the night.

For two centuries now Egypt has led a Sisyphean struggle for modernity, for a place among the nations worthy of its ambitions. It has not fared well, and the lamentations all around bespeak of a disappointment with the dismal economic and cultural results. Yet another false detour can only compound the grief of Egypt. On August 3, 2011, there happened a scene that could give Egyptians a measure of solace. The country's last pharaoh—may it be so—came to court on a gurney: "Sir, I am present," the former ruler said to the presiding judge. Mubarak was not pulled out of a drainage pipe, as was Qaddafi. And unlike Bashar al-Assad, he had not hunkered down with his sect and his family murdering his people at will. Outsiders who have savored and thought they have known this land have always fallen back on the ability of this country—the words are those of E. M. Forster—to harmonize contending assertions. If this attribute quits Egypt, there shall be endless suffering for a country that has known more than its share of heartbreak.

* * *

Egypt's journey out of the dictatorial past was to put on display the difficulty of surmounting tyrannical legacies. In the space of some thirty months the country was to know the excitement and complications of a new season of liberty, a brief ascendency by the Muslim Brotherhood, and then an odd mix of a popular insurrection and a military seizure of power that upended the rule of the Brotherhood. The "democratic" experiment that had issued in the presidency of Mohamed Morsi turned out to be a brief interregnum. The ballot had not resolved the contradictions of a deeply divided society. Egypt had become ungovernable, and a military coup d'état on July 3, 2013, offered a way out of the great impasse between the Brotherhood and a broad secular coalition. Dictatorship rests on a measure of consent: an ordinary man obliges, and the crowd projects onto him its need for a redeemer. There was nothing unusual about General Abdel Fattah el-Sisi. He had been a man of military intelligence, the product of a vast officer corps. Yet the crowd—the secularist crowd—anointed him as a savior. In truth, there had been no urgencies to the sacking of Morsi. All the levers of power were beyond his writ. The army was a force all its own, the judiciary was a truculent establishment by Mubarak holdouts, and the police was a rogue force that Morsi had tried to conciliate with very little success. A strong case could have been made for letting the Morsi presidency play out, but the young who had tasted power in Tahrir Square and the officer corps had come together to bring the interlude of the Brotherhood to an end.

Vengeance stalked the land. An irreverent young physician and satirist, Bassam Youssef (he has been repeatedly dubbed the Jon Stewart of his country), in an essay on July 16, gave Egyptians an honest rendition of their crisis. Youssef mocked the secularists' dream of a "normal country" of "good-looking people" without veils or beards. The liberals of Egypt, he said, were on a "victory high," their media outlets "full of discrimination and inciting rhetoric." The satirist cut to the heart of things: the liberal secularists averting their gaze from the transgressions of the army and the police were no different from the "Islamists who think that their enemies' disappearance off this planet would be a victory for the rule of God." The army had broken the stalemate between the secularists and the Brotherhood, but the rancor of politics had not ended. "We have replaced the enemies of Islam with the enemies of the state," Youssef said. The army and the police can rout the Brotherhood and overturn the verdict of the ballot, but there can be no total victory over the Brotherhood. "These people are never going to disappear. . . . They will return to their homes full of hatred, frustration and disappointment," Youssef said. They will pay back the rulers with "more violence and determination."

The secularists who were willing to cast their loyalty aside in order to be rid of the Brotherhood insisted that it hadn't been a military coup that had overthrown Morsi. These erstwhile liberals were strident: Morsi had been brought down by "popular impeachment," they said. People who had loathed the police were now singing their praise.

The surrender of the liberals, now gripped by a spirit of vengeance, was the shameful surprise of this moment of Egyptian history. "This is not us. It's not Egypt at all. We are not happy with death and blood," said Israa, an Egyptian woman who gave only her first name to a foreign reporter. Israa gave voice to a reflexive, unexamined pride—the good, peaceful land whose life has been regulated, since the dawn of history, by a steady, gentle river.

Now go tell that old, timeless idea of Egypt to Mohamed ElBaradei, the celebrated Egyptian liberal who, as the former director of the International Atomic Energy Agency, had returned to his country crowned with a Nobel Peace Prize. He was glorified on the Egyptian street for having frustrated, as best he could, the George W. Bush administration's resort to war in Iraq.

ElBaradei had given his blessing to the July 3 coup. He had given the interim regime a respectable façade when he accepted the vice presidency. He opposed the storming of the two encampments of the Brotherhood, which took place six weeks after the coup. The estimates as to the number killed ranged between 230 and 421. ElBaradei had foreseen the bloody outcome and sought to distance himself from it.

His resignation was the only honorable thing open to him. After that decision, his secular allies wanted him tried for treason: he was a Freemason, a tool of the Americans, an enemy of the valiant Egyptian army, a covert ally of the Muslim Brotherhood determined to use it for his own bid for power. ElBaradei has reportedly left Cairo for Vienna, his old domicile.

Egypt was done with patience and compromise. On November 4, some four months after his forced disappearance, Morsi turned up at court. He had refused to dress in prison clothing;

he had declared himself Egypt's lawful president and rejected the legitimacy of the trial. Whatever his faults, he had been duly elected. But now this didn't matter. Egypt had given itself over to a military strongman.

* * *

In the scheme of modern Arab history, this tumult, this awakening, is the third of its kind to wash upon the Arabs. The first, a political-cultural renaissance born of a desire to join the modern world, came in the late 1800s. Scribes and reformers, lawyers, would-be parliamentarians, and Christian intellectuals in the lead sought to reform political life, separate religion from politics, emancipate women, walk away from the debris of the Ottoman centuries. Fittingly enough, that great movement, with Cairo and Beirut at the head of the pack, was chronicled by George Antonius, a Christian writer of Lebanese birth, Alexandria youth, Cambridge education, and service in the British administration in Palestine. His book *The Arab Awakening*, published in 1939, three years prior to his premature death, remains the principal manifesto of Arab nationalism and of the high hopes of those years.

The second awakening came in the mid-1950s and gathered force in the 1960s. This was the era of Gamal Abdel Nasser in Egypt, Habib Bourguiba in Tunisia, and the early leaders of the Baath Party. No democrats, the leaders of that time were intensely political men engaged in the great issues of the day. They were men of the broad middle class. They had dreams of power, of industrialization, of ridding their people of the sense of inferiority hammered into them by the Ottomans and then aggravated by colonial rule. In a reflection on his upbringing, Bourguiba (1903–2000) remembered his time at the *lycée*, his

French instructor reading Racine and the students moved to tears by the reading. Say what you will about Bourguiba—he was vain and pompous—but he puts to shame the thieves and policemen who replaced him in 1987. No simple audit could do these men justice: they had monumental accomplishments, and then an explosive demography and their own authoritarian proclivities and shortcomings undid a good deal of their work. Political Islam and plain police rule came forth to fill the void when these leaders faltered.

This third awakening came in the nick of time. The Arab world had grown morose and menacing, and the people no longer claimed their own nation-states. The populations hated the rulers and wished them ill, loathed the foreign patrons and backers of these rulers, and bands of jihadists, forged in the cruel prisons of these dreadful regimes, scattered about everywhere looking to kill and be killed. A Tunisian vendor, in the most horrific of ways, summoned the Arabs, particularly the young among them, to a new history. In Tahrir Square, and in those places that wanted a Tahrir Square of their own, Arabs were now reclaiming their countries. "Realists" in distant lands, and skeptics among the Arabs made weary by the failures of the past, were prophesying disaster for this bold, new awakening. Luckily for the Arabs engaged in this tumult, they were paying no heed to the realists.

SOURCE NOTES:

Translation of "A Mohammed Bouazizi" (An Open Letter to Mohamed Bouazizi), by Boualem Sansal was first published in *Le Monde*, June 15, 2011. An English translation can be found at www.wordswithoutborders.org.

For a classic account of Egypt, see Emil Ludwig's *The Nile in Egypt: The life-story of a river*, first edition (Allen & Unwin, 1937).

For more detail about Syria, see French political geographer Fabrice Balanche's *La region alaouite et le pouvoir syrien* (The Alawi Region and Power in Syria) (Karthala, 2006).

For a view of Egypt in the early twentieth century, see British novelist and humanist E. M. Forster's *Pharos and Pharillon* (Hogarth Press, 1923).

The full-length op-ed by satirist and television host Bassam Youssef can be found in *Al-Shorouk*, an Egyptian newspaper, "Alas Nobody Lives There Anymore," July 16, 2013. An English translation can be found at TahrirSquared.com (retrieved on July 17, 2013).

For further reading on the Arab condition, see George Antonius's *The Arab Awakening: The Story of the Arab National Movement* (Simon Publications, 1939).

Chapter 2

The Honor of Aleppo

A Syrian Novel and a Syrian Revolution

I.

In November of 2011, some eight months into the Syrian rebellion, a protester on the outskirts of Damascus held up to the cameras a placard that mocked the people of Aleppo: "URGENT! ALEPPO REBELS—IN 2050!" It was hardly heroic, the caution of Aleppo, particularly against the background of a rebellion that had scorched Deraa and Hama and Homs and Baniyas and so many unheralded Syrian towns. Aleppo was known for its practicality and its dourness and its prudence: as an old expression had it, *halabi chalabi*, "the Aleppine is a gentleman." Another adage was at once a rebuke and a boast: the Damascene and the Cairene are impetuous, but the Aleppine acts only after consulting his mother.

Aleppo has a special identity among Syria's cities and towns. The most populous city in the country, it has a history of rivalry

This essay originally appeared in *The New Republic*, March 1, 2012, and is republished here in slightly different form with the cooperation and consent of the original publisher.

with Damascus. In the Ottoman centuries, the two cities were the seats of provinces that answered directly to Istanbul. They had entirely different mental geographies: Damascus, the gathering point of the annual pilgrimage to the holy cities, looked eastward to the Hijaz and westward to Beirut as its port, but Aleppo's world was oriented northward toward Anatolia and to southwest Iraq. Its port was Alexandretta, which would be lost to the Turkish state in 1939. If political and religious primacy belonged to Damascus, the edge in commerce belonged to Aleppo.

In the early years of the past century, Damascus carried the banner of Arab nationalism and Aleppo was slow to stir to the movement. The urban cultures differed: Damascus was sure of itself and its political and religious mission, whereas the Aleppines were more flexible and supple—the Anatolian world was near, the hinterland was Kurdish, and the city was favored by Western consuls and merchants. Only grudgingly did the Aleppines, in the course of the struggle for independence, and the development of the Syrian state in the aftermath of World War II, come to accept the primacy of Damascus. There remained in them the pride of memory and the stubborn conviction that they had been shortchanged by the rise of Damascus. Politics trumped economics and trade in Syria's turbulent history, and there settled upon the Aleppines a subdued sentiment that this new political world was unkind to their beloved home.

With his brilliant flamboyance, T. E. Lawrence thought that he divined the ways of Aleppo:

Aleppo was a great city in Syria, but not of it, nor of Anatolia, nor of Mesopotamia. There the races, creeds, and tongues of the Ottoman Empire met and knew one another in a spirit of compromise. The clash of characteristics, which made its streets a kaleidoscope, imbued the Aleppine with a lewd thoughtfulness which corrected in him what was blatant in the Damascene. Aleppo had shared in all the civilizations which turned about it: the result seemed to be a lack of zest in its people's belief.

And another traveler, Robin Fedden, a generation later, in his book *Syria: An Historical Appreciation,* saw Aleppo as "a stage; though a large, permanent, and important one upon a road somewhere else: a useful junction, rather than the home and term of imagination and ambition." Fedden was bewitched instead by Damascus: "Thus while Damascus is the town of the Arab, Aleppo is the town of the merchant. Merchants are serious men and have perpetually urgent matters to consider. Aleppo therefore lacks the heady irresponsible effervescence of Damascus. It has less politics and less fanaticism; it has also undoubtedly less gaiety."

We know now that these chroniclers erred. For several terrible years, sobriety and practical reason would quit Aleppo, as its souks became warrens of rebellion and its people prayed for the rains of deliverance that never came. In the late 1970s and early 1980s, Aleppo became the battleground for a grim struggle between the Muslim Brotherhood and the regime of Hafez al-Assad. The refined old world of Aleppo came face-to-face with the brutal new rulers who had seized power and intended never to relinquish it.

During that bitter struggle, Damascus let Aleppo twist in the wind. Khaled Khalifa, an immensely talented writer who was born in Aleppo in 1964, has recalled that grim Aleppine time. In an interview with Robert F. Worth of *The New York*

Times in 2008, he recollected that "for me, Aleppo was the main struggle, because the violence there happened over a long time, not overnight, like in Hama." Khalifa came of age during that cruel era, and the violence that he witnessed nourished his writing.

Khalifa has now produced a genuinely important novel, even a great novel, the kind of novel that makes us see in patient and exacting detail what the world is really like. *Madih al-Karahiyah (In Praise of Hatred)* was published in Beirut in 2008. (A French translation, *Eloge de la Haine*, rendered by Rania Samara, appeared in Paris last year. A portion of the book has been skillfully translated into English by Marlin Dick in the University of Iowa's writing program.) Aleppo was Khalifa's universe. He was in his early teens when a political hell descended on his city. A war was fought there, but it was Hama—in his words, *al-madina al-saghira*, the small city—that had become the bearer of that war's sorrow and its memory. *In Praise of Hatred* complicates that picture of Syria's recent torments, and enriches it and darkens it. I will tell its story in some detail, because it sheds considerable light on the present-day excruciations of Syria.

II.

The narrator of Khalifa's tale—she is not named in the novel—is a young woman of ease and manners who lives in a sprawling house, her maternal grandfather's manse, in an old Aleppo neighborhood. This is the bourgeois Sunni world before the storm. Khalifa's heroine is young and in secondary school, and she lives with her aunts. She is bound by the discipline of the traditional world: strict hours for meals, trips to the *hammam* (bath) every Thursday evening, and an obligatory Friday evening in the company of the older women. Her grandfather, a rug merchant, now deceased, had known adventure in distant lands, as far as Samarkand and beyond. His business was now divided among his three sons, and the big house was given to his daughters. It is a cocoon, this world, and Khalifa's beautiful portrayal of it is but a preparation for the storm about to tear it apart.

The Aleppine schoolgirls are given to daydreaming, and a dance by an Egyptian actress in a popular film has hypnotized them. But already there is trouble: they are consumed by hatred for the "report writers," or informers, who are noisy in their expression of loyalty to the ruling party. A classmate named Nada is the mistress of an officer from the "battalions of death," the dreaded Defense Battalions headed by the ruler's brother, so she is free to come and go in school as she wishes. No one dares to question Nada's liberties, because they all remember the teacher who flunked the daughter of a man who worked for military intelligence: she was dragged into the streets in front of her neighbors, and her clothes were torn up by the *Mukhabarat* as her children watched and wept. There is also Ghada, another student, who is picked up daily from school by a man in his fifties in a Mercedes-Benz, feared and saluted by the battalions of death. Bakr, the youngest of the narrator's uncles, who is religiously devout, orders her to stay away from those girls no matter what.

The Aleppine world, in Khalifa's telling, was changing. The rug business had slowed down—Persian and Kashmiri rugs were no longer coveted as they once were; and the old families were now coming into partnerships with the intelligence barons and the army officers. Those officers, now regulars in the posh restaurants, had become smugglers of electronics and foreign cigarettes. Sometimes they would feud among themselves over the distribution of the spoils, and gunshots would be heard, and then the presidential palace would intervene and issue its binding commands. Peace would be restored, and the officers would return to the mistresses and the restaurants, marveling at the authority they had acquired. People trembled in their presence. "Thus did the city that was once a twin of Vienna become a desolate place, peopled by frightened ghosts. The sons of the old families had lost their influence and now grieved for the old world. They were forced to become in-laws of the sons of the countryside, joining them at backgammon, overlooking their crude ways."

Intimations of the political loyalties of the narrator's family come early in Khalifa's story. A gathering is held in their home: there is a well-known religious preacher, big merchants and industrialists, a political man who had been a player in the postindependence governments, men known for their membership in the Muslim Brotherhood, an army officer, a Saudi, and a Yemeni in his mid-forties who sits in the middle of this gathering. The Yemeni is there for political reasons, but he is also a suitor of one of the aunts, whom he wants for his second wife, and finally he secures her hand in marriage. The Yemeni is a bottomless source of knowledge about Islamic parties, and about the martyrs who died in prisons or on the battlefield. The young narrator is hooked on his tales. She has real gifts for the sciences and was destined for medical school, but now this ruinous interest in politics and religion tugs at her. The Yemeni had been one of the leaders of the Marxists in Aden, but he had broken with his colleagues, taken to the road, and found a whole new political faith in Islam. This was the calling that had brought him to Bakr, the narrator's devout uncle.

The Yemeni, it turns out, was bringing money to Bakr and his companions in the Muslim Brotherhood. And the narrator herself, this fine young woman, is drawn into the dark web. A girl her age with "cold eyes" is the leader of a cell that takes her in, and speaks to her of the moral corruption that has descended on the women in the city. Meanwhile, in front of the Umayyad Mosque, young men gather and then head out to the forest close to the sea, as though on a picnic, to train in weapons and the martial arts. The narrator's brother is one of these militants. In the textbooks that he passed on to her, she saw his obsessions: sketches of pistols and bombs. She ponders what he has scribbled in the margins: "spying on his dreams." What he dreamed of was the day of retribution for the unbelievers. On the narrator's seventeenth birthday, she thinks aloud to herself: "We need hatred to give meaning to our lives."

Hatred is being drummed into her by the group of militants to which she belongs. One day her brother comes home with his shirt stained with blood. An air force officer with "green eyes," a neighbor, had been killed, and her brother had committed the deed. The *Mukhabarat* search the neighborhood, her family home included. She contemplates her brother, once a silent boy, good at mathematics, now quietly putting his gun away and burning his bloodstained shirt. A wave of assassinations is taking place in the city, and so the commanders of the battalions of death are more careful in their movements. The narrator's hatred momentarily lets go of her, but she is rebuked by the other girls and reminded of the transgressions committed by the officers and their sect, who had turned the country into a big plantation of their own. And so she coldly shakes off the pity that she had felt for the murdered man and his family. Her uncle Bakr had made a fateful choice: he was the leader of a team responsible for assassinating men of the regime. He had "friends and allies in neighboring countries" who understood his cause and wished to return the country to its "normal course" and to punish the infidels and the ruling party who had thrown Syria into the camp of the communist powers.

The horrors multiply. One day a military man who had been a guest of her family performs the morning prayer in the mosque, reads from the Quran, quietly selects seventeen cadets in the military academy, lines them up against a wall, and executes them. (The cadets are obviously Alawis.) He slips away with his partners into the outskirts of Aleppo, where he is given a heroic welcome for bringing grief to the "other sect." "No one knows why these men who had come down from the mountains so full of ambition and drive had died." Sixty armed men, soldiers and men of the *Mukhabarat*, storm the house, looking for Bakr and for the narrator's brother. They break the locks and shatter pictures and souvenirs. A blind servant rebukes the soldiers, reminding them of the standing of the deceased merchant, telling them that this house is inhabited by women. "He is pushed aside," our young narrator relates, "by a soldier who curses my grandfather and his ancestors, says that this is a house of whores now. I nearly wished that Bakr had remained a rug merchant, outdoing other families with his wealth, making a life out of the trivialities of daily happenings." But this was a passing thought: after all, there was the war with the "other sect" and the ruling party. She dreamed of punishing the unveiled girls of Aleppo without mercy, making them pay for their liberties. Righteous men were going willingly to the gallows of the *Mukhabarat*, and "we envied them because they were getting to paradise before us."

Death stalks the city. Aleppo becomes a city of lamentations and funerals, a place under siege. Forty thousand soldiers enforced a dusk-to-dawn curfew. When Aleppo's troubles reach the presidential palace in the capital, the president of the republic appears on television, summoning his party and his military units into the fight. And Hama, at some remove, "*al-madina al-saghira*, the small city, [becomes] a war zone, its people dreaming of the restoration to leadership of our sect." This is 1982, and "the Hamawis [are] counting their dead." Hajja Souad, a militant old woman who had recruited the narrator into the cause, is terrified by the news from Hama. The battle seems to be nearing its end, as some families flee into the countryside and corpses are dumped in the streets, with no one claiming them. Then the call comes for a final showdown, and the rebels in Hama bring out weapons that had been hidden in the wells of their homes. The narrow streets are soon surrounded by tanks that—in Khalifa's unforgettable image—block the flight of birds. "It was left to future generations to tell that all this was madness that could have been avoided so as to give life to children who loved to jump into the Orontes river from waterwheels whose sound was the one true expression of yearning for the past. The bereaved mothers would don black garments that they swore they would never take off. Many mothers went out into the streets, half-naked, lamenting the city in poetry that would make the stones weep."

Khadija, one militant in this cell, telling the Hama story in Aleppo, swears that she is done with the narrator's group of radicals. She packs up her things in a bundle and disappears like a "piece of salt dumped into a parched river." Bakr also abandons the cause: he flees to Jordan on a fake passport and from there to London. He arrives at night to its fog and walks slowly along the banks of the Thames, "a man determined not to look back lest he remember the hundreds of young boys who swore on the Koran and went out in search of a road to paradise and to a certain death." He writes home from the safety of his distance; and to assuage his guilt, he accuses the leaders of the Brotherhood of leaving Hama to its fate.

But back in Aleppo the madness descends further upon the miserable city. A young militant named Samir is caught in a shoot-out with security officers, and when he runs out of ammunition he jumps in despair into the oven of the neighborhood bakery. The soldiers are stunned, and keep firing at the burned corpse. The baker, who cannot believe what he has seen, abandons the city for his village. It was the narrator's brother Hussam, a year older, who had changed Samir from a boy who loved to flirt with the girls into a fierce fighter, and Samir's mother now vows eternal hatred—more hatred!—for the narrator's family and for the battalions of death. Banned from leaving her home, Samir's mother would open the windows every morning and curse all the protagonists of the tragedy, until her sudden death from a heart attack.

Death, now all around, mocks all the taboos. The security forces no longer bother to deliver the dead to their families: they just cast the corpses aside or bury them in shallow graves. "Death re-covered its real attributes, a sudden absence, a complete harmony with the elements of nature. The living were too busy staying alive, they had no time to mourn and praise the dead in a city known for its excessive respect for the dead." One day, the *azan*, the call to morning prayer, was not made. Soldiers stormed the neighborhood homes, "spat in the faces of the men, made them kneel for several hours, no one dared move or object. Most of the city residents began to say that this battle was no affair of theirs. After noon prayers, the battalions of death left the neighborhood, to everyone's relief." A soldier distributes free of charge the local paper, the front page of which shows pictures of twelve swollen faces, a charred corpse, and soldiers flashing victory signs and dancing around the corpses and the weapons.

An Al-Azhar University–educated cleric named Shaykh Jamil now makes his appearance in this minefield. His father had been a revered man of the guild, ascetic and disinterested in worldly belongings, and all of Aleppo bade him farewell when he died. But the son was different: he pined for wealth and power. He had spent some years in Saudi Arabia, where he had gone to make his fortune. He had written a book on the Wahhabis, defending them against their detractors, and made a gift of it to the Saudi monarch, stressing the need for obedience to the monarch and praising the services the royal family had rendered to the two holy mosques of Mecca and Medina. Shaykh Jamil waited and waited for a royal audience, but he was instead given a sum of $10,000, well below his expectations. Finally he wearied of waiting for crumbs in the courts of princes and went back to Aleppo.

The men of the *Mukhabarat* took to him, this man of the clergy who was willing to do their bidding, who would issue fatwas exonerating the men of the regime of whatever deeds they committed. It did not take Shaykh Jamil long to see the hopelessness of his situation: the Brothers now regarded him as a traitor to the faith. He did his best to mediate between the two sides, quoting scripture, the tradition of the Prophet, and historical precedent, but it was all to no avail: the *Mukhabarat* had a thick file on him, six hundred pages long, and his sons were notoriously corrupted by power. The Brothers were in need of a victory, and Shaykh Jamil was their target. Four masked men entered his home one morning as he was readying himself for prayer. They slit his throat and left him by the corner where he took his evening coffee. The narrator is fixed on the shaykh's story—the son of a pious scholar becoming "a turbaned man of the regime who justified the domination of the other sect and the repression of our own." (This part of Khalifa's fictional story became reality in October, when the son of the mufti of the republic, Shaykh Ahmad Badr al-Deen Hassoun, was killed. His father, an Aleppine, is a man of unwavering commitment to the regime.)

III.

But one night the Aleppines catch a break. It is the beginning of summer, and a lunar eclipse gives the city a chance to release itself from all that had befallen it. People went to the roofs of their houses to see the eclipse, beating their tambourines, beseeching Allah for mercy. They readied themselves to practice rituals that had been lost in the expansion of their city, as it took in "hundreds of thousands of villagers in search of an appropriate place in a city once beloved by travelers and savored by consuls who never forgot its uniqueness." The moon began its eclipse, turned crimson red and bewitching. The battalions of death had never seen this before. Chants of *"Allah-hu Akbar"* filled the city, and both the Aleppines and the battalions of death accepted this respite.

All this may sound fantastic, but Khalifa has no need of magical realism. He invents no extravagant flights of fancy. His novel is a faithful reconstruction of his tormented city. His literary recovery of the Aleppine torments is uncannily accurate. For example: an assassination attempt was made on the life of Hafez al-Assad. The battalions of death readied themselves for revenge. The president of the republic had not been harmed, because a devoted bodyguard had thrown himself over the bomb and saved the tyrant. Nazir, the Alawi officer who had married into "the other sect," was summoned before the commander of the battalions—an obvious fictional surrogate for Rifaat al-Assad, the ruler's notorious younger brother. Known for his love of pleasure and a temperament that made his extreme cruelty seem like the most natural of things, he coldly said: "Tonight we shall attack the desert prison, don't let the sun rise on any of them." A decision was made to storm the Palmyra prison and murder the political prisoners, "attack them like dogs in a closed ring, swat them like flies." In less than an hour, Nazir thought, the planes will be on their way toward the desert, heavily armed soldiers heading there "as though they were hunting for wild ducks, or chasing deer in the desert."

Nazir made a decision and approached a colonel who was a distant relative of his. He informed the colonel that he could not take part in this mission, and he removed his officer's insignia and announced that he was ready to be tried before a military court or to attack any Israeli position. As he walked away, he watched the soldiers lift their fists in the air, proclaiming their loyalty to the commander of the battalions, and ascend the ten planes lined up on the tarmac. On the Aleppo road, in a taxi with three passengers, Nazir thought of the impending horror in the desert.

The land awoke on that hot summer day to rumors, spread like lightning, about the soldiers descending from the planes, entering the desert prison, and opening fire on the prisoners whose "brains were scattered to the ceilings, whose bodies were piled up in the corridors, like sacks of rotten oranges thrown haphazardly aboard a ship crossing the ocean in total boredom." Black flags were raised over the balconies of countless homes: more than eight hundred prisoners had been killed in less than an hour. Bulldozers carried the corpses and dumped them in a pit. "Whoever entered Hama or Aleppo that day," Khalifa writes, "thought that a festival of grief had begun in the early evening hours, to be followed by a carnival reminiscent of the rituals of sorrow for Imam Hussein, which had stirred the imagination of artists and Orientalists and strangers who had passed by Karbala." The narrator's mother is overcome with grief, because her son Hussam was in that desert prison. She sits in the courtyard, with a picture of Hussam, ululating and dancing like a woman possessed.

The character of Nazir is Khalifa's instrument for a memorable portrait of Rifaat al-Assad. Nazir is summoned before the commander of the battalions, who had been his friend and his classmate. "Why did you betray me?" asks the commander. He strains for an answer that would not offend. "Sir, I did not betray you. I only wanted to remind ourselves of a military code of honor that would not permit us to attack unarmed prisoners." A pause follows, before the commander, looking directly at him, says: "Didn't you think they are criminals who want to wipe out our sect?" It was all about the sect, always. Nazir remembers a time when the two of them were young boys, on their way to school, together sheltering from the winter rain under a plastic tarp. A sudden burst of courage comes to him, and he addresses the commander by his first name, without the burden of titles or protocol: "Why do you wish to destroy our sect, and weigh it down with crimes it did not commit? Do what you wish, but leave the sect alone. You will smuggle your wealth abroad, leaving the poor to pay the price of all this." The commander calmly fiddles with his pistol, then brings the meeting to an end. Nazir had been spared. The commander was reined in by his desire to avoid a split in the ranks of the sect— an outcome he wanted to avoid as he plotted to remove his older brother from power and take his place. Nazir is relieved of his duties and returns to his village, to the farming life and the companionship of his wife.

The legend of the commander of the death battalions would grow: a powerful and mighty man who loved life, and gave his battalions license to do what they wished. He plundered at will and stashed his wealth in European and American banks. He was like a pampered boy who is granted his every wish "lest he ruin the evening for everyone." News spread of his sexual scandals, of his men kidnapping comely young women off the streets and carrying them off to the swanky quarters of Damascus and then casting them away in the wretched streets. He cut in on the business of rich merchants, and one of his partners fell to his death from the seventh floor onto the cold pavement. "The next day there was a funeral for the deceased, a wreath of flowers in the name of the commander was paraded at the head of the funeral procession. The commander offered his condolences to the merchant's sons. They thanked him, and sought no justice for the blood of their father. They attributed his death to a loss of balance, something that would befall any man who had stood on his terrace, on the seventh floor, waiting for the moon to appear." The commander's wealth grew as a reward for his deeds—the killings of the Brotherhood, the murder in cold blood of prisoners, "the destruction of a city that loved cotton candy and sweets more than it loved death."

It is Nazir, in the simplicity and the clarity of his village life, who advises the narrator to give up on the *Gamaa*, her Islamist group, and turn her back on all this, and focus on her studies in medical school. But it is too late. She returns home one evening to find the *Mukhabarat* waiting for her. They handcuff her as her family looks on. She is carried off to prison.

Khalifa's prison pages are brilliant. Syria's prisons came with independence and its corruption, as the heroes of yesteryear were sent to perish in them. The two prisons—one in the desert in Palmyra and the other in Mezze on the outskirts of Damascus—begat their own distinct and horrific narratives. A rival of Hafez al-Assad, a fellow Alawi coup-maker, went to prison in 1970 and died there in 1993. A head of state, who was in actuality a Sunni frontman for Assad, was to spend twenty years in prison, until 1992, when he was released on a stretcher and permitted passage to Paris, where he died a few weeks later of cancer. Syrian prison memoirs are plentiful, but Khalifa's pages are unusually valuable and strong because they describe the women's prisons.

A baby is born in the prison to Suheir, a beautiful and defiant woman who is proud to be the widow of a martyr to the cause, and the child becomes beloved by all the prisoners. In the prison there are Marxist women, who are granted family visits once a month, and women from the *Gamaa*, who are granted this privilege every three months. There are old whores, and they fare best. The guards are extortionists and blackmailers; the wardens are perverts, spying on the women. Tuhama, a prisoner from Hama, is hanged in the courtyard. She is a mute, but the authorities believed that she was faking it: they charged her with blowing up an armored car in the streets of Hama and then feigning the disability to escape punishment. Umm Mamdouh, an older prisoner, herself from Hama, tells Tuhama's story: her three brothers had been killed, and she went out in search of "two meters of earth" where she could bury them. "Gunfire surrounded her from every direction. She made her way through it unaware, dragging her brothers one at a time, as though she were in an ancient Greek drama. She buried all three of them on the banks of the Orontes, and prayed over them, only to discover when she tried to recite the *al-fatiha* [the opening chapter in the Koran] that she had lost the capacity of speech after two nights with the bodies. She didn't care that she could not speak. Above her the helicopters circled the city, paratroopers falling from the sky like heavy rain."

Our narrator spends seven years in prison. As her twenty-sixth birthday approaches, she is about to be released into the world she had left as though she had gone out for a "bundle of parsley." A jailer who had praised the murders in the desert prisons sees her off. The jailer himself was seriously ill. He speaks to her of the "benevolence of the merciful leader," hoping that the years in prison will now lead her to the straight path. He tries to convince her that the *Gamaa* were criminals and that he and his colleagues are patriots who were trying to defend the country. She did not utter a word. "He stood up and gave me my release papers. He stretched out his hand, I stretched out mine to pass onto him the poison of my hatred. I shook the hand of an enemy, looked into his eyes, and saw his imminent death."

It was a nightmare, her return to her old world. The commander of the death battalions had left the country, emptying the state treasury and departing with it. (Rifaat al-Assad now makes his home in Marbella. He surfaced of late, to preach the gospel of democracy and to offer himself as an alternative to his nephew. Not much really happened in Hama in 1982, he now says. It was just a small quarrel between the regime and the Brotherhood.) The narrator now practices medicine and works in the city morgue. The house with the courtyard, in the Old City, has fallen on hard times. The Old City has been abandoned by the well-off for new neighborhoods. A different breed has moved in, people who keep goats and sheep in rooms with high ceilings. It was time for her, too, to go. She is done with Aleppo. She has no world of her own. The *Gamaa* women cannot accept her refusal to don the veil, and the young men and women of the regime look on her as an enemy. Like her devout uncle Bakr before, she leaves for London, far from the city of sorrow.

* * *

Aleppo's luck was not destined to last, it turned out. The prudent city may have wanted to sit out the rebellion, but it was the country's economic powerhouse, and it had an impoverished countryside. All along, the rebels were convinced that they could break the regime were they to come into control of Aleppo. Sixteen months into this dreadful war, the peace of Aleppo was shattered. There was no place for neutrality amid the bloodletting. The practicality of the souk and the merchants could not withstand the fury of this war. The boys of *Rif Halab* (rural Aleppo) struck into the city in late July 2012, and the regime was not far behind. The rebels had been right: the dictatorship would not let go of Aleppo. An enterprising reporter for Reuters,

Erika Solomon, had made her way to Aleppo, and her dispatches of late July, early August, catch the truth of what befell the city. An unnamed rebel commander, from a nearby village, described the fight to Solomon in stark terms: "We liberated the rural parts of the province. We waited and waited for Aleppo to rise, and it didn't. We couldn't rely on them to do it for themselves so we had to bring the revolution to them. About 80 percent of the fighters in this city came from the countryside. Aleppo is a business town, people wanted to stay neutral. But now that we have come, they seem to be accepting us."

This rebel had been optimistic, and this was still the month of July. The full fury of the regime had not yet been unleashed on Aleppo. The helicopter gunships and the fighter jets were still to come. Bashar al-Assad and his killers had not bothered to conceal the brutal logic of this war. It was there scribbled on the armored cars and tanks of the regime: Al-Assad or the burning of the country. The merchants of Aleppo who had made their grudging peace with Bashar would not be spared. In late September fire swept through Aleppo's old souk, and somewhere between 700 and 1,000 shops were consumed in the blaze. This struggle was indifferent to beauty and history. UNESCO had designated Aleppo, with its medieval market of vaulted stone alleyways, and the accretion of history's artifacts and culture, a World Heritage site, but Aleppo knew no reprieve now. What indulgence had been given the rebellion had vanished. Hunger and privation came to Aleppo, and the ethnic sectarian fissures of the place made their appearance. The Kurds threw in their lot with the regime, as did most of the Christians. The Armenians—ever alert to persecution—thought it best to take up arms in defense of their neighborhoods. The regime had always insisted that it was a shield against chaos, and that claim was finding a measure of vindication. This was trench warfare with no conclusion, no victory over the horizon. In the early months of the rebellion, there had been idle hopes, fed by religious passion, that all would be settled during the holy month of Ramadan, in August of 2011. But the regime held on and defied the odds. Ramadan came and went, and then another Ramadan. In the scripture and belief of Islam, there is a Night of Destiny in Ramadan that falls on the twenty-seventh night of that holy month. The Quran exalts that night. "Better is the Night of Destiny than 1,000 months. On that night the angels and the spirits by their Lord's leave come down with his decrees." The foreign powers had deserted the Syrians, and God's mercy had not made its appearance.

It is mid-October, and so much of Aleppo had been reduced to rubble. The Aleppines and the countryside folks with guns were beyond claims of camaraderie. Hamza Hendawi, a reporter for the Associated Press, recorded a rebel commander's sentiments about the Aleppines. "They have been breast-fed cowardice and their hearts are filled with fear. With their money, we could buy weapons that could enable us to liberate the city in a week."

In an earlier war, Picasso memorialized the Basque town of Guernica for the air raids it endured. Guernica was a forgotten town of some 7,000, while Aleppo is a large metropolis of well over three million people. German and Italian pilots had done the raids over Guernica, but it was Syrians who were laying to waste this most ancient and heralded of cities. Vengeance was vowed. An Internet posting circulated by the Free Syrian Army on August 9 listed the names, ranks, and cell phone numbers of eleven pilots who took part in the air raids. There would be no forgiveness here. But no Syrian Picasso stepped forth to do justice to Aleppo. And in our decidedly unromantic time, no Lincoln Brigade of passionate men and women rushed to the defense of the Syrian rebellion. True, some Sunni Islamists, Libyans, and others made their way to Syria. But the Syrians were fighting alone. They were invoking Allah more often than they did at the beginning of their struggle—a fair and accurate reading of their solitude in the world of nations. We shall never know what that protester on the outskirts of Damascus, who taunted Aleppo about its quiescence, a good long year earlier, now thought of the Aleppines amid their grief and ruin.

SOURCE NOTES:

For further reading on the Arab revolt, see T. E. Lawrence's classic, *Seven Pillars of Wisdom*, 1922.

Another traveler to the East, Robin Fedden wrote of his insights into the Arab world of the time in his book *Syria: An Historical Appreciation* (Robert Hale Limited, 1946).

Khalifa Khaled wrote a rich and heartbreaking novel, *Madih al-Karahiya* (In Praise of Hatred) (Beirut: Dar al adab, 2008).

Part II

Chapter 3

The Sorrows of Egypt

A TALE OF TWO MEN

A generation after that day of October 6, 1981, when Anwar el-Sadat was struck down, a strange bond has been forged between Sadat and his assassin, Khalid Istanbuli. A place has been made in the country's narrative for both men. The history of Egypt, her very identity, is fluid enough to claim the wily ruler who swallowed his pride to deal with Israel and the United States, and also the assassin appalled by the cultural price paid in the bargain. In a sense, Sadat and Istanbuli are twins, their lives and deeds one great tale of the country's enduring dilemmas and her resilience amid great troubles, about the kind of political men Egypt's history brought forth when her revolutionary experiment of the 1950s and 1960s ran aground.

It is not hard for Egyptians to recognize much of themselves and their recent history in Istanbuli, the young lieutenant who

This essay originally appeared in *Foreign Affairs*, Vol. 74, No. 5, September/October 1995, and is republished here in slightly different form with the cooperation and consent of the original publisher.

proclaimed with pride that he had shot the pharaoh. He was in every way a son of the Free Officers Revolution of Gamal Abdel Nasser, on July 23, 1952, when Egypt cast aside her kings and set out on a new, nonaligned path. Istanbuli was born in 1957, a year after the Suez crisis, during what seemed to be a moment of promise in the life of Egypt. He was named after Nasser's oldest son. His father was a lawyer in a public-sector company that was a product of the new, expanding government. He was ten years old when calamity struck Egypt in the Six Day War, and the Nasser revolution was shown to be full of sound and fury and illusion. The country had been through a whirlwind, and Istanbuli's life mirrored the gains and the setbacks.

He had not been particularly religious; he had attended a Christian missionary school in his town in Middle Egypt. Political Islam entered his life late in the hour, not so long before he was to commit his dramatic deed of tyrannicide. An older brother of his, a religious activist, had been picked up in a massive wave of arrests that Sadat ordered in September 1981. All sorts of political men and women had been hauled off to prison: noted men and women of the elite, from the law, journalism, the universities, former ministers, Muslims and Copts alike. The wave of arrests had been a desperate throw of the dice by Sadat, and it had backfired. It broke the moral contract between Sadat and his country. In taking revenge, Istanbuli did what normal society could not do for itself. "Khalid," an admiring author wrote in tribute to the assassin, "I spoke and you did, I wished, and others wished, and you fulfilled our wishes."

But Sadat, too, has a place, and an increasingly special one, in the country's memory. Sadat, it is true, had died a loner's death. Presumably victorious in October 1973 in the war against Israel, he was yet judged a lesser figure than his predecessor, who was defeated in 1967. But a certain measure of vindication has come Sadat's way: he had broken with Arab radicalism, and the years were to show that Arab radicalism's harvest had been ruin and bankruptcy. He had opted for peace with Israel; the Palestinians and other Arabs, so many of them shouting treason and betrayal, had followed in his footsteps. The crafty ruler, to his fingertips a wily man of the countryside with a peasant's instinctive shrewdness and wisdom, was able to see before it was evident to others that the Soviet Union was no match for American power.

It has not been lost on his people that Sadat had foreseen American primacy and had placed his bets on American power, making the sort of accommodation with America that his proud predecessor would have never been able to pull off. And then there is, of course, the gift he bequeathed his country: the liberation of the land that his legendary predecessor had lost in 1967. Indeed, ten days after Istanbuli was put to death with four of his fellow conspirators on April 15, 1982, Israel returned the Sinai Peninsula to Egyptian sovereignty.

This tension in the psyche and politics of Egypt will persist between Sadat's world, with its temptations and its window on modernity, and Istanbuli's world, with its rigors and its furious determination to keep the West at bay. A fissure has opened, right in the heart of Egypt's traditionally stoic and reliable middle class. A wing of this class has defected to theocratic politics. The rest are disaffected and demoralized. There is no resolution in sight for this dilemma.

But we misconstrue Egypt's reality and the nature of its malady if we see it as another Islamic domino destined to fall, if we lean too hard on the fight between the regime and the Islamist challengers. For all the prophecies of doom and the obituaries written of the Egyptian state, the custodians of political power have ridden out many storms. This is a country with a remarkable record of political stability. Only two regimes have governed modern Egypt over the past two centuries: the dynasty of the Albanian-born Muhammad Ali, the soldier of fortune, who emerged in the aftermath of the chaos unleashed by Napoleon Bonaparte's invasion of the country in 1798, and the Free Officers regime of Nasser and Sadat and their inheritors. The sorrow of Egypt is made of entirely different material: the steady decline of its public life, the inability of an autocratic regime and of the middle class from which this regime issues to rid the country of its dependence on foreign handouts, to transmit to the vast underclass the skills needed for the economic competition of nations, and to take the country beyond its endless alternation between false glory and self-pity.

THE THEOCRATIC CHALLENGE

We must not exaggerate the strength of the theocratic challenge or the magnitude of the defection of the middle class. In our fixation on Iran's revolution—the armed imam chasing Caesar out of power—we have looked for it everywhere and grafted its themes and outcomes onto societies possessed of vastly different traditions and temperaments.

There never was a chance that Shaykh Omar Abdel Rahman, the blind Egyptian preaching fire and brimstone in Brooklyn, would return to his land, Khomeini-like, to banish the secular powers and inherit the realm. Even the men who gunned down Sadat were under no illusions about their own power in the face of the state. No fools, these men knew the weight of the state, the strength of all they were hurling themselves against. They sought only the punishment of "the tyrant," sparing the lives of his lieutenants (Hosni Mubarak included), who stood inches away on the reviewing stand. Sadat's inheritors, the assassins hoped, would be humbled by what they had seen; they would refrain from playing with fire and from the kinds of violations Sadat (and his wife, Jehan) had committed against the mores of the land.

Nor should we project Algeria's descent into hell onto Egypt. Look at Algeria with its terror and counterterror: armed Islamic groups campaigning against all perceived Francophiles, secularists, and emancipated women; reprisals by the state and its "eradicationists" who pass off their violence as the defense of modernity itself, state-sponsored killer squads, the ninjas with their ski masks. This politics of zeal and cruelty so reminiscent of Argentina and Chile in the 1970s is alien to the temperament of Egypt. The chasm between the Francophiles and the Arab-Islamists at the root of the terror in Algeria has no parallel in the experience and the life of Egypt. There is plenty of contempt for the government in Egypt today, but the political and cultural continuity of the place has not ruptured. No great windfall was squandered by the Egyptian elite the way the nomenklatura in Algeria blew the oil revenue of the past three decades. Most important, unlike the shallow roots of the Algerian state—a postcolonial entity that rose in the 1960s—central authority in Egypt reaches back millennia.

The recent troubles began in 1992 when a small war broke out between the state and the *Gamaat Islamiyya*, the Islamic groups, as the loosely organized underground of the forces of political Islam call themselves. The armed bands treated the country to a season of wrath and troubles. But the state fought back; it showed little mercy toward the insurgents. It pushed their challenge to remote, marginal parts of the country, in provincial towns in Middle and Upper Egypt, the country's poorest areas. There, beyond the modernity of Cairo and Alexandria, away from the glare of publicity, the running war between the police and the Islamists degenerated into the timeless politics of vengeance and vendettas, an endless cycle of killings and reprisals. The campaign of terror against foreign tourists, the targeting of men of letters, the killing in the summer of 1992 of Farag Foda, a brave secularist commentator, the attempt on the life of the venerated and aging Naguib Mahfouz two years later—all played into the hands of the state. Men of the regime were also targeted by the insurgents. In 1993 there were three separate attempts, over the space of six months, on the lives of the minister of information, the minister of the interior, and the prime minister.

Thus faced with a relentless campaign of subversion, the regime responded by showing no mercy. The state apparatus was given a green light to root out armed Islamic groups and to do it without the kinds of protections and restraints a society of laws honors and expects. The governors and police officers dispatched to Middle and Upper Egypt, the hotbeds of religious strife, have invariably been men known for their willingness to use force. Massive searches and arrests have been routine there, as they have been when deemed necessary in the poorer and more radicalized parts of Cairo. The military tribunals were swift. Nearly 70 death sentences were decreed and carried out.

Tough police work was one side of the response to the terror of the Islamists; the other was a discernible retreat on the part of the regime from secular politics and culture. Historically the agent of social change, the one great instrument for transforming this old land and pushing it along, the state now seems to have slipped into a cynical bargain with some devoted enemies of the secular idea. It granted these preachers and activists cultural space as long as the more strictly political domain (the police power of the regime, its hegemony over defense and foreign affairs) was left to it.

The custodians of the state drew a line between the legitimate and moderate Islamic groups and the armed Islamists. While the regime hunted down the latter, it made its peace with the former. A regime anxious for religious credentials of its own and for religious cover bent with the wind. Preachers and religious activists drawn from the ranks of the old Muslim Brotherhood, an organization now sanitized and made respectable in comparison with the younger, more uncompromising members of the *Gamaat,* were given access to the airwaves and the print media and became icons of popular culture. They dabbled in incendiary material, these respectable sorts, careful to stay on the proper side of the line. They advocated an Islamic state but said they would seek it through legitimate means. They branded as heretics and apostates noted secular figures in politics and culture. (One such influential preacher, Shaykh Muhammad Ghazali, a figure of the original Muslim Brotherhood and its clone, so branded all believers in Western law.) They hounded the Copts and made no secret of their view that the best the Copts, a community of no less than six million people, could hope for in a would-be Islamic state was the protected but diminished status of a subordinate community. To all this the state turned a blind eye.

The country's leading center of Islamic learning and jurisprudence, Al-Azhar University, has been given greater leeway and authority than it has possessed at any time this century.

Where Al-Azhar had been on the defensive during the Nasser years as an institution that had to be modernized and reformed, it now speaks with self-confidence on the social and cultural issues of the day. A wide swath of the country's cultural life is now open to the authorities of Al-Azhar. The theological alternative has seeped into the educational curriculum. Until the state caught on a year or two ago and set out to reclaim some of this lost ground, whole schools had been ceded to the Islamists. There the advocates of political Islam, their apparent zeal and devotion a marked contrast to the abdication all around, had gone to work, weaning the young from the dominant symbols and outlook of the secular political order. In schools captured by the Islamists the national anthem and the Egyptian flag were banned for they were, to the religious radicals, the symbols of an un-Islamic state. "Political Islam had been checked in its bid for power," the shrewd analyst and observer Tahseen Bashir said, "but the Islamization of society has gained ground."

It did not come on the cheap, this victory of the state over the political Islamists. The country feels trapped, cheated, and shortchanged in the battle between an inept, authoritarian state and a theocratic fringe. The tough response of the state did its work, but important segments of the population in the intellectual, political, and business classes drew back in horror at the tactics. Some of the very men and women sheltered by the regime against the fury of the Islamists were taken aback by the number of executions ordered and the speed with which they were carried out. "Mubarak orders the executions but loses no sleep over them," a prominent figure of the opposition said to me. It has come down to this, because the regime has little else in its bag. It is no consolation to Egyptians that they have been spared the terror visited on less fortunate places like Syria or

Iraq or the Sudan. This is a country where lawyers and the rule of law had an early footing, a society with a rich syndicalist tradition and associational life and an independent judiciary with pride in its legacy. The terror had given Mubarak a splendid alibi and an escape from the demands put forth by segments of the middle class and its organizations in the professional syndicates—the lawyers, the engineers, and the journalists—for a measure of political participation. Mubarak had done the order's work; it had become easy for him to wave off the tangled issues of economic and political reform.

ET IN ARCADIA EGO

At the heart of Egyptian life there lies a terrible sense of disappointment. The pride of modern Egypt has been far greater than its accomplishments. The dismal results are all around: the poverty of the underclass, the bleak political landscape that allows an ordinary officer to monopolize political power and diminish all would-be rivals in civil society, the sinking of the country into sectarian strife between Muslim and Copt, the dreary state of its cultural and educational life.

A country of sixty million people, the weekly magazine *Al Mussawar* recently revealed, now produces a mere 375 books a year. Contrast this with Israel's four thousand titles, as the magazine did, and it is easy to understand the laments heard all around. *Al Ahram*, the country's leading daily—launched in 1876 and possessed of a distinguished history—is unreadable. There is no trace of investigative journalism or thoughtful analysis on its pages, only the banal utterances of political power. No less a figure than the great novelist Naguib Mahfouz, a product of the ancien régime (he was born in 1911), has spoken with sorrow and resignation about this state of affairs. "Egypt's culture is declining fast," he wrote. "The state of education in our country is in crisis. Classrooms are more like warehouses to cram children in for a few hours than places of education. The arts and literature are barely taught in these institutions, which are run more like army barracks than places where cultural awareness and appreciation can be nurtured." In more apocalyptic terms, the commentator Karim Alrawi warned that the modernizing imperative that has dominated and driven Egypt since the early 1800s after its encounter with Europe is being reversed.

It is out of this disappointment that a powerful wave of nostalgia has emerged for the liberal interlude in Egyptian politics (the 1920s through the revolution of 1952), for its vibrant political life, for the lively press of the time, for the elite culture with its literati and artists, for its outspoken, emancipated women who had carved a place for themselves in the country's politics, culture, and journalism. Some of this is the standard nostalgia of a crowded, burdened society for a time of lost innocence and splendor; some, though, is the legitimate expression of discontent over the mediocrity of public life. Egypt produced better, freer cinema in the 1930s than it does today. Its leading intellectual figures were giants who slugged out the great issues of the day and gave Egyptian and Arabic letters a moment of undisputed brilliance. When the critic and writer Louis Awad, a Copt, a prolific and independent man of letters born in 1915, died in 1990, an age seemed to come to a close. The Egypt of the military has produced no peers for Awad and Mahfouz and their likes.

Curiosity about this bourgeois past and its contemporary relevance led me to the home of Fouad Pasha Serageddin, a nearly legendary figure of that era, born in 1908, a man of the ancien régime, who was the boy wonder of his time, rising to become a minister at age thirty-two. On the eve of the Free Officers revolt, he was the ancien régime's largest landholder: he was secretary-general of the Wafd Party, the repository of bourgeois Egyptian nationalism from 1919 until the military revolt of 1952. The Free Officers regime had imprisoned and then exiled him; he had returned in the 1970s when Sadat opened up the life of the country; in no time his political party under its revered old name, the Wafd, became a force to reckon with. It was in many ways a natural home for the professionals and the Copts and the men and women of private industry and commerce. Sadat had derided the Pasha, had called him Louis XVI, but the figure from the prerevolutionary past made a place for himself in the new political order.

The Pasha—the country knows him by no other name—lives in a palace in Garden City, one of Cairo's neighborhoods that still has patches of what the city was in more quaint and less crowded times a half-century ago: villas once grand but now shabby and covered with dust, homes with gardens where the great bourgeois families once lived secure in their sense of place and order. The Pasha's palace, built by his father in 1929, speaks of bygone splendor. Dark and decaying inside, with the thread-bare furniture of the era, it has the grand entrance and the marble columns of its time. The staff and servants, too, old and bent by the years, must have been with the Pasha's household since better times.

A scent of old Egypt, the Egypt of the Grand Tour, the country celebrated by Lawrence Durrell in his book *The Alexandria Quartet*, blows in with the Pasha when he enters the reception room. He has spanned decades and worlds of Egypt's contemporary history. Nostalgia and a scathing judgment of the military regime drive the Pasha's vision. He ridicules the government-controlled press; he now reads *Al Ahram*, he says, for the obituaries of his old friends; there is nothing else to read in the subservient press. He has a jaundiced view of the American role in Egypt. The Americans, he believes, feel quite comfortable with authoritarianism. The American fear of a fundamentalist takeover, he observes, plays into the hands of Mubarak's regime.

The Pasha's world, the world of his Wafd Party, has deep roots in this conservative land. But after a moment of genuine enthusiasm, the Wafd lost much of its lure. A bargain it made to contest the parliamentary elections in 1984 in alliance with the Muslim Brotherhood seemed like a betrayal of the party's secular heritage. The Pasha's age was another handicap. The memories his presence evoked were increasingly his alone. He reintroduced into the political world a measure of courage in the face of the state and launched a daily paper infinitely better than the official organs of the regime, but Egypt's troubles seemed beyond his scope. Sixteen million people have been added to the population since Mubarak came to power in 1981. This increase alone is more than the combined total populations of Jordan, Israel, Lebanon, and the Palestinians of the West Bank and Gaza. The facts of Egypt's poverty and need are so well known that one hardly need state them. One set of figures reveals the trouble: four hundred thousand people enter the job market every year; seventy-five percent of the new entrants are unemployed; ninety percent of these people have intermediate or higher education diplomas. That is why some of Mubarak's critics concede the burden the regime has to carry. The task of keeping the place afloat and intact is like plowing the sea. This crowded land has gone beyond that pleasant bourgeois age and its houses with gardens.

THE PAST IS ANOTHER COUNTRY

In one of the country's best recent works of fiction, *War in the Land of Egypt*, Yusuf al-Qa'id, a novelist of the younger generation, expresses the sense of siege and failure among his contemporaries:

> Every generation has a particular fate, and our fate, we the sons of Egypt, is that our ambitions were greater than our possibilities. We stepped forward but we found no ground underneath us; we lifted our heads to touch the clouds and the sky disappeared from above us. And at the very moment we divined the truth of our time our leader [Nasser] deserted us with his death right when we needed him. Let us look carefully at our land and our country. It is a strange place, at once dangerous and safe, hard and accommodating, harmonious and full of envy, satiated and hungry. The age of wars has ended; in Egypt today it is the age of words, and because words feed off one another the land of Egypt will only know the reign of words.

This is a jaded country that has known many false starts and faded dawns. Modern Egyptian history telescopes easily: from the time Napoleon Bonaparte's armada turned up off the coast of Alexandria in the summer of 1798, Egypt's history has in the main been its Sisyphean quest for modernity and national power. The ease with which the modern artillery of the French shredded the Mamluk soldiers who had conquered and possessed Egypt was the great dividing line in Egypt's history and the great spur of its political class. A quintessential romantic who knew texts and understood the power of memory,

Bonaparte evoked Egypt's former splendor and greatness: "The first town we shall come to was built by Alexander. At every step we shall meet with grand recollections worthy of exciting the emulation of Frenchmen," he told his soldiers. From Cairo, in a later dispatch, the great conqueror noted a paradox: "Egypt is richer than any country in the world in corn, rice, vegetables, and cattle. But the people are in a state of utter backwardness."

The paradox the outsider saw may have been the self-serving justification of a commander who had happened onto a foreign adventure that had gone badly for him and was seeking a way out. But it would be fair to say that this paradox has engaged Egyptians over the past two centuries. Egypt has thrashed about in every direction, flirted with ideologies of all kinds—liberal ways, Marxism, fascist movements, Islamic utopias—but the urge for national progress, and the grief at being so near and yet so far, have defined the Egyptian experience in the modern world.

Dreams of national power and deliverance have visited Egypt no less than four times in its recent history, and they all ended in frustration. Muhammad Ali (who ruled 1805–1848) made a bid of his own, a classic case of revolution from above, but he overreached and ran afoul of his nominal Ottoman masters and of Pax Britannica; his attempt to build a powerful state and a national manufacturing base came to naught. His descendant, the vainglorious Ismail Pasha (who ruled 1863–1879) gave it another try when cotton was king and a windfall came Egypt's way. Ismail built boulevards, railways, and an opera house; he declared on one occasion, "My country is now in Europe; it is no longer in Africa." But Ismail's dream ended in bankruptcy and ruin and led to the British conquest of Egypt in 1882.

The liberals of the 1920s and 1930s had their moment and flirted with a native capitalist path and parliamentary politics of sorts. But theirs was a fragile liberalism, prone to corruption, outflanked by collectivist ideologies (it was here in this period, in 1928, that the Muslim Brotherhood was formed), a liberalism in the shadow of an occupying foreign power. Then came Nasser's bid, perhaps Egypt's most heartbreaking moment of false promise: import substitution, Pan-Arabism, a place in the non-aligned world, a national army that looked imposing and fierce before the whole edifice of Nasserism came crashing down.

Egyptians who know this narrative by heart see all these bids as brushes with success. This is part of the country's self-image. To rule Egypt is to rule against the background of these expectations and disappointments. Pity the air force officer who now presides over a country groaning under the weight of its numbers, scrambling to pay for its food imports, reconciling its claims to greatness with the fact of its dependence on American power and largesse. Egyptians are not blind to what has befallen their country. They can see the booming lands in Asia, countries that were once poorer than Egypt, digging out of the poverty of the past. No way out has materialized for Egypt. The dreams of liberal reform, the hopes for revolution from above, the socialist bid of Nasser all withered away. The country drifts. No Lee Kuan Yew has risen here to make the place orderly and efficient even at a price in political and cultural freedom. The economy remains a hybrid. It combines a wild form of laissez-faire capitalism for the sharks and fat cats who raid the place with subsidies for the poorer classes. There is endless talk of economic reform. But the state has chosen the path of least resistance and stays with the status quo. The push for privatization that raised the share of the private sector from twenty-three percent of industrial output in 1974 to thirty percent a decade later has stalled. Four decades of positioning the country for foreign assistance from the Soviet Union, the Arab oil states, and the United States have done terrible damage to Egypt. A political economy and a mentality of dependence have set in.

THE GENDARME

Chroniclers of the Mubarak regime may look back at his rule as ten good years followed by lean years of trouble and drift. By his own early accounts and self-portrayal as an ordinary man with no claims to greatness, Mubarak appeared to heed the fate of his predecessor. A cautious man, he drew back from the precipice, stitching back together as best he knew how the fault line between the state and the mainstream opposition. He rebuilt bridges to the Arab world burned by Sadat; he gave every indication that the fling with America and the West that had carried Sadat away would be reined in, that a sense of proportion and restraint would be restored to Egyptian politics. He presented himself as a man with clean hands who would put an end to the crony capitalism and economic pillage of the Sadat era.

But Mubarak was no great reformer bent on remaking the political landscape. To begin with, he labored against the background of an adverse set of changes in the economic domain. The 1980s proved to be a difficult decade for Egypt's economy. The rate of annual growth plummeted; in 1989–90 the economy grew a mere two percent, less than the growth in the population. Egypt dropped from the World Bank's group of lower-middle-income countries to its lower-income category; inflation rose and the real income of industrial workers eroded. A regime unable to reverse this decline fell back on its powers of coercion when the *Gamaat* took on the state.

In retrospect, the choice that mattered was made by Mubarak with his coronation for a third term in 1993. A modest man (a civil servant with the rank of president, a retired army general of Mubarak's generation described him to me) had become president for life. Mubarak had broken a pledge that he would limit himself to two terms in office. Though outsiders may have a romantic view of Egyptians as patient fellahin tilling the soil under an eternal sky in veritable awe of their rulers, in fact a strong sense of skepticism and a keen eye for the foibles of rulers pervade Egyptian political culture. No one had the means to contest Mubarak's verdict; a brave soul or two quibbled about the decision. An open letter was sent to Mubarak by Tahseen Bashir, one of the country's most thoughtful and temperate public figures, questioning the wisdom of the decision. Autocracy prevailed, but a healthy measure of the regime's legitimacy seemed to vanish overnight.

That keen eye for the ruler's foibles now saw all of Mubarak's defects. He had hung around too long. An inarticulate man, he had done it without bonding with the country. The national elections he presided over became increasingly fraudulent and transparent. Worse still, Mubarak ran afoul of his country's sense of propriety by refusing to designate a successor or help develop a process of orderly succession. His two predecessors, much larger historic figures with far greater claims to political legitimacy, their personal histories deeply intertwined with their country's, never dared go that far. Supreme in the political domain, Nasser always ruled with a designated successor in place. And Sadat had chosen Mubarak in homage to generational change. Mubarak had no claim to inheritance when Sadat picked him from a large officer corps; it was Sadat's will that made him. In contrast, Mubarak rules alone: the glory (what little of it there has been of late) and the burdens are his. He stands sentry against the armed Islamists, but the expectations of the 1980s—modernizing the polity, giving it freer institutions, taking it beyond the power of the army—have been betrayed. At heart he is a gendarme determined to keep intact the ruler's imperative. Is it any wonder that those rescued from the wrath and the reign of virtue promised by the Islamists have no affection for the forces of order and feel no great sense of deliverance?

The defects of a political system without an orderly succession in place and reliant on the armed forces as a last arbiter were laid bare last June when Mubarak, in Addis Ababa to attend a meeting of the Organization of African Unity, escaped unhurt from an armed attack on his motorcade. He rushed back home full of fury against the Sudanese, whom he accused of masterminding the attempt on his life; he was eager, as well, to tell of his cool under fire, the man of the armed forces who had known greater dangers. The play of things was given away in the scripted celebrations of Mubarak's safety. The men of the religious establishment hailed Mubarak as a just ruler who kept the faith. The military officers renewed their pledge of allegiance and warned that they were there to ward off the dangers to the regime. The minister for municipalities said the crowds from the provinces who had wanted to come to Cairo would have covered the "face of the sun." The one obvious lesson that was not drawn, the danger that went unexamined and unstated, was the vacuum, the uncertainty, that would have been left behind had Mubarak been struck down in Ethiopia. Egyptians were no doubt relieved to have Mubarak back: that is not the kind of tragedy they would want for him or for themselves. But no staged celebrations and no display of bravado on the Egypt-

Sudan frontier could hide the stalemate of the Egyptian political order.

PAN-ARABISM REDUX

A pan-Arab wind, a pan-Arab temptation, has lately emerged in Egypt. It is the return of an old consolation that brought Egypt failure and bitterness. From her pundits and intellectuals can now be heard a warmed-over version of the pan-Arab arguments of the 1960s, a disquiet over the country's place in the region. And for all the vast aid the United States has poured into Egypt over the past two decades, there is in the air as well a curious free-floating hostility to American ideals and interests, a conviction that the United States wishes Egypt permanent dependency and helplessness, a reflexive tendency to take up, against America's wishes, the cause of renegade states like Libya and Iraq, a belief that the United States is somehow engaged with Israel in an attempt to diminish and hem in the power and influence of Egypt. The peace with Israel, we know, stands, but it is unclaimed and disowned by the professional and intellectual class in the country; the pharaoh's peace, concluded by Sadat a generation ago, was kept to a minimum by his inheritors.

This new version of pan-Arabism, we are told, would be pragmatic whereas the old movement led by Nasser was romantic and loud and strident. Egypt would lead other Arabs, she would help defend the security of the Persian Gulf states (against Iran) and set the terms of accommodation with Israel, but she would do all this without shrillness, without triggering a new ideological war in the Arab world. She would use her skills and her vast bureaucratic apparatus to balance the power of Israel.

In truth, the pan-Arabism that the Egyptian state (and the intellectual class) wishes to revive is a mirage. Egypt's primacy in Arab politics is a thing of the past. Arabs have gone their separate ways. Egypt was the last to proclaim the pan-Arab idea, and the first to desert it. If Egypt succumbs again to that temptation as a way of getting out of its troubles, the detour will end in futility. To borrow an old expression, pan-Arabism will have visited twice: the first time as tragedy, the second as farce. Egypt cannot set the terms or the pace of the accommodation in the Fertile Crescent between Israel and each of its neighbors. These terms will be decided by the protagonists. The irony was not lost on the Jordanians when the Egyptians began to deride them for their forthcoming peace with Israel. It was under Egyptian command during those fateful six days in 1967 that Jordan lost the West Bank and East Jerusalem. Jordan then had to wait on the sidelines for an entire generation after the Camp David Accords as Egypt garnered the wages of peace and the vast American aid that came with it.

Egypt cannot render services that are no longer in demand: her doomed and quixotic campaign, waged earlier this year, against the extension of the Nuclear Nonproliferation Treaty and the attempt to hold the treaty hostage to new controls over Israel's nuclear capabilities offers a cautionary tale. The campaign rolled together Egypt's panic about its place in the region, the need to demonstrate some distance from American power, and the desire to reassert Egypt's primacy in Arab politics. The regime threw everything it had into the fight. For months it was high drama: Egypt against the elements. But it was to no avail. There were no Arab riders eager to join the Egyptian posse. The passion had gone out of that old fight.

Nor is there a special assignment for Egypt in securing the sea-lanes of the Persian Gulf or defending the Arabian Peninsula. To balance the two potential revisionist states, Iran and Iraq, the conservative states of the Gulf will rely on American power and protection. This is an assignment for an imperial power; it is now America's, as it had been Britain's. In that kind of work Egypt has a minor role, as it did in Desert Storm, providing an Arab cover for American power. There could be gains for Egypt here, but they are at best marginal ones.

Egyptians who know their country so well have a way of reciting its troubles and then insisting that the old resilient country shall prevail. As an outsider who has followed the twists of the country's history and who approaches the place with nothing but awe for its civility amid great troubles, I suspect they are right. The country is too wise, too knowing, too tolerant to succumb to a reign of theocratic zeal. Competing truths, whole civilizations have been assimilated and brokered here; it is hard to see Cairo, possessed of the culture that comes to great, knowing cities, turning its back on all that. The danger here is not that of sudden, cataclysmic upheaval, but of the steady descent into deeper levels of pauperization, of the lapse of the country's best into apathy and despair, of Egypt falling yet again through the trapdoor of its history of disappointment.

Some two decades ago, in the aftermath of the October war of 1973, the influential journalist Mohamed Heikal, Nasser's main publicist, set out to explain to Henry Kissinger that Egypt was more than a state on the banks of the Nile, that it was an idea and a historical movement. Yet that is all that remains.

Both the Mediterranean temptation of Egypt being a piece of Europe and the pan-Arab illusion have run aground.

To rule Egypt today is to rule a burdened state on the banks of the Nile and to rule it without the great consolations and escapes of the past.

SOURCE NOTES:

Anwar el-Sadat's legacy was given its due in a work of fiction by Naguib Mahfouz, *Before the Throne*, first U.S. edition (American University of Cairo Press, 2009).

The demographic weight of the Copts is one of the great riddles of Egypt. "We count everything in Egypt: cups, shoes. The only thing we don't count are the Copts. They have been two million since 1945. No one has died; no one has been born," political historian Rifaat Said observed. The political Islamists prefer a low estimate of two million Copts. The number was given to me by Adel Hussein, a noted figure in the Islamic political movement. Other estimates run as high as ten million.

Lawrence Durrell lived and worked in Alexandria in the mid-1940s and his book *The Alexandria Quartet* (Penguin Books, 1961), though a work of fiction, reflects his own experiences and his encounters with those who inhabit that city during the age of the Grand Tour.

Yusuf al-Qa'id's brilliant work of fiction, *War in the Land of Egypt* (Interlink Pub Group, November 1997), leads us into the world of frustration and failure felt by a younger generation of Egyptians.

Chapter 4

The Secular Inheritance

It is time that Saturns ceased dining off their children;
time, too, that children stopped devouring their parents . . .
—ALEXANDER HERZEN

It was in the mid-1980s that a whole world slipped through the fingers of the Arab elite, formed on the secular ideals of nationalism and modernity. A city that had been their collective cultural home—Beirut—was lost to them. A political culture of nationalism that had nurtured them had led to a blind alley and been turned into a cover for despotism, a plaything of dictators. A theocratic temptation blew into the political world like a ferocious wind, and the secular Arabs were left thrashing about. Nothing today, no ship of sorrow, can take these men and women of the secular tradition back to the verities of their world. A political inheritance has been lost.

This essay originally appeared in *Foreign Affairs*, Vol. 76, No. 5, September/October 1997, with the title "The Arab Inheritance"; it is republished here in slightly different form with the cooperation and consent of the original publisher.

Modern Arabs came into that secular inheritance with relative ease. It came to them the way dominant ideas are transmitted and received when they are ascendant. The labor that had gone into that grand edifice reached back into the late years of the nineteenth century. In the barracks and the academies, in *al-mahjar,* the lands of emigration in Europe and the New World, and in Cairo, a national movement had taken shape, a product of the cities and of the intellectual class. And though anti-Western in its rhetoric, it was given force and expression by thinkers who had been formed by the ideals of the West. When George Antonius gave this national movement its manifesto, *The Arab Awakening*, in 1939, he was true to all that: he was a son of Mount Lebanon, a Greek Orthodox from a trading family, raised there and in the polyglot world of Alexandria, and educated at Cambridge. He had behind him years of service in the British colonial administration. He had written his famous tract thanks to the financial patronage of Charles R. Crane, a Chicago industrialist and philanthropist, a dilettante and a crank who always seemed in search of exotic causes in distant lands. It was for an Anglo-American audience that Antonius had written his book. He had told that defective tale of Western betrayal that lies at the heart of Arab nationalist historiography, the partition of the Arab world in the diplomatic settlement that followed the First World War—but he had written it as an appeal to the judgment of the West. It could not have occurred to him that a way—or a world—could be found beyond that of the West. It was in the schools of the Anglo-American missions, and in the flagship of those missions, the Syrian Protestant College (later renamed the American University of Beirut) that Arab nationalism had its start.

The dream of that national "awakening" had been a dream of social emancipation as well. Ten years prior to the appearance of Antonius's book, a Muslim woman of Beirut, Nazira Zayn al-Din, a child of the upper bourgeoisie, had written a daring book of her own, *al-Sufur wa al-Hijab* (*Unveiling of the Veil*). In it she had staked out the right of Muslim women to shed their veils yet remain within the faith. Nazira had not given an inch to the religious obscurantists. There were four veils in the land, she had written: veils of cloth, of ignorance, of hypocrisy, and of stagnation. She wanted no favors; she wanted for her land, and for the women in her land, the freedom of "civilized nations." There was nothing shameful to her and her generation about this quest for modernity. They wanted to find their way out of poverty and out of "the past." Not far from her was Mustafa Kemal Ataturk's project of remaking a Muslim society, and Nazira Zayn al-Din wanted for the Arabs the political and cultural renewal the Turkish leader had introduced in his land.

BLISS WAS IT IN THAT DAWN

For a young Arab, it was heady in the 1950s and 1960s to come into this tradition that the early modernists had worked out. To be awakened to politics by the Suez War of 1956 was to be given a dream of social and political renewal, to partake of a new psychological order of things. But this was not destined to last. The beginning of the end came with the Six Day War in June of 1967. In retrospect, it is fitting to say that the retreat of the secular ideal began on the seventh day of the Six Day War. That defeat wrecked the hopes of one generation, and branded a younger one raised in its shadow. The universal truth of Arab nationalism—that large idea of a common political inheritance and a common destiny, that belief that the national boundaries of the Arab world were contrived—had cracked. That truth had only itself to blame. It had been willful, and it looked past historical facts and realities it did not like and could not cope with. It papered over the antagonism between Muslim and Christian Arabs, and it looked away from the "compact communities" in the Fertile Crescent and the Gulf: the Alawis, the Druze, the Shia. A project of the cities, it had been silent about the hinterland and its people. Having relied on the power of Egypt in the preceding decade, it was devastated by Egypt's retreat into its own world.

There was a partial recovery in October of 1973—the windfall of oil wealth, the decent military outcome of the war with Israel. The pull of money seemed as if it might deradicalize the political tradition. But by the end of that decade, a pied piper had risen in the East. Ayatollah Ruhollah Khomeini rallied the excluded in Arab politics and exposed the terrible secret that lay at the heart of Islam in the Fertile Crescent and the Gulf—the fault line between Sunni and Shia Muslims. Beyond the Shia who saw the "armed Imam" as their avenger, Khomeini made theocratic politics glamorous for all Arabs. By the time Khomeini made his appearance, the secular nationalist movement in the Arab world had long cast aside its liberal beginnings and been overtaken by the autocrats. Arabs were delivered into a world that the likes of Antonius had not foreseen: the political culture of charismatic command that prevailed in Egypt and the unbridled military autocracies of Syria, Iraq, and Libya. Two French-educated pundits and intellectuals had conceived of the Baath Party.

They could not have imagined the regimes in Syria and Iraq that their movement had hatched.

A brigand's gift was offered to the Arabs in August of 1990 when Saddam Hussein swept into Kuwait with, amid the pillage and terror, a dream of historical revisionism. His soldiers' drive to the gold souk of Kuwait was an offering to all those Arabs thwarted by an era of wealth that had taunted and then been denied them. A hound with an instinct for his own small world, the Iraqi had been a faithful son of the clan. He had held up a mirror to that Arab era. A decade earlier he had treated Arabs to an anti-Persian, anti-Shia campaign. He had been the "sword of the Arabs." No limits had been drawn for him. Now he struck again; it was the "springtime of nations," that annus mirabilis in Eastern Europe, and the Iraqi despot intuited the Arab despair and confusion in that time of change. But Saddam was defeated and despair persisted.

The doors were flung wide open in Arab lands: from one side entered Pax Americana, from the other political Islam. The foreigner had called up the ancestors, as it were, and the writ of the ancestors was sharpened like a sword by men and women who insisted that they could cut the tradition to their own needs. This was the break with the nationalism of the preceding era. The hero who had dominated Arab politics, Gamal Abdel Nasser, the man at the helm of the Egyptian state from 1954 to 1970, had fought both at once political Islam and American primacy. He had all but decimated the Muslim Brotherhood in his own country, showing it no mercy. The West and the past had both been kept at bay, but that battle was now lost, and the secular project had come apart. The secular nationalists were on the run. Arabs had traveled far only to arrive at desolation.

Arabs had known troubles aplenty, but there had been political and cultural—and moral—limits, notions of what was *halal* (permissible) and *haram* (impermissible). Now these limits were transgressed with abandon. In Syria and Iraq, in the city of Hama, and in the hill country of Kurdistan, Arabs saw levels of violence they had not known in earlier times. In Beirut, a city of the Arab liberal age and once a showcase of Arab enlightenment, they saw communal carnage and religious vendettas that had been covered up by a veneer of modernity and worldliness.

The great Arab inheritance had wound its way to two destinations: autocracy and political Islam. Cynicism and nihilism overtook the political world. Arabs took to the road, to Europe and the United States. The castaways who had made Beirut their home were forced into a second migration. An emigre journalism put down roots in Paris and London. In exile, that journalism grew shrill and embittered, as though to compensate for the distance from home. A century ago, in the long twilight of Ottoman despotism, an Arab political and literary tradition had also thrived in exile. A circle was closed.

A THWARTED GENERATION

"They are sons without fathers," the Lebanese Waddah Charara has written of the theocratic brigades that had risen in Beirut—a Mediterranean parody of the events in Iran. The sociologist could have cut a wider swath with that description, taking in the boys of the intifada in Gaza and the West Bank; the activists of Hamas; and, on the other side of the Arab world, in North Africa, the armed Islamists of Algeria who had launched a deadly war of their own, a second battle of Algiers, against their rulers. The Islamists have described it as a battle between Hezbollah (the Party of God) and Hizb Franca (the Party of France), the pious against the wicked. The sociologist's observation was true as well for that smaller war in Egypt between the inheritors of the Nasserist legacy and the Islamists, who broke with the "godless" revolution of the Free Officers and let loose their uncompromising notions of theocratic politics.

The boys of the intifada and the suicide drivers in Beirut were embraced by their weary elders. A thwarted generation of secular nationalists now offered the cruel, angry young the homage of a generation that conceded its own defeat. "The children of the stones have scattered our papers, spilled ink on our clothes, mocked the banality of our old texts," wrote the Syrian-born Nizar Qabbani, the Arab world's most widely read poet. "What matters about the children of the stones is that they have rebelled against the authority of the fathers, that they have fled the house of obedience, disobeyed our commands and our wishes. . . . Oh children of Gaza, don't refer to our writings. We are your parents, don't be like us; we are your idols, don't worship us." Qabbani was giving voice to the abdication of the secularists. The thwarted generation was writing its own political obituary, ceding the political domain to the wrath of the new theocrats.

There is a portrait that bears an uncanny resemblance to the generational war that beset the Arab world in the 1980s: Ivan Turgenev's arresting novel, *Fathers and Sons*, published in 1862. In that work, Turgenev sketched the struggle in mid-nineteenth-century Russia between a feeble liberalism and a merciless Jacobin revolt. In Bazarov, the novel's central character, Turgenev left a universal portrait of the confident young: cruel, fanatical, and unbent. Bazarov scorned the accomplishments that a westernizing elite had secured in Russia against the background of autocracy and a peasant culture steeped in custom and superstition: "Aristocratism, liberalism, progress, principles—think of it, what a lot of foreign and useless words! To a Russian they are not worth a straw," Bazarov rails to Nikolai Petrovich, a middle-aged provincial notable of a "liberal" outlook. The ground had to be cleared, Bazarov believed, for there was nothing in public life "which does not call for absolute and ruthless repudiation." Turgenev had no illusions about Bazarov: "I conceived him," he wrote, "as a somber figure doomed to destruction because he still stands only in the gateway of the future."

The Arab Bazarovs could not win: they, too, were only in the gateway of the future. In time the intifada would drown in its own blood and degenerate into a Night of the Long Knives, a hunt for demons and collaborators, and the millennium in Beirut would end in stalemate and in the triumph of the cold-blooded soldier next door, the Syrian ruler, who stepped in and inherited the ruins. The young bearers of this new politics of cruelty and wrath had bloodied the status quo; they had trampled over precious things and fed off the self-doubts of the generation that preceded them. But they could not prevail in the test of arms against the regimes in power.

Members of this new breed were literalists in the way they read the scripture and the faith. There had been allegory and subtlety aplenty in Islam. In Baghdad during the High Middle Ages, in Islamic Spain in its heyday, philosophers had quarreled about the balance between reason and revelation, perfecting an art of doublespeak that permitted them enormous leeway while keeping the pretense of piety. There had developed a consensus of sorts that the mass of ordinary people can be left to their faith, while the philosophers and the skeptics gave free rein to the rule of reason.

But the literalists had no patience for all that. They were half-educated. They could read the text and were often the first in their families to become literate. That literacy empowered them. Education—rote learning—had remade all Arab and Muslim societies. A new generation could now read and write, but the learning came without the habits and the attitudes of tolerance. Elite culture—emancipated women, daring writers, young people under the spell of new forms of expression—was under surveillance. The new enforcers could look into that elite culture and take it apart. Even in the lands of the Muslim diaspora, in Western Europe and later in North America, the literalists were alert to the slights they looked for and saw everywhere.

The faith had become portable. It was British Muslims who first burned copies of Salman Rushdie's *The Satanic Verses*; they were the ones who gave Ayatollah Ruhollah Khomeini, on the rebound from a disastrous war with Iraq, the inspiration for his fatwa on the life of Rushdie.

The angry protesters in Bradford, West Yorkshire, in 1989 weren't readers of fiction. It was enough for them that a man raised in a Muslim home had taken liberty with the faith. In the same vein, a barely literate Egyptian electrician stabbed Mahfouz, the greatest writer in Egypt and the Arab world, and paralyzed his writing hand in 1994. The electrician had been offended by a novel he could not penetrate, a Mahfouzian work of allegory that had long antagonized the keepers of Islamic orthodoxy.

The traditional folks awed by the learning of the modernist elites had been replaced by their angry offspring. Islamism gave power and a sense of militant virtue to an unsettled generation exposed to a modernity it can neither master nor reject. An explosive demography and a literacy disconnected from critical inquiry had given rise to a culture of brittle pride: young men exalt the faith, as they grapple with its inability to contain their lives or keep them at home.

The literalists had come into their own. For them, there was no way back to a cozy past, and the way forward, to a new world, was blocked by the vast magnitude of their numbers, their material disinheritance, and the very inabilities they carry with them.

THE POVERTY OF POLITICAL ISLAM

We have exaggerated the strength of the brigades of political Islam. All they could do was mount a rearguard action against an encircling civilization they could neither control nor ignore. Much to their own pain, no doubt, they had that dominant civilization of the West under their skin. It was from France that the Algerian Islamists wanted to wage their campaign against the regime of the military and the ruling party; it was from Jersey City and Manhattan that the blind preacher Omar Abdel Rahman and his band of young followers wanted to unseat the regime of Hosni Mubarak. And it was from London, by fax, from *bilad al-Kufr* (the land of unbelief) that Muhammad al-Massari, a German-trained Saudi dissident with an American wife, plotted against the House of Saud. That dissident vowed to extirpate the power and presence of the "infidel" from the sands of Arabia. But the rebel was fooling himself: the self-sufficiency of that desert world now belongs to an irretrievable past.

We have looked to the heavens, and we have looked in the scripture, for explanations for the appeal of political Islam. We have spent a generation speaking of "Islamic fundamentalism," of that theocratic force that has come into Arab life. But the truth lies in material circumstances. Theocratic politics blew in when economic growth faltered. As an authoritative World Bank report, *Claiming the Future*, documents, 1960–85 was a "golden age" of economic growth and income equality in Arab lands. Infant mortality halved, life expectancy rose by ten years, primary school enrollment increased dramatically from sixty-one percent in 1965 to ninety-eight percent in 1985, and adult literacy rose. The levels of poverty were far lower in Arab countries than in East Asia and Latin America. Oil prices quadrupled in that great event in October 1973—perhaps the single largest transfer of world wealth in modern history. The place was living beyond its means and its skills. Urbanization was in full swing: the share of agricultural labor had declined from fifty percent to thirty percent in the span of three decades. But the urban population's hold on the new prosperity was tenuous. When a deep recession hit in the mid-1980s, due to the fall of oil prices, a politics of panic and resentment overtook the newly urbanized and newly prosperous. The population had been growing at a yearly rate of 2.7 percent (the highest of any developing region), the working-age population at 3.3 percent. In the cities and in the no-man's-land trapped by the recession, the newly urbanized were strangers living on their nerves. Their children were available to the politics of millenarianism and turmoil.

THE LOST DECADES

In the privacy of their own language, when "Orientalists" and other "enemies" are not listening in, in their searing fiction and poetry, Arabs today circle their own tradition. Round and round they go in their attempt to divine the causes of their malady. They are not blind to what has befallen them. They may take the consoling testimonies of their "foreign friends," who tell them of the "moderation" that lies deep inside these Islamic movements, but they know better. They know of the men and women of letters and culture who have quit Arab lands and taken their work and their memories to distant shores. The poet Nizar Qabbani left for London, where he was to die in 1998; the celebrated Syrian-Lebanese critic and writer Adonis went to Paris; and the Egyptian philosopher Nasr Hamid Abu Zeid headed for the Netherlands. Arabs could see that broken chain of transmission between the modernism of the interwar years and the political and cultural thought of today. The plain truths that earlier generations had seen—the separation between religion and politics, the primacy of reason—were lost in the course of a harsh decade. In allegory, the men and women of the secular tradition have struck back of late, traveled into the *turath* (heritage) itself in search of their own ancestors—philosophers and thinkers who upheld the rule of reason and honored the place of dissent in public and intellectual life. Once proud of their place in the world of nations, Arabs are well aware of the sea of autocracies surrounding them. It was not for political orders like those that prevailed in the national security states—Iraq, Libya, Syria—that the early generation of nationalists had toiled. A modern political tradition that begot the rulers of these states, that begot the terror of Algeria, was clearly a tradition gone awry.

THE LETHAL TRADITION

For the fourth time in 30 years, Arabs faced a moment of truth, a turning point, forced on them this time by the global marketplace. In many ways, this fourth crisis is the most difficult. The first moment of truth was the outcome of the Six Day War of 1967, and it was handled with skill. The "Arab Cold War" between the republics and the monarchies was liquidated, a new war was launched six years later, and a cunning *ibn balad* (son of the land), Anwar el-Sadat, proceeded to use the verdict of that war to extricate his country from the captivity of pan-Arab politics. Egypt came to terms with the world after 1973, and a measure of inter-Arab peace prevailed. The stridency of Pan-Arabism and its challenge to the ruling regimes were moderated.

The second crisis was Iran's revolution and its rulers' war against the dominant order. The Arabs waited out that revolution, bought time for themselves, and paid off the gendarme in Baghdad who had stepped forth and offered his services as a man who would quarantine the theocratic upheaval. The strategy worked. The enthusiasm of that revolution blew over: a revolt that could not offer happiness to its own people could hardly export it to others. But the strategy had a price. The gendarme was emboldened.

The third challenge came with Saddam Hussein's bid for mastery of the Gulf in 1990. In retrospect, this crisis ended up as a war between a local despot and a foreign savior (Pax Americana). What truth came with this war, what lessons the Arabs should have drawn from it—the shattering of the legend of Arabism—soon dissipated. The region worked its will on the foreign power's victory, and five or six years later, there emerged in Arab lands second thoughts about the foreigner's rescue and about the foreign power that had won that brilliant military campaign. There was new sympathy for Iraq, and there was a sly suspicion of the foreign protector. "Each stranger made his own poor bed among them," T. E. Lawrence once wrote of the Arabs, and the great power standing sentry in the Gulf was to prove no exception to this rule. A power that had let a dictator off the hook but maintained an embargo on his people could not convince others of its wisdom. The solitude of that foreign power, and the doubts about its intentions, were laid bare in a crisis in the summer of 1996, when Saddam Hussein struck into Kurdistan, into the "safe haven" that American power had marked out for the Kurds after Desert Storm. This time, America was on its own. The earth had shifted: the two volleys of missiles that were fired against Iraqi air-defense installations had to be launched from American ships in the Persian Gulf and B-52 bombers flying in from Guam. Those missiles were fired in the hope that America would hear no more from its nemesis in Baghdad. No one was fooled; no one believed that American power would be deployed to unseat the Iraqi leader. The people of those skeptical lands had a knack for knowing when strangers fire their guns as a cover for their retreat back to their own world.

This fourth crisis was made of different material. The very political economy that saw the Arab world through that quarter-century of growth (1960–85) will have to be cleared away. The bases of that political economy—the bias against agriculture, protected markets, the public sector, a top-down educational system—have eroded. This massive adjustment to a new world will have to be done in a merciless era of capital. The balance of skills and the terms of trade have turned against the lands of the Middle East and North Africa. The World Bank report sounded the alarm: the economies of the lands of the Middle East and North Africa have stagnated. Some 260 million people in that region, we are told, export fewer manufactured goods than Finland's five million people. The average laborer was earning no more in real terms in the mid-1990s than in 1970. A mere one percent of the private capital flowing into the developing world finds its way into these lands. And the crisis is endemic: since 1986, per capita income has fallen by two percentage points a year, the largest decline in any developing region. Not even the oil countries have been spared: the GDP per capita in these countries declined by four percentage points a year between 1980 and 1991. These Arab states of the Gulf have run down their foreign reserves, and their populations have doubled over the past two decades. Poverty had not come to the oil lands, but the ability of these states to maintain the entitlements of the past and absorb the surplus labor of their neighbors has come to an end.

This economic decline is a cruel twist of fate for a region with a deep mercantilist tradition. The cultural interpretation that attributes Russia's economic troubles to the absence of a capitalist tradition does not hold for the Arab lands. The fault lay not in scriptures and traditions but in public policies. The regime of state ownership, subsidies, and protectionism is in part to blame. The ruin caused by the wars and violence of the past two decades drove some $350 billion in private capital for deposits abroad, closing the circle of misfortune.

The last time that the age of capital intruded into Muslim domains, their bureaucratic states had not been able to hold their own against the political power and cheaper manufactures of Europe. Foreign debt overwhelmed them; and then came political subjugation. "What wealth we have we spend on injuring one another," a Druze emir of Mount Lebanon told a foreign visitor in the mid-nineteenth century, when the European economy was devastating the traditional crafts in Ottoman domains. That lethal tradition has yet to end. In the trade-off between the interests and the passions, the latter—sectarian, nationalist, ethnic—have had the upper hand. Nations beget the history they deserve and want. Arab society has sought from its politics satisfactions more precious than social peace and economic welfare.

There is a danger worse than subjugation in this new era of capital: irrelevance, the danger that capital will have no interest in these lands, that their labor cannot be productive enough, that their products cannot be competitive enough. A sobering lesson is supplied by Algeria: while the dirty war rages in the north and in the cities between the "eradicationists" of the regime and the terrorists of the Armed Islamic Group, the work goes on in the oil and gas fields of the Sahara, and the oil production zone has been cordoned off by the army. Algerians need special passes to enter that zone. Whole countries could be written off and forgotten, their skills overtaken, in this new era of global capitalism. No incantations about authenticity will stop the slide into obsolescence.

The authoritarian state, the nihilistic opposition: the middle ground has been scorched in the two decades behind us. The ruler claiming everything, the oppositionist dispensing with all that has been built and secured by those who came before. On pain of poverty and decay, nations can persist with ruinous ways. An encrusted tradition has its own ways, a thicket of consolations and alibis shelter it from the world. Beyond economic repair (really a precondition of it), a modernist impulse will have to assert itself if rescue is to materialize. "We can't look for the future in the caves of the past, and we can't make the future with ready-hewn stones," an Egyptian thinker, Mahmoud Amin al-Alim, has written in a book on Arab thought between "authenticity" and "globalization." The romance with the Islamic past is illusion, a detour: that romance had filled the void when a national tradition faltered, when new classes, half-educated and bewildered, sought to simplify the world around them.

It could be tougher going for the rulers of the Middle East in a post-Islamist phase: on the whole, their present modus operandi—counterinsurgency—is easier than economic and political reform. A frightened middle class, desperate to hold on to its small cultural liberties against the Islamists' reign of virtue and terror, is willing to sanction and live with autocratic rule. Reform of the Arab political culture will begin when a system of limited authority encounters the oppositionist with limited, realizable goals—half-steps of reform. The one Arab land that offers the best chance of a political reclamation of this sort is Egypt. It is there, in a society with genuine political experience, an innate temperament of moderation, and the security of centralized rule, that a politics of restraint and pragmatism could break the vicious circle of total rule and nihilistic opposition. If Egypt found a way out of this dilemma, Arabs would then have a model of their own of a more accommodating, more merciful political world. Egyptians had their gaze on Iran for a good generation, but they were not fooled; they did not want for themselves the theocratic culture of Iran. But they were wistful about their own condition, and there lies deep within them a reverence for the parliamentary politics they had known in the interwar years.

PAX AMERICANA: SATAN'S REDEEMER

Failure can drape itself in ways both religious and secular. For a modernist Arab alternative to work and stick, the obsessive themes of the Arab political tradition—a historiography that lays every blame at the doorstep of the West—will have to be shed. It will not be easy, and the odds weigh against a modernist path. There is a widespread belief that the new global order and its civic religion of fiscal rectitude, privatization, and competitiveness, and high tolerance for inequality is made in America's image and cut to its needs. In the workshops of the Pacific, this perception has no resonance. There is a self-confident swagger in East Asia, a belief that the "East Asian way"—markets, political autocracy, and a hierarchical social order—is made out of that region's own cultural material. No such confidence is to be found among the Arabs.

The shadow of American primacy lay on Arab lands; inescapably, onto the new reforms, onto the whole structure of contemporary international order for that matter, were projected the resentments that the intellectual class harbors toward Pax Americana. The Egyptian Mohamed Heikal, perhaps the most influential expositor of the tradition of Pan-Arabism and Nasserism, gave voice to this distrust of the new order of things: nothing of value could come out of this American primacy, he wrote. A "new order" was being hatched for the region that could bring in its train greater ruin for the Arabs than the diplomatic settlements that carved up the Arab dominions of the Ottoman Empire in the aftermath of the First World War. Arabs could come out empty-handed, he warned, in this new order of nations, let down by feeble states and "kept in the dark in this age of satellites and mass information." No wonder the economic reforms that the Egyptian state undertook in the mid-1990s—slashing the budget deficit, a beginning to privatize public-sector companies, liberalizing the land rent laws in favor of the landholders—were written off by economic nation-

alists as a capitulation to an American policy bent on disman-
tling the public sector and undoing what had been built
during the high tide of Nasserism and Arab nationalism.

It is a curious presence that America casts across the Arab
landscape. America is simultaneously the agent of political
order and social revolution. It has befriended the status quo and
has, for good reasons, taken a skeptical view of the opposition-
ists in Arab lands. The irony has not been lost on those on the
receiving end of American power. The twin deities in this
American civic religion, ballots and markets, have been decou-
pled in Arab lands. The American enthusiasm for the forms of
democracy in other lands has been reined in here. (That enthusiasm is kept in check in the case of Turkey as well, and for the
same reasons: fear that secularism may lose out, in open contest,
to the Islamists.) Clarity will begin when the political class
acknowledges the true and modest dimensions of the American role in Arab public life. The American presence in the Arab
world has a long trail behind it: it stretches back to the late
years of the nineteenth century with the arrival of the mission-
aries and the educators. In the intervening decades, America
has been the thing and its opposite: Satan and redeemer; it has
nurtured Arab nationalism and sustained Israel; its pop culture
and media have disseminated social emancipation while its
official weight has been thrown on the side of the ruling orders.
But this American imperium is now part real, part pretense. No
imperial vocation beckons America in Arab lands.

The Arab political imagination will also have to steal away
from Israel. That grand alibi for every failure under the sun has
worn thin and ought to have lost what force it had in the time
of the wars and of nationalism. But a foul wind has greeted
Israeli-Palestinian peace, and the Arab intellectual class has, by

and large, taken a dark view of the peace of Oslo and of the wider process of normalization with Israel. To the critics, this peace of Yasir Arafat, the Egyptian state, and Jordan is one large deed of surrender to American designs, an acknowledgment that the race with Israel has been lost. Palestine has become another Andalusia, Anton Shammas wrote. He mourned a lost homeland, "a construct of nostalgia, a territory without a map."

The accommodation with Israel was delegitimized, branded as the rulers' peace. That peace could not be overturned, but the keepers of the Arab political truth—the men and women of the professional guilds, the émigré intellectuals, the world of letters, secularists, and Islamists alike—would not sanction or embrace this peace. To its opponents the peace was a Pax Hebraica or a joint Israeli-American project that a feeble Arab world had been unable to resist. An odd, ironic destiny had overtaken Arafat after Oslo: the man who had been followed through thick and thin by his own people as he took them on endless detours had lived to see the same charges of "treason" leveled at him that had once been the unhappy possession of men like King Abdullah of Jordan and Anwar el-Sadat. After settling for what he could get, Arafat had walked away from the refugees of 1948 who had been his old constituency and from their claims to Jaffa and Haifa and Acre to lead the Palestinians of the West Bank and Gaza. Now that old pre-1948 Palestine rose like an apparition to rebuke this practical peace.

A messy history was in the making west of the Jordan River in the aftermath of Oslo; a Palestinian political enterprise had risen in the West Bank and Gaza (a state in all but name), and Israel had outgrown the tower-and-stockade Zionism of its youth. But the dominant stream in the Arab intellectual world looked past all those changes, because the peace had come during a time of sorrow and disarray. The old pan-Arab truth could not be reconstituted, and the émigrés could not find their way back to their old homes and lost cities. The intimacy of the Arab past and the cozy certainties of nationalism could not be retrieved. The one sure way to the old fidelities was the enmity with Israel, which harked back to a past that memory has rearranged and turned into a time when the world was whole and right. As the world makes obsolete all the rest of the Arab inheritance, this one, anti-Zionism, becomes too precious to cast away.

In the memory of a simpler time, there were collection boxes in the schools of the Arab east for money to contribute to a struggle that raged in a distant Arab land, that first battle of Algiers against French rule, and there were celebrations when the colonialists had packed up and left and a proud Algerian state emerged and strutted on the world stage. An altogether different terror stalks Algeria today. The pain of the Arab condition in the modern world persists. But this time, one undeniable truth the early Arab nationalists had yearned for has come to pass: what destiny awaits the Arabs, what history comes their way, is now made with Arab hands.

SOURCE NOTES:

For further reading on the Arab condition, see George Antonius's *The Arab Awakening: The Story of the Arab National Movement* (Simon Publications, 1939).

A courageous young woman of the Arab world in the early years of the twentieth century, Nazira Zayn al-Din, wrote a daring book, *al-Sufur wa al-Hijab* (*Unveiling of the Veil*), published in Beirut in 1928.

The popular poet of romance, Nizar Qabbani wrote "The Trilogy of the Children of the Stones" (Beirut: Nizar Qabbani Publications, 1988).

My analysis of this generational revolt draws on Isaiah Berlin's exquisite essay, "Fathers and Children: Turgenev and the Liberal Predicament," in his book *Russian Thinkers* (New York: Penguin Books, 1979).

For further reading on the Arab revolt, see T. E. Lawrence's classic, *Seven Pillars of Wisdom*, 1922.

The Arab Marxist thinker on politics and culture, Mahmoud Amin al-Alim wrote "Arab Thought Between Privacy and Globalization," Dar al-Mustaqbal al-Arabi, STADT, 1996.

For Mohamed Heikal's views, I drew on the text of a lecture, available to me, which he gave to the students of the American University of Cairo, October 19, 1993. See also his "Misr wa al-Qarn al-Wahid wa al-Ishrin," ("Egypt and the Twenty-First Century"), Cairo, 1994.

For the truth of the entanglement between Israel and Palestine, see the dazzling work of fiction by the Arab-Israeli novelist Anton Shammas, *Arabesques* (Harper & Row, 1988).

Chapter 5

The Sentry's Solitude

Pax Americana in the Arab World

F rom one end of the Arab world to the other, the drumbeats of anti-Americanism had been steady. But the drummers could hardly have known what was to come. The magnitude of the horror that befell the United States on Tuesday, September 11, 2001, appeared for a moment to embarrass and silence the drummers. The American imperium in the Arab-Muslim world hatched a monster. In a cruel irony, a new administration known for its relative lack of interest in that region was to be pulled into a world that has both beckoned America and bloodied it.

History never repeats itself, but when Secretary of State Colin Powell came forth to assure the nation that an international coalition against terrorism was in the offing, Americans recalled when Powell had risen to fame. "First, we're going to cut it off, and then we're going to kill it," he had said of the Iraqi army in 1991. There had been another coalition then, and Pax Americana had set off to the Arab world on a triumphant cam-

This essay originally appeared in *Foreign Affairs*, Vol. 80, No. 6, November/ December 2001, and is republished here in slightly different form with the cooperation and consent of the original publisher.

paign. But those Islamic domains have since worked their way and their will on the American victory of a decade ago. The political earth has shifted in that world. The decade was about the "blowback" of the war. Primacy begot its nemesis.

America's Arab interlocutors have said that the region's political stability would have held had the United States imposed a settlement of the Israeli-Palestinian conflict—and that the rancid anti-Americanism now evident in the Arab world has been called up by the fury of the second intifada that erupted in September 2000. But these claims misread the political world. Long before the second intifada, when Yasir Arafat was still making his way from political exile to the embrace of Pax Americana, there was a deadly trail of anti-American terror. Its perpetrators paid no heed to the Palestinian question. What they thought of Arafat and the metamorphosis that made him a pillar of President Bill Clinton's Middle East policy is easy to construe.

The terror was steady, and its geography and targets bespoke resourcefulness and audacity. The first attack, the 1993 truck bombing of the World Trade Center, was inspired by the Egyptian cleric Shaykh Omar Abdel Rahman. For the United States, this fiery preacher was a peculiar guest: he had come to *bilad al-Kufr* (the land of unbelief) to continue his war against the secular regime of Egyptian President Hosni Mubarak. The shaykh had already been implicated in the 1981 murder of Mubarak's predecessor, Anwar el-Sadat. The young assassins had sought religious guidance from him—a writ for tyrannicide. He had provided it but retained a measure of ambiguity, and Egypt let him leave the country. He had no knowledge of English and did not need it; there were disciples and interpreters aplenty around him. An American imperium had incorporated

Egypt into its order of things, which gave the shaykh a connection to the distant power.

The preacher could not overturn the entrenched regime in his land. But there was steady traffic between the United States and Egypt, and the armed Islamist insurgency that bedeviled Cairo inspired him. He would be an Ayatollah Ruhollah Khomeini for his followers, destined to return from the West to establish an Islamic state. In the preacher's mind, the world was simple. The dictatorial regime at home would collapse once he snapped its lifeline to America. American culture was of little interest to him. Rather, the United States was a place from which he could hound his country's rulers. Over time, Rahman's quest was denied. Egypt rode out the Islamist insurgency after a terrible drawn-out fight that pushed the country to the brink. The shaykh ended up in an American prison. But he had lit the fuse. The 1993 attack that he launched was a mere dress rehearsal for the calamity of September 11, 2001. Rahman had shown the way—and the future.

There were new Muslim communities in America and Europe; there was also money and freedom to move about. The geography of political Islam had been redrawn. When Khomeini took on American power, there had been talk of a pan-Islamic brigade. But the Iranian revolutionaries were ultimately concerned with their own nation-state. And they were lambs compared with the holy warriors to come. Today's warriors have been cut loose from the traditional world. Some of the leaders—the Afghan Arabs—had become restless after the Afghan war. They were insurrectionists caught in a no-man's-land, on the run from their homelands but never at home in the West. In Tunisia, Egypt, and Algeria, tenacious Islamist movements were put down. In Saudi Arabia, a milder Islamist challenge was contained. The counterinsurgencies had been effective, so the extremists turned up in the West. There, liberal norms gave them shelter, and these men would rise to fight another day.

The extremists acquired modern means: frequent-flier miles, aviation and computer skills, and ease in Western cities. They hated the United States, Germany, and France but were nonetheless drawn to them. They exalted tradition and faith, but their traditions could no longer give them a world. Islam's explosive demography had spilled into the West. The militant Islamists were on the move. The security services in their home countries were unsentimental, showing no tolerance for heroics. Men such as Abdel Rahman and Osama bin Laden offered this breed of unsettled men a theology of holy terror and the means to live the plotter's life. Bin Laden was possessed of wealth and high birth, the heir of a merchant dynasty. This gave him an aura: a Che Guevara of the Islamic world, bucking the mighty and getting away with it. A seam ran between America and the Islamic world. The new men found their niche, their targets, and their sympathizers across that seam. They were sure of America's culpability for the growing misery in their lands. They were sure that the regimes in Saudi Arabia and Egypt would fall if only they could force the United States to cast its allies adrift. Terror shadowed the American presence in the Middle East throughout the 1990s: two bombings in Saudi Arabia, one in Riyadh in November 1995 and the other on the Khobar Towers near Dhahran in June 1996; bombings of the US embassies in Tanzania and Kenya in 1998; the daring attack on the *USS Cole* in Yemen in October 2000. The US presence in the Persian Gulf was under assault.

In this trail of terror, symbol and opportunity were rolled together—the physical damage alongside a political and cultural message. These attacks were meant for a watchful crowd in a media age. Dhahran had been a creature of the US presence in Saudi Arabia ever since American oil prospectors turned up in the 1930s and built that city in the American image. But the world had changed. It was in Dhahran, in the 1990s, that the crews monitoring the no-fly zone over Iraq were stationed. The attack against Dhahran was an obvious blow against the alliance between the United States and Saudi Arabia. The realm would not disintegrate; Beirut had not come to Arabia. But the assailants—suspected to be an Iranian operation that enlisted the participation of Saudi Shia—had delivered the blow and the message. The foreigner's presence in Arabia was contested. A radical Islamist opposition had emerged, putting forth a fierce, redemptive Islam at odds with the state's conservative religion.

The *ulama* (clerics) had done well under the Saud dynasty. They were the dynasty's partners in upholding an order where obedience to the rulers was given religious sanction. No ambitious modernist utopia had been unleashed on them as it had in Gamal Abdel Nasser's Egypt and Iran under the Pahlavis. Still, the state could not appease the new breed of activists who had stepped forth after the Gulf War to hound the rulers over internal governance and their ties to American power. In place of their rulers' conservative edifice, these new salvationists proposed a radical order free from foreign entanglements. These activists were careful to refrain from calling for the outright destruction of the House of Saud. But sedition was in the air in the mid-1990s, and the elements of the new utopia were easy to discern. The Shia minority in the Eastern Province would be decimated and the Saudi liberals molded on the campuses of

California and Texas would be swept aside in a zealous, frenzied campaign. Traffic with the infidels would be brought to an end, and those dreaded satellite dishes bringing the West's cultural "pollution" would be taken down. But for this to pass, the roots of the American presence in Arabia would have to be extirpated—and the Americans driven from the country.

The new unrest, avowedly religious, stemmed from the austerity that came to Saudi Arabia after Desert Storm. If the rulers could not subsidize as generously as they had in the past, the foreigner and his schemes and overcharges must be to blame. The dissidents were not cultists but men of their society, half-learned in Western sources and trends, picking foreign sources to illustrate the subjugation that America held in store for Arabia. Pamphleteering had come into the realm, and rebellion proved contagious. A dissident steps out of the shadows, then respectable critics, then others come forth. Xenophobic men were now agitating against the "crusaders" who had come to stay. "This has been a bigger calamity than I had expected, bigger than any threat the Arabian Peninsula had faced since God Almighty created it," wrote the religious scholar Safar al-Hawali, a master practitioner of the paranoid style in politics. The Americans, he warned, had come to dominate Arabia and unleash on it the West's dreaded morals.

Saudi Arabia had been free of the anticolonial complex seen in states such as Algeria, Egypt, Syria, and Iraq. But the simplicity of that Arabian-American encounter now belonged to the past. A fatwa of the senior religious jurist in the realm, Shaykh Abdelaziz ibn Baz, gave away the hazards of the US presence in Arabia. Ibn Baz declared the Khobar Towers bombing a "transgression against the teachings of Islam." The damage to lives and property befell many people, "Muslims and others alike," he wrote. These "non-Muslims" had been granted a pledge of safety. The shaykh found enough scripture and tradition to see a cruel end for those who pulled off the "criminal act." There was a saying attributed to the Prophet Muhammad: "He who killed an ally will never know the smell of paradise." And there was God's word in the Quran: "Those that make war against Allah and his apostle and spread disorder in the land shall be put to death or crucified or have their hands and feet cut off on alternate sides; or be banished from the country. They shall be held to shame in this world and sternly punished in the next." The shaykh permitted himself a drapery of decency. There was no need to specify the identity of the victims or acknowledge that the Americans were in the land. There had remained in the jurist some scruples and restraints of the faith.

In ibn Baz's world, faith was about order and a dread of anarchy. But in the shadows, a different version of the faith was being sharpened as a weapon of war. Two years later, bin Laden issued an incendiary fatwa of his own—a call for murder and holy warfare that was interpreted by the historian Bernard Lewis. Never mind that by the faith's strictures and practice, bin Laden had no standing to issue religious decrees. He had grabbed the faith and called on Muslims to kill "Americans and their allies . . . in any country in which it is possible to do so." A sacred realm apart, Arabia had been overrun by Americans, bin Laden said. "For more than seven years the United States has been occupying the lands of Islam in the holiest of its territories, Arabia, plundering its riches, overwhelming its rulers, humiliating its people, threatening its neighbors, and using its peninsula as a spearhead to fight the neighboring Islamic peoples." Xenophobia of a murderous kind had been dressed up in religious garb.

The attack on the *USS Cole* on October 12, 2000, was a case apart. Two men in a skiff crippled the ship as it docked in Aden to refuel. Witnesses say the assailants, who perished with their victims, were standing erect at the time of the blast, as if in some kind of salute. The United States controlled the sea-lanes of that world, but the nemesis that stalked it on those shores lay beyond America's reach. "The attack on the U.S.S. Cole . . . demonstrated a seam in the fabric of efforts to protect our forces, namely transit forces," a military commission said. But the official language could not describe or name the furies at play. The attack on the *USS Cole* illuminated the US security dilemma in the Persian Gulf. For the US Navy, Yemen had not been a particularly easy or friendly setting. It had taken a ride with Saddam Hussein during the Gulf War. In 1994, a brutal war had been fought in Yemen between the north and the south, along lines of ideology and tribalism. The troubles of Yemen were bottomless. The government was barely in control of its territory and coastline. Aden was a place of drifters and smugglers. Moreover, the suspected paymaster of anti-American terror, bin Laden, had ancestral roots in Hadramawt, the southeastern part of Yemen, and he had many sympathizers there.

It would have been prudent to look at Yemen and Aden with a jaundiced eye. But by early 1999, American ships had begun calling there. US officials had no brilliant options south of the Suez Canal, they would later concede. The ports of call in Sudan, Somalia, Djibouti, and Eritrea were places where the "threat conditions" were high, perhaps worse than in Yemen. The United States had a privileged position in Saudi Arabia, but there had been trouble there as well for US forces: the terrorist attacks in 1995 and 1996, which took 24 American lives. American commanders and planners knew the hazards of Yemen, but the US Navy had taken a chance on the country. Terrorists moved through Yemen at will, but American military planners could not find ideal refueling conditions in a region of great volatility. This was the imperial predicament put in stark, cruel terms.

John Burns of the *New York Times* sent a dispatch on October 28, 2000, of unusual clarity from Aden about the *USS Cole* and the response on the ground to the terrible deed. In Yemen, the reporter saw "a halting, half-expressed sense of astonishment, sometimes of satisfaction and even pleasure, that a mighty power, the United States, should have its Navy humbled by two Arab men in a motorized skiff." Such was imperial presence, the Pax Americana in Arab and Muslim lands.

There were men in the shadows pulling off spectacular deeds. But they fed off a free-floating anti-Americanism that blows at will and knows no bounds among Islamists and secularists alike. For the crowds in Karachi, Cairo, and Amman, the great power could never get it right. A world lacking the tools and the political space for free inquiry fell back on anti-Americanism. "I talk to my daughter-in-law so my neighbor can hear me," goes an Arabic maxim. In the fury with which the intellectual and political class railed against the United States and Israel, the agitated were speaking to and of their own rulers. Sly and cunning men, the rulers knew and understood the game. There would be no open embrace of America—and no public defense of it. They would stay a step ahead of the crowd and give the public the safety valve it needed. The more pro-American the regime, the more anti-American the political class and the political tumult. The United States could grant generous aid to the Egyptian state, but there would be no dampening of the anti-American fury of the Egyptian political class. Its leading state-backed dailies crackled with the wildest theories of US-Israeli conspiracies against their country.

On September 11, 2001, there was an unmistakable sense of glee and little sorrow among upper-class Egyptians for the distant power—only satisfaction that America had gotten its comeuppance. After nearly three decades of American solicitude of Egypt, after the steady traffic between the two lands, there were no genuine friends for America to be found in a curiously hostile, disgruntled land.

Egyptians have long been dissatisfied with their country's economic and military performance, a pain born of the gap between Egypt's exalted idea of itself and the poverty and foreign dependence that have marked its modern history. The rage against Israel and the United States stems from that history of lament and frustration. So much of Egypt's life lies beyond the scrutiny and the reach of its newspapers and pundits—the ruler's ways, the authoritarian state, the matter of succession to Mubarak, the joint military exercises with US and Egyptian forces, and so on. The animus toward America and Israel gives away the frustration of a polity raging against the hard, disillusioning limits of its political life.

In the same vein, Jordan's enlightened, fragile monarchy was bound to the United States by the strategic ties that a skilled King Hussein had nurtured for decades. But a mood of anger and seething radicalism had settled on Jordan. The country was increasingly poorer, and the fault line between Palestinians and East Bankers was a steady source of mutual suspicion. If the rulers made peace with Israel, "civil society" and the professional syndicates would spurn it. Even though the late king had deep ties with the distant imperial power, the country would remain unreconciled to this pro-American stance. Jordan would be richer, it was loudly proclaimed, if only the sanctions on Iraq had been lifted, if only the place had been left to gravitate into Iraq's economic orbit. Jordan's new king, Abdullah II, could roll out the red carpet for Powell when the general turned up in Jordan recently on a visit that had the distinct sense of a victory lap by a soldier revisiting his early triumph. But the throngs were there with placards, and banners were aloft branding the visitor a "war criminal." This kind of fury a distant power can never overcome. Policy can never speak to wrath. Step into the thicket (as Bill Clinton did in the Israeli-Palestinian conflict) and the foreign power is damned for its reach. Step back, as George W. Bush did in the first months of his presidency, and Pax Americana is charged with abdication and indifference.

The power secured during Desert Storm was destined not to last. The United States could not indefinitely quarantine Iraq. It was idle to think that the broad coalition cobbled together during an unusually perilous moment in 1990–91 would stand as a permanent arrangement. The demographic and economic weight of Iraq and Iran meant that those countries were bound to reassert themselves. The United States had done well in the Persian Gulf by Iraq's brazen revisionism and the Iranian revolution's assault on its neighboring states. It had been able to negotiate the terms of the US presence—the positioning of equipment in the oil states, the establishment of a trip wire in Kuwait, the acceptance of an American troop presence on the Arabian Peninsula—at a time when both Iran and Iraq were on a rampage. Hence the popular concerns that had hindered the American presence in the Persian Gulf were brushed aside in the 1990s. But this lucky run was bound to come to an end. Iraq steadily chipped away at the sanctions, which over time were seen as nothing but an Anglo-American siege of a brutalized Iraqi population.

The campaign against Saddam Hussein had been waged during a unique moment in Arab politics. Some Muslim jurists in Saudi Arabia and Egypt even ruled that Saddam had run afoul of Islam's strictures, and that an alliance with foreign powers to check his aggression and tyranny was permissible under Islamic law. A part of the Arabian Peninsula that had hitherto wanted America "over the horizon" was eager to have American protection against a "brother" who had shredded all the pieties of pan-Arab solidarity. But the Iraqi dictator hunkered down, outlasting the foreign power's terrible campaign. He was from the neighborhood and knew its rules. He worked his way into the local order of things.

The Iraqi ruler knew well the distress that settled on the region after Pax Americana's swift war. All around Iraq, the region was poorer: oil prices had slumped, and the war had been expensive for the oil states that financed it. Oil states suspected they were being overbilled for military services and for weapons that they could not afford. The war's murky outcome fed the belief that the thing had been rigged all along, that Saddam Hussein had been lured into Kuwait by an American green light—and then kept in power and let off the hook—so that Pax Americana would have the pretext for stationing its forces in the region. The Iraqi ruler then set out to show the hollowness of the hegemony of a disinterested American imperium.

A crisis in 1996 laid bare the realities for the new imperium. Saddam Hussein brazenly sent his squads of assassins into the "safe haven" that the United States had marked out for the

Kurds in northern Iraq after Desert Storm. He sacked that region and executed hundreds who had cast their fate with American power. America was alone this time around. The two volleys of Tomahawk missiles fired against Iraqi air-defense installations had to be launched from US ships in the Persian Gulf and B-52 bombers that flew in from Guam. No one was fooled by the American response; no one believed that the foreign power would stay. US officials wrote off that episode as an internal Kurdish fight, the doings of a fratricidal people. A subsequent air campaign—"fire and forget," skeptics dubbed it— gave the illusion of resolve and containment. But Clinton did not have his heart in that fight. He had put his finger to the wind and divined the mood in the land: there was no public tolerance for a major campaign against Saddam Hussein.

By the time the Bush administration stepped in, its leaders would find a checkered landscape. There was their old nemesis in Baghdad, wounded but not killed. There was a decade of Clintonianism that had invested its energy in the Israeli-Palestinian conflict but had paid the Persian Gulf scant attention. There was a pattern of half-hearted responses to terrorist attacks, pinpricks that fooled no one.

It was into this witch's brew that Arafat launched the second intifada last year. In a rare alignment, there had come Arafat's way a US president keen to do his best and an Israeli soldier-statesman eager to grant the Palestinian leader all the Israeli body politic could yield—and then some. Arafat turned away from what was offered and headed straight back into his people's familiar history: the maximalism, the inability to read what can and cannot be had in a world of nations. He would wait for the "Arab street" to rise up in rebellion and force Pax Americana to redeem his claims. He would again let play on his people the old dream that they could have it all, from the river to the sea. He must have known better and he must have known the scales of power, it is reasonable to presume. But there still lurks in the Palestinian and Arab imagination a view, depicted by the Moroccan historian Abdallah Laroui, that "on a certain day, everything would be obliterated and instantaneously reconstructed and the new inhabitants would leave, as if by magic, the land they had despoiled." Arafat knew the power of this redemptive idea. He must have reasoned that it is safer to ride that idea and that there will always be another day and another offer.

For all the fury of this second intifada, a supreme irony hangs over Palestinian history. In the early 1990s, the Palestinians had nothing to lose. Pariahs in the Arab councils of power, they made their best historical decision—the peace of Oslo—only when they broke with the maximalism of their political tradition. It was then that they crossed from Arab politics into internal Israeli politics and, courtesy of Israel, into the orbit of Pax Americana. Their recent return into inter-Arab politics was the resumption of an old, failed history.

Better the fire of an insurrection than the risks of reconciling his people to a peace he had not prepared them for: this was Arafat's way. This is why he spurned the offer at Camp David in the summer of 2000. "Yasir Arafat rode home on a white horse" from Camp David, said one of his aides, Nabil Shaath. He had shown that he "still cared about Jerusalem and the refugees." He had stood up, so Shaath said, to the combined pressure of the Americans and the Israelis. A creature of his time and his world, Arafat had come into his own amid the recriminations that followed the Arab defeat in 1948. Palestine had become an Arab shame, and the hunt for demons and sacrificial lambs would shape Arab politics for many years.

A temporizer and a trimmer, Arafat did not have it in him to tell the 1948 refugees in Lebanon, Syria, and Jordan that they were no more likely to find political satisfaction than were the Jews of Alexandria, Fez, Baghdad, and Beirut who were banished from Arab lands following Israel's statehood. He lit the fuse of this second intifada in the hope that others would put out the flame. He had become a player in Israeli politics, and there came to him this peculiar satisfaction that he could topple Israeli prime ministers, wait them out, and then force an outside diplomatic intervention that would tip the scales in his favor. He could not give his people a decent public order and employ and train the young, but he could launch a war in the streets that would break Israel's economic momentum and rob it of the normalcy brought by the peace of Oslo.

Arafat had waited for rain, but on September 11, 2001, there had come the floods. "This is a new kind of war, a new kind of battlefield, and the United States will need the help of Arab and Muslim countries," chief Palestinian negotiator Saeb Erekat announced. The Palestinian issue, he added, was "certainly one of the reasons" for the attacks against the United States. An American-led brigade against terrorism was being assembled. America was set to embark on another expedition into Arab-Muslim domains, and Arafat fell back on the old consolation that Arab assets would be traded on his people's behalf. A dowry would have to be offered to the Arab participants in this brigade: a U.S.-imposed settlement of the Israeli-Palestinian conflict. A cover would be needed for Arab regimes nervous about riding with the foreigner's posse, and it stood to reason that Arafat would claim that he could provide that kind of cover.

The terror that hit America sprang from entirely different sources. The plotters had been in American flight schools long before the "suicide martyrs" and the "children of the stones" had answered Arafat's call for an intifada. But the Palestinian leader and his lieutenants eagerly claimed that the fire raging in their midst had inspired the anti-American terror. A decade earlier, the Palestinians had hailed Saddam Hussein's bid for primacy in the Persian Gulf. Nonetheless, they had been given a claim on the peace—a role at the Madrid Conference of October 1991 and a solicitous U.S. policy. American diplomacy had arrived in the nick of time; the first intifada had burned out and degenerated into a hunt for demons and "collaborators." A similar fate lies in wait for the second intifada. It is reasonable to assume that Arafat expects rescue of a similar kind from the new American drive into Arab and Muslim lands.

No veto over national policies there will be given to Arafat. The states will cut their own deals. In the best of worlds, Pax Americana is doomed to a measure of solitude in the Middle East. This time around, the American predicament is particularly acute. Deep down, the Arab regimes feel that the threat of political Islam to their own turfs has been checked and that no good can come out of an explicit public alliance with an American campaign in their midst. Foreign powers come and go, and there is very little protection they can provide against the wrath of an angry crowd. It is a peculiarity of the Arab-Islamic political culture that a ruler's authoritarianism is more permissible than his identification with Western powers—think of the fates of Sadat and of the Pahlavis of Iran.

Ride with the foreigners at your own risk, the region's history has taught. Syria's dictator, Hafez al-Assad, died a natural death at a ripe old age, and his life could be seen as a kind of success. He never set foot on American soil and had stayed within his world. In contrast, the flamboyant Sadat courted foreign countries and came to a solitary, cruel end; his land barely grieved for him. A foreign power that stands sentry in that world cannot spare its local allies the retribution of those who brand them "collaborators" and betrayers of the faith. A coalition was in the offing, and America had come calling, urging the region's rulers to "choose sides." What these rulers truly dread has come to pass: they might have to make fateful choices under the gaze of populations in the throes of a malignant anti-Americanism. The ways of that world being what they are, the United States will get more cooperation from the ministers of interior and the secret services than it will from the foreign ministers and the diplomatic interlocutors. There will be allies in the shadows, but in broad daylight the rulers will mostly keep their distance. Pakistan's ruler, Pervez Musharraf, has made a brave choice. The rulers all around must be reading a good deal of their worries into his attempt to stay the course and keep his country intact.

A broad coalition may give America the comfort that it is not alone in the Muslim world. A strike against Afghanistan is the easiest of things—and far away from the troubles in the Persian Gulf and Egypt, from the head of the trail in Arab lands. The Taliban are the Khmer Rouge of this era and thus easy to deal with. The frustrations to come lie in the more ambiguous and impenetrable realms of the Arab world. Those were not Afghans who flew into those towers of glass and steel and crashed into the Pentagon. They were from the Arab world, where anti-Americanism is fierce, where terror works with the hidden winks that men and women make at the perpetrators of the grimmest of deeds.

"When those planes flew into those buildings, the luck of America ran out," Leon Wieseltier memorably wrote in *The New Republic.* The 1990s were a lucky decade, a fool's paradise. But we had not arrived at the end of history, not by a long shot. Markets had not annulled historical passions, and a high-tech world's electronic age had not yet dawned. So in thwarted, resentful societies there was satisfaction on September 11 that the American bull run and the triumphalism that had awed the world had been battered, that there was soot and ruin in New York's streets. We know better now. Pax Americana is there to stay in the oil lands and in Israeli-Palestinian matters. No large-scale retreat from those zones of American primacy can be contemplated. American hegemony is sure to hold—and so, too, the resistance to it, the uneasy mix in those lands of the need for the foreigner's order, and the urge to lash out against it, to use it and rail against it all the same.

There was now the distinct thunder of war. The first war of the twenty-first century is to be fought not so far from where the last inconclusive war of the twentieth century was waged against Iraq. The war will not be easy for America in those lands. The setting will test it in ways it has not been tested before. There will be regimes asking for indulgence for their own terrible fights against Islamists and for logistical support. There will be rulers offering the bait of secrets that their security services have accumulated through means at odds with American norms. Conversely, friends and sympathizers of terror will pass themselves off as constitutionalists and men and women of the "civil society." They will find shelter behind pluralist norms while aiding and abetting the forces of terror. There will be chameleons good at posing as America's friends but never turning up when needed. There will be one way of speaking to Americans, and another of letting one's population know that words are merely a pretense. There will step forth informers, hustlers of every shade, offering to guide the foreign power through the minefields and alleyways. America, which once held the world at a distance, will have to be willing to stick around eastern lands. It is both heartbreaking and ironic that so quintessentially American a figure as George W. Bush—a man who grew up in Midland, Texas, far removed from the complications of foreign places—must be the one to take his country on a journey into so alien, so difficult, a world.

SOURCE NOTES:

For more insights into the Saudi religious scholar Shaykh Safar al-Hawali and his anti-American rants, please see Mamoun Fandy's article, "Safar al-Hawali: Saudi Islamist or Saudi Nationalist?" *Islam and Christian Muslim Relations*, 9, March 1999.

For Bernard Lewis's interpretation of Osama bin Laden's fatwa and a translation of some passages, please see "License to Kill: Usama bin Ladin's Declaration of Jihad," *Foreign Affairs*, November/December 1998.

An electronic copy of the redacted investigation by the military commission on the *USS Cole* can be found at http://www.foia.mil/usscole.

Abdallah Laroui's remarks come from his book *The Crisis of the Arab Intellectual*, Berkeley, University of California Press, 1976.

Leon Wieseltier's article about 9/11, "It Happened Here," the editors, *The New Republic*, September 24, 2001.

Chapter 6

The Making of a Hijacker

*The Banal Lie and Barbarous Deeds of a
9/11 Terrorist*

Of the 19 young Arabs who struck the United States on September 11, 2001, the Lebanese-born Ziad Jarrah, who is thought to have been at the controls of the plane forced down by its heroic passengers in Shanksville, Pennsylvania, has always been of greater interest to me than the others, and for strictly parochial reasons: we were both born in the same country, but two generations apart. For me, the contours of his life are easy to make out. He hailed from a privileged Sunni family from the Bekaa Valley and was raised in Beirut. He had gone to an elite French lycée, Collège de la Sagesse, one of the country's most prestigious. In the fashion of the Lebanese families of means, great hopes were pinned on him and nothing was denied him. He was his parents' only male child. There was little if any religious observance in his family. His sisters were modern young women of Beirut; they hit the beaches of the city in the summer, and they and their brother were carefree souls. The boy

This essay originally appeared in *The New Republic*, September 15, 2011, and is republished here in slightly different form with the cooperation and consent of the original publisher.

wanted to be a pilot; his father had vetoed that choice, so he settled for a course in aeronautical engineering and aircraft design. In a place like Beirut, that occupational ambition was glamorous. It was never easy making one's way in Lebanon. The country was crowded, and there wasn't enough to go around for all the dreams and ambitions swirling about.

Jarrah's life—the details of which were chronicled by two Beirut dailies, *An Nahar* and *L'Orient-Le Jour*, as well as the *Der Spiegel* staff in a 2002 book titled *Inside 9–11: What Really Happened*—began in 1975. And the year of his birth was of no small consequence to the journey he made. It was the year the long and bloody Lebanese civil war broke out, the war that would last a good generation. All the verities gave way; the bourgeois dreams of prosperity and safety rested in the palms of the devil, as the Arabs would say. The Lebanese continued to say the usual things about their country—that the wars in their midst were inflicted on them by others, that Lebanon was a secular, modern place where the crescent embraced the cross, and that no one bothered with the religious identity of their neighbors. All the while, the religious and sectarian slaughter went on unabated, and Beirut became a divided city at war with itself. Some Lebanese held onto the old ways. The Jarrah family's sending of their only son to a Catholic school was of a piece with that fidelity and with the ambition they had for him.

At age 20, Jarrah would leave his birthplace—nothing unusual about that, as the Lebanese are the quintessential migrants. Their country was poor, but the people consoled themselves, saying that they were Phoenicians and that adventures and voyages abroad were in their blood. Jarrah's destination was Germany. There, his good looks, charm, and ease of manners—Beirut taught that to the young, particularly to the young on their way to foreign lands where they would depend on the kindness of strangers—served him well. A German landlady was taken with him. She was an artist and painted his portrait. Aysel Senguen—a young woman of Turkish descent, fiercely irreligious, and a medical student—fell in love with him, and there were plans for marriage.

But there was a great rupture in Jarrah's life. The boy who never missed a party in Beirut would now never miss a prayer in Hamburg. The turn to religion announced itself in small ways—this is standard in the biographies of Islamic militants. His girlfriend remembered him suddenly growing irritated with her choice of clothing, with her drinking. He enrolled at the University of Applied Science in Hamburg; in nearby Harburg, he drifted into a circle of Muslim students. There he met the Egyptian Mohamed Atta, who, in time, would lead the death pilots. This was freelance religion—faith without the mediation of religious authorities, faith in *bilad al-Kufr* (the land of unbelief), a militant faith offered as penance for a party boy who had never known, or practiced, the rituals of the faith. He would journey to Afghanistan and offer a pledge of loyalty to Osama bin Laden in 1999. He kept his family in the dark about this turn in his life. We have no record of what he thought of Afghanistan, but he had his Beirut snobbery, and, doubtless, he would have seen the stark surroundings through the prism of his upbringing in that polished city by the Mediterranean.

The journey to the United States in the summer of 2000 was the journey of a jihadist in preparation. He would take a course in martial arts and attend a flight school in Venice, Florida. He set off no alarms. Always with Jarrah, there was the polish of his background; bin Laden had chosen his killers well. They were taught to slip into the world of the infidels undetected. A boy educated in a Catholic school was now ready to kill and die for the faith.

Jarrah's new piety can be glimpsed in the farewell letter he wrote to Senguen on September 10: "I did not leave you alone. Allah is with you, and with my parents. If you need anything, then ask Him for what you need. He listens and knows what is within you. Hold on to what you have until we meet again. And then we will have a very beautiful eternal life, where no problems exist and where there is no mourning." For Jarrah, there had been no immersion in the scripture and the sources, no stultifying education in a madrassa. He would have had no time for the tracts of Sayyid Qutb. The textualism of the Islamists was not for him. There was the confusion hurled at him by the tumult of Beirut. There was the effect of the storefront mosques that had sprouted in Europe and North America. There were the attachments formed with fellow Arabs in an alien European setting. That fellowship appears to have mattered greatly to him; he had never been a loner.

The haunting thing about Jarrah is the banality of his journey and the barbarism of his deed. He did not come from poverty; he had an allowance of $2,000 a month from his family. There had been no evidence of a deep religious attachment, no indication of some burning hatred of the United States. There is no aversion to women, no trace of the misogyny that Atta gave voice to in his last will and testament. Atta had not wanted women to pray over him, or to come to his graveside and rend their garments and grieve for him. In contrast, Jarrah's final and most felt sentiments were the consoling words he had sent to his intended bride. Modernism offended Atta and was alien to the 15 young Saudis, most of whom came from the insular southwestern hinterland of that country. This Lebanese young man of 26, who boarded United Airlines Flight 93 in Newark and took it to its grim end, was at ease with the modern world. The very normalcy of his upbringing and the old hedonism giving way to a sudden need for absolution are much more unsettling than the warning signs and the zeal of a true believer. No sooner does he come into focus for me—the familiarity of his life, the ways of the city where we both were brought up—than I lose him, and he becomes a man possessed, a stranger.

SOURCE NOTE:

For further reading on the events of September 11, 2001, see *Inside 9–11: What Really Happened*, by the Reporters, Writers, and Editors of *Der Spiegel* Magazine (St. Martin's Press, 2002).

Chapter 7

Writing Iraq

REVIEW:

The Occupation of Iraq: Winning the War, Losing the Peace,
by Ali A. Allawi

I.

ay what you will about the American experience in Vietnam, that war was well written. *A Bright Shining Lie* by Neil Sheehan had a character who could have stepped out of the pages of a Graham Greene novel. John Paul Vann was an even more arresting figure than Alden Pyle in *The Quiet American.* "The odds, he said, did not apply to him," Sheehan wrote of the unforgettable man who embodied the war's hubris and the war's undoing. Michael Herr's *Dispatches* became a cult book—it described the hallucinatory war, the first rock-and-roll war—and therefore suffered the fate of cult books, but there can be no denying its magic and power. Frances FitzGerald, in *Fire in the Lake,* attempted to give Vietnamese culture the respectful, close reading it deserved: what interested her about our war was not merely that it was ours. She wrote about our Other. And we do not need to guess what the men of the New Frontier who waged that war were really up to, thanks to David Halberstam's lasting portrait of "the best and the brightest":

This essay originally appeared in *The New Republic*, April 23, 2007, with the title "Blind Liberation"; it is republished here in slightly different form with the cooperation and consent of the original publisher.

He was Bob, Bob McNamara, taut, controlled, driving—climbing mountains, harnessing generals—the hair slicked down in a way that made him look like a Grant Wood subject. The look was part of the drive: a fat McNamara was as hard to imagine as an uncertain one. The glasses straight and rimless, imposing; you looked at the glasses and kept your distance. He was a man of force, moving, pushing, getting things done, Bob got things done, the can-do man in the can-do society, in the can-do era.

So in this way, too, pity our venture into Iraq: its literary yield has fallen way short of the Vietnam standard. No doubt this land in Araby where we have planted our truth, and our armor, is a truly arcane and forbidding place; but still the poverty of the literature of this American expedition begs for an explanation. In the books about the war, it became the norm to decry the faults of the American viceroy, Paul Bremer, and to note that the man, a gourmand with diplomatic assignments in Norway and Holland behind him, a man who marked time in Iraq but pined for his retreat in Vermont, could not find his way into the recesses of the Iraqi culture. True enough about the American, but what about Iraq? The military correspondent Thomas Ricks had a success with his book about the "fiasco" of the American military campaign, but no Iraqis walk out of his pages. This was not a man who had "embedded" himself with the people of the Anbar province.

This was certainly not war in the Jimi Hendrix era. Iraq was lethal, and outsiders had difficulty moving about outside the safety of the American enclave. The women, available everywhere in Vietnam, were off-limits here. In most of the American chronicles, Iraq is hunkered down and hidden, its people and ways and language inaccessible. (France had left its language behind in Vietnam, which provided Western writers with a kind of entry into the culture.) In Iraq the outsiders were on their own, captives of the Green Zone, of the "minders" and the interpreters.

It was hard, practically impossible, to bond with the place. Shiism was not waiting to be deciphered or understood; Muqtada al-Sadr had no time, and no desire, to explain the origins of his worldview, his noble pedigree, the high clerical tradition of his family, to foreign reporters. It was enough for him that his devoted followers knew the magic of his lineage. The reclusive Grand Ayatollah Ali al-Sistani, in his modest home on a lane in Najaf's souk, kept the invading power—and the press that came with it—at bay. In one of my favorite anecdotes of Iraq, an American diplomat of considerable sway asked an Iraqi interlocutor what the term *hawza* (a Shia study group and academic circle) meant. "It's amazing," the Iraqi academic answered. "You send a huge army to this country, but you don't know the most rudimentary thing about its life."

We had made our way into a land that had been hermetically sealed to outsiders. We never had the slightest interest in Iraq. There were Americans who knew Beirut and the Palestinians; there were the expats, the oil prospectors and engineers who had bonded with the people of the Peninsula; and there came a time, in the 1970s, when Egypt was incorporated into the American orbit. The late King Hussein of Jordan had made his realm accessible and familiar to us—he even married a Princetonian. But Iraq had never figured in the American imagination, or in the American scheme of things. We were invading the most insular of countries.

But invade it we did, and so we had to talk ceaselessly of Iraq. The travelers and the journalists and the talking heads made the obligatory visit to the Green Zone and returned with a spurious authority. This was how you staked a claim to the airwaves; it was important to go over there if you were to be listened to over here. Iraq became a background, a credential. A kind of "nonaggression pact" was entered into by the instant experts: no one called anybody else's expertise into question. In this way, Iraq became the subject of some of the darkest hours in the history of expertise. We were on the lookout for the deficiencies of our soldiers and our bureaucrats in Iraq. We had taken the Iraqis out of the Iraq story, and we settled in for another bout of American narcissism—our deeds, our failures, our war.

It fell to Dexter Filkins to give the Iraq war its most haunting rendition by an American writer. *The Forever War* is in every way the equal of the best works on Vietnam. Michael Herr's *Dispatches* has nothing on the reporting of Filkins. Indeed the latter has the advantage of poise and control. Filkins does not strain for impact; the terrible war does this on its own. His book aptly opens with an epigraph from the great novelist Cormac McCarthy, and this book has the morals and sensibility and cadence of McCarthy's prose. Filkins didn't go to Iraq to become a television commentator. The war, in all its unforgiving cruelty, took him there. He held nothing back, and his opening is a masterpiece of writing. It is Fallujah, the "city of mosques," in November 2004. The jihadists who had held this town for seven months had come to take it back. From the loudspeakers of the minarets, there was a call for a holy war against the infidels. "And then, as if from the depths, came a new sound: violent, menacing and dire." He recognized it right away, it was AC/DC, an Australian heavy metal band.

There is no sentimentalism in the work of Mr. Filkins. But the intimacy with which he works produces vignettes of heartbreaking power. He jogged in Baghdad—a madness all its own. On one run, an Iraqi boy by the name of Hassan started running next to him in his bare feet. The boy, nine years old, stayed with him for the full two-and-a-half miles and then dropped off to wave goodbye. A few days later, at twilight, the boy appeared again. He pointed to the Republican Palace. "Saddam House," the boy said. "Now, Bush House." He never saw the boy again on his runs. Later in the summer, another Iraqi youngster pulled up alongside him, a girl by the name of Fatima, also nine years of age. "She wore sandals, and she was very dirty. She kept up the pace. . . . After a time, she indicated that she needed a rest. We stopped at one of the open-air fish restaurants. A man put a hand on Fatima's shoulder and ran a finger across his neck. Mother, father finished. He pointed to the sky, as if to suggest that they had been killed by bombs. Fatima lived here. . . . Then a second man walked up, twisted Fatima around and gave her a long, ugly kiss on her lips. He laughed and walked away. Fatima looked at me with very sad eyes, and I suggested it was time to go. We ran some more and then, after a time, Fatima stopped. Bye-bye tomorrow, OK? Fatima said, and she turned and walked up the street. I never saw her again."

II.

Ali A. Allawi's magnificent book arrives not a moment too soon. Here, finally, is a man of Iraq who knows its history and its wounds. He can write with deep understanding about its poets, its intellectuals, its clerics. He thoroughly grasps its peculiar place in its neighborhood, caught as it has been for several centuries between an Arab sense of belonging and currents from the

Persian state to its east. A man of the Shia aristocracy—a cousin of Ayad Allawi, and a maternal nephew of Ahmad Chalabi—and a man of Baghdad, Allawi was marked for exile. His father had been one of the country's most respected physicians and had served as minister of health under the monarchy. His family left Iraq after the revolution of 1958, when he was a boy of ten. He was sent to boarding school in "deepest Sussex," then to MIT and Harvard. He found a big world outside Iraq, and financial success. But his country would continue to tug at him.

Allawi was active in the politics of the exiles and made his return to his homeland shortly after the destruction of the regime of Saddam Hussein. This was no carpetbagger who had come back for the loot. By all reports a man of exacting integrity, he has served, at one time or another, as minister of trade, defense, and finance, and as a member of parliament. A man with a literary bent and a feel of his country's torments, Allawi has now come forth with a testimony that will endure. Away from home for decades, he brought with him what Leon Wieseltier once called the "stranger's wakefulness." But he is invested in his country's ordeal as no stranger could be.

After three decades—many lifetimes in a country that has been through what Iraq endured in wars and despotism and devastating economic sanctions—Allawi returned to a country altered beyond recognition. In our image of it, Iraq had been a Sunni dominion, but there always was a special place in it for the Shia aristocracy of Baghdad into which Allawi was born. There had been a pact that marked out the political life, which he ably describes:

Essentially, it was based on the recognition by the Shi'a elite that they might have some share of central power, within limits that would satisfy the more ambitious of their leaders. But they should not aspire to control or run the state, even though their numbers might warrant this. At the same time, the state, dominated by the Sunni Arabs, would recognize and acknowledge the props of Shi'a identity, and would not move to alter or shrink them in any significant way. Essentially, the Sunni Arabs controlled the state, while the Shi'a were allowed to keep their civil, mercantile and religious traditions. It was a precarious balance, but it held the potential for improvement and progress towards a common sense of citizenship, duties and entitlements. Successive governments in the 1960s and 1970s, however, foolishly destroyed this. The state removed the elements that kept a vigorous Shi'a identity alive in parallel to a Sunni-dominated state. Nationalizations, emigration and expulsions destroyed the Shi'a mercantilist class; the state monopoly on education, publishing and the media removed the cultural underpinnings of Shi'a life; and the attack on Najaf and the religious hierarchy came close to completely eliminating the hawzas of Iraq. When the state embarked on the mass killings after the 1991 uprisings, Iraq became hopelessly compromised in the minds of most Shi'a.

The restraints of the ancien régime had given way. From afar, the exiles and the Anglo-American planners of the coming war talked of the modernism of Iraq and of the promise of its vast middle class. But the country of memory had ceased to exist.

There had been, Allawi observes, something of a brief "golden period" of the middle class in the 1970s. It was a time of official brutality; but oil income had given Iraqis a shot at a new life.

This was not destined to last. The 1990s—the years of sanctions and hyperinflation—had devastated the bourgeoisie. Proud men and women auctioned off their movable assets to survive. There was a mass exodus of professionals to any country that would have them. A "faith campaign" launched by Saddam Hussein when all was lost and compromised—a time of false piety, when the hijab spread in ever-greater numbers and a show was made against the consumption of liquor—hid the misery and the moral collapse. Some women, now heads of households as never before, were driven into prostitution. The pride of this country, a relatively advanced educational system, cracked. By 2000, a quarter of school-age children had given up on school, and children scrambled to help support eroding family incomes. By 2003, nearly half the adult population was illiterate. So the liberating power had its work cut out for it: it swept into a brutalized country.

More problematic still, the past of this land was everywhere in its present. A past deeper and older than the sanctions, older even than the regime of the Baath, haunted Iraqis. Allawi finds his way into his country's temperament and its tradition through the work of Iraq's most distinguished and controversial sociologist, the scholar Ali al-Wardi (1913–1995), a US-educated Shia writer who spent a lifetime trying to decipher his country's ways. Intuitive, anecdotal, dismissive of the statistical pretensions of Anglo-American social science, Wardi left behind a huge body of writing. Inspired by the work of the great fourteenth-century North African scholar Ibn Khaldun, Wardi believed that the process of urbanization, indeed modernism itself, was skin-deep in Iraq. For Wardi, and for Allawi after him, the country's turbulent history rested on a "pervasive dichotomy between the city, representing urban civilized values, and the steppes, representing the prevalence of nomadic, tribal values."

Back and forth, Iraqis oscillated between the desert and the town. "The sense of the impermanence of the source of their values drove Iraqis into developing their noted schizoid qualities," Allawi observes. "The desert could actually or metaphorically encroach on the city, while at the same time, the city could tame the desert by harnessing the country's waters and cultivating its soil." The struggle between town and country took on a special deadly meaning here, for it lay across the fault line between the Sunnis and the Shia. In Wardi's classification, the southern part of the country, the heartland of Shiism, was a settled urban world, while Sunnism, with its nomadic and tribal culture, was based in the western steppes of Iraq.

The Anglo-American war planners were unaware of this history. But this was the actual country that awaited its foreign liberators. In Allawi's elegant summation: "When the Coalition arrived in Baghdad on 9 April, 2003, it found a fractured and brutalized society, presided over by a fearful, heavily armed minority. The post 9/11 jihadi culture that was subsequently to plague Iraq was just beginning to take root. The institutions of the state were moribund; the state exhausted. The ideology that had held Ba'athist rule had decayed beyond repair."

In the best of circumstances, it would have been extremely difficult to repair this country and to hold it together. But Iraq was soon to become the battleground of an ideological war, and a turf war, between different wings of the American national security bureaucracy. The "realists" in the Central Intelligence Agency and in the State Department lost the early rounds, but they soon struck back. The victory that would come their way shortly after the fall of Baghdad would set the pattern of the

American venture in Iraq. On May 6, 2003, as Allawi narrates it, George W. Bush announced that Paul Bremer would be the top civilian administrator in Iraq. Two days later, the United States and Britain announced that they were sponsoring a resolution that would grant them the status of occupying powers. On May 12, Bremer landed in Baghdad, the proconsul of an occupation regime. This, Allawi remarks, had come like a "thunderbolt out of the blue" to the Iraqi political class. The Iraqi leaders had expected a sovereign government of their own. But Colin Powell and the CIA had fought an effective rearguard battle: the "American project" in Iraq would be stripped of the ideological promise of an independent Iraq that would be a showcase for other Arabs. In no uncertain terms, Bremer would make it clear to the principal Iraqi leaders that his writ would run in Iraq and that genuine authority was invested in him and in the Coalition Provisional Authority (CPA) over which he presided.

But Bremer was no Douglas MacArthur, and this was not America in an age of self-confidence born of a great, decisive war. The American occupiers were not of one mind as to what ought to be done with this imperial acquisition. Wild-eyed schemes for remaking the country, recasting it as a bastion of free enterprise and participatory politics, clashed with bouts of reticence and the hard-boiled sentiment that Iraq was what it was and therefore was best dealt with through incrementalism. An old totalitarian bureaucracy soon found the cracks in the occupying powers' authority and knowledge. "The CPA did not demolish the state that it had inherited and then start to rebuild it along the lines that it prescribed," Allawi writes. "This was the usual way of working in countries that had been totally defeated in war and then occupied. But the CPA insisted on keeping the form and most of the content of Iraq's government intact."

The proconsul made sweeping declarations, but the Iraqi bureaucracy stalled and waited him out. In a telling metaphor, Allawi likens the CPA reforms to a demolition ball that struck a huge, decrepit building but unevenly inflicted minor damage on the edifice: "The foundations, and a considerable part of the superstructure of the dysfunctional state, remained." A huge amount of cash was sloshing around the country, and the old networks of corruption and inside dealing would reconstitute themselves in record time. This was the perfect playground for carpetbaggers and profiteers.

A show was made of Iraq's independence, a transparent cover for the occupation with the formation of a Governing Council, a twenty-five-member body drawn from the exiles and the political parties that had staked a claim to the new order. Oddly, the American regency had no sooner midwifed this Governing Council than it set out to undermine it. It was said of this council that it was unrepresentative of Iraq, and thus would not be granted sovereignty or power. This was in part the bureaucratic imperative of the CPA; but the Americans had perhaps caught the bias in the Sunni Arab world against this body. In Amman, in Cairo, in the Peninsula, in the circles of the Arab League, there was a fierce hostility to the Governing Council. It was written off as a group of quislings and "collaborators."

This was peculiar, for the entire region lay within the American orbit of power, and American security arrangements bound virtually all the ruling regimes to the Pax Americana. Yet the council, with a bare Shia majority, was singled out for abuse by the domesticated media of the Arab world and its satellite channels. When, in May 2004, an American-led raid on the home of Governing Council member Ahmad Chalabi took place, the play in Baghdad was laid bare. Chalabi had emerged over the preceding year as a relentless advocate of Iraqi sovereignty; but the American regency was bent on having its way. And beyond this raid, the shape of things to come had crystallized in the first year of the occupation: the CPA, for all its pretensions to absolute power, was being driven into what Allawi aptly describes as a "physical and psychological ghetto." Outside the bubble of the Green Zone, a violent insurgency was taking shape. This insurgency was an affair of a thousand discontents: hostility toward an occupation, the anger of the Sunni Arab "supremacists" (a fitting word for the extreme elements in that community) at the loss of power, the desire for plunder and revenge, the conviction among the Shia that this was their chance to make the Iraqi state in their own image and to claim it for themselves.

III.

It is the gift of Allawi's narrative that his is not merely a story of American incompetence or the CPA follies. (He leaves this to the self-regarding Americans.) For beyond Bremer and the "wet behind the ears" crowd that came with the occupation and quickly gave up when Iraq confounded or "disappointed" them, there were deep changes within Iraq itself; and they would in the end determine Iraq's destination. The ghost of Wardi would make its appearance with a vengeance: desert and town would descend into a new war. And this war would be fought in an Arab world where swords—and identities—were being sharpened and drawn in a new fight between the old Sunni hegemony and the Shia outcasts now pressing for a new place in the sun.

We owe to Allawi a clear account of the impact upon Shia consciousness—and its subsequent radicalization—of the discovery of mass graves during the first year of the occupation. The brutality of the regime toward the Shia, and the Kurds, was well known. But the mass graves—and the documentary evidence: the Baathists were meticulous about keeping records of their grim atrocities—were to "harden the determination of the Shi'a to carve for themselves a commanding role in the new Iraq." The estimates of the scale of the terror were not precise. Human rights organizations put the victims at 300,000, while the American estimates ran to 400,000. Either way, the psychological impact of these mass graves on the Shia sense of righteousness and violation was immense.

These great crimes had taken place, the Shia knew, against the background of wider Arab indifference. The years since 1991, when Saddam's regime survived the first American-led war and turned its wrath on the Shia and the Kurds, had been a time of great terror. The Kurds had made their way out of Iraq, psychologically and physically; the Anglo-American coalition had secured for them a separate state in all but name. But the Shia had remained in the big prison, and what little traces of mercy and restraint existed in Saddam's domain had vanished. The psychological and physical terror unleashed on the Shia dwarfed the "traditional" brutalities of preceding Iraqi regimes.

Moreover, the Shia who had taken refuge in Iran had returned with accounts to settle. In an important distinction, Allawi remarks that the Shia had been loyal to the country but not to the state. Now the country was to be made fully theirs. Power would drift to the Islamists among the Shia; and men such as

Chalabi and Ayad Allawi, Baghdad aristocrats with years of exposure to the West, would scramble to keep their place. The men of the Dawaa Party—the party of Nuri Kamal al-Maliki, the current prime minister—came into their own. The Baghdadi Shia, heirs to an urban mercantile tradition, would cede their primacy to political men born and reared in the Shia heartland of the southern and middle Euphrates.

This new Islamism among the Shia did not transpire overnight. The crucible had been the cruel interlude between the onset of the Iranian revolution in 1979–80 and the fall of Baghdad in 2003. In 1980 there occurred a searing crime against the Shia: the execution by the Baath regime of Iraqi Shiism's brightest star, Ayatollah Muhammad Baqir al-Sadr. A philosopher of deep modernism, a writer of exquisite talent, a genuinely charismatic figure, he was marked for destruction by the Baath regime, which was locked in an ideological battle with Ayatollah Ruhollah Khomeini. An example was to be made of him; he and his sister, Bint al-Huda, a poet and a scholar in her own right, were put to death shortly before the regime plunged into its catastrophic war with Iran. (Sadr came to be called "the first martyr"; another Sadr, Ayatollah Muhammad Sadiq al-Sadr, Muqtada al-Sadr's father, was assassinated in 1999 and given the designation "the second martyr.")

In the decade of unrestrained terror that followed the first Gulf War, the life of the Shia seminarians had atrophied. Shiism had been pushed into the underground. The *ulama* (clerics) who survived had opted for quiescence—the traditional *taqiyya* (dissimulation) of the Shia. But another current of Iraqi Shiism, bearing the brand of persecution, had been waiting for deliverance. In its zeal for hegemony, the regime assaulted the reed beds, the very ecology, of the marshes in the south. The Shia of the marshes sought shelter in Baghdad, in the slums that would become known as Sadr City. It was in this culture, and to this yearning for vengeance, that young Muqtada al-Sadr was to find his role. His father, an ayatollah who had arranged his own détente with the regime only to break with it, had been killed, along with two of his older brothers. Muqtada would take the gift of this American war, but without incurring any debt to the liberating power. Perhaps America came too late for gratitude on the part of the Shia. The American betrayal in 1991 had already become part of the Shia narrative of righteousness and defeat.

The chaos of Iraq after 2003 and the virulence of the Sunni attack on the Shia would give the Shia diehards their opportunity to push for their own utopia. In seclusion in Najaf, Grand Ayatollah Ali al-Sistani struggled mightily against these gale winds. He gave the presence of the coalition his tacit approval. He forbade revenge killings. He did his best to keep the poise of Shiism against the background of a relentless assault against his community. The young hothead Muqtada al-Sadr bristled against the controls thrown up by the *Marjiiyya* (the official religious institution of the Shia jurists) of Sistani. He probed the limits of his community's religious and political order with attacks on Sistani for his quietism in the days of the terror and hints that the great jurist was an Iranian and so an outsider to Iraq, all of this balanced by professions of loyalty to the great man. The center of Shiism has so far held, though the Islamists have staked their claim to the spoils of power.

The world of the Sunni Arabs was undergoing its own transformation. In a rational world, the Sunni Arabs might have let well enough alone; they had ruled, and had been cruel, and the crimes of the Tikriti despotism could be laid at their doorstep.

In a world of reason, they might have traded their old privileges, and the chance for redemption offered them by the occupation authorities, for a place in the new Iraq, a role short of their old dominion but a place of honor and influence nonetheless. But this the Sunni Arabs would not do. They had the habits and the memories of power, and they had their sense of entitlement to it. They had the Sunni Arab states, and the jihadists—the suicidals, as they are called by Iraqis—beyond and around Iraq spoiling for a war against the American infidels and the Shia heretics. The Sunnis claimed Saddam and did not claim him at the same time. For them, de-Baathification was synonymous with de-Sunnification.

In the starkest and simplest of terms, the American war had robbed the Sunni Arabs of their primacy and their patrimony, and delivered them to the Iranians and to their "fifth columnists" within Iraq. Nor would the Sunni Arabs accept the basic arithmetic of the land. They were wedded to the legend that Iraq was a country of minorities, and that they, the Sunni Arabs, constituted a plurality of forty-two percent of its population. There was a weird precision about that figure; national and communal myths always include a touch of precision.

In no time, the Sunni Arabs would raise the standard of rebellion against the occupation. They had not been excessively pious, but their mosques now emerged as centers of opposition to the occupation. Fallujah, a town in the Anbar province known for its religious conservatism—it is called *madinat al masajid* (the city of mosques)—was the first to declare a virtual rebellion against the new order. Fallujah would become the stuff of legends; the Arab satellite channels outside Iraq would celebrate its heroism (as a few years earlier they had celebrated the doomed and pointless radicalism and violence of Jenin, in the West Bank). A full-fledged insurgency had "crystallized," Allawi writes. Yet the American regency was in denial. The mounting violence was written off as the work of "dead-enders" and former regime elements. "The insurgency began to gel in the summer of 2003. . . . The infrastructure war began in earnest in the summer of 2003, aimed at creating a fuel shortage inside Iraq, reducing the revenue base of the country and impeding the supply of power to the public. The political advantages of such terrorist attacks would multiply as they began to reveal the inability of the occupying power to provide a basic level of services to the public."

The Sunni Arabs had declared war against the new Iraq. By a "freak of history," Allawi says, a dominant order, the order of several centuries, was unnaturally overturned. Arab jihadists, misfits at war with their own regimes in Jordan and Algeria, Saudi Arabia and Sudan—the unwanted of the Arab world—made their way to Iraq to kill and be killed. The borders were porous, for the CPA had not fully secured them. The jihadists were deadly. But in truth, the insurgency had deep roots in the Anbar province and Mosul, and in the outskirts of Baghdad, which despotism had nurtured as a protective shield against domestic upheaval. "The insurgency was not inevitable by any stretch of the imagination," Allawi declares, "even though some form of on-going resistance would have been probable. But there was no reason why it could not have been contained, and possibly defeated, at its inception." (There is plenty of room for disagreement here. Perhaps the insurgency was fated from the start, given the will to rule on the part of the Sunni Arabs; but then, too, the kind of punishment needed to thwart the Sunni Arab insurgency was not in the cards, given the deference shown by the Pax Americana to the Sunni Arab states around Iraq.)

The Iraqi army and the security services of the old regime had not fought back; they had melted away and lived to fight another day. Given sustenance by a wider Arab world that had seen this new order in Iraq as an assault on all things Arab, the insurgents grew more brazen by the day.

IV.

A year into the time of the Americans, the regency of Paul Bremer had run its course. In an astounding development that gave away the incoherence of the American enterprise in Iraq, the Bush administration sought deliverance through the auspices of Kofi Annan and an Algerian troubleshooter of his named Lakhdar Brahimi. The latter had been a functionary of the League of Arab States; he had never bonded with the Kurds or the Shia, and they in turn were excessively wary of him. Moreover, Brahimi, who made his home in Paris, partook of the standard anti-Americanism of his political class. He looked with a jaundiced eye on the American war in Iraq and made no secret of his views. His arrival in Baghdad was, to the Shia and the Kurds, a sign that the American regency, battered and shocked by the virulence of the insurgency and the hostility of the Sunni Arabs, was embarking on a compromise with the Sunni insurgents and their fellow travelers in the political class. "I am a U.N. man," Brahimi said in protest against the enmity that welled up among the Shia. He was entrusted with the task of choosing an interim prime minister and a government that would inherit the CPA. "I will not say who was my first choice, and who was not my first choice. . . . I will remind you that the

Americans are governing this country," Brahimi declared as he tipped the scales toward the old CIA favorite Ayad Allawi.

On the face of it, Allawi was an attractive choice. He was the oddest of Shiites—a man with a bent for secrecy and an eagerness to assume and exercise power. His political beginnings had been in the Baath Party; he was tight with the security services in Jordan and Egypt. His political party, the Iraqi National Accord, drew from the Baathists who had fallen out with the regime of Saddam Hussein. His relations with the clerical institution in Najaf were correct but distant. He distrusted Iran and made no secret of what he had in mind: a national security state in the Arab mold. For defense minister, he made an ill-fated choice: Hazem Shaalan, a Shia political man who staked out an uncompromising position against the Shia religious class and against Iran.

This interim government made security its raison d'être. It would fight inconclusive campaigns in Najaf against the forces of Muqtada al-Sadr, and in Fallujah against the Sunni insurgents. This was part of Ayad Allawi's message: that he was an Iraqi patriot not given to the call of sectarianism. A man of the shadows— that is what Ali Allawi calls him—Ayad Allawi was not someone who thrilled to the cause of democracy. Left to his own devices, he would have called off the parliamentary elections scheduled for January 2005; he had the pretext of the security situation and the wide sentiment among the Sunni Arabs against turning out to vote. But he could not hold back the tide. Bush had made these elections a showcase of the war and of its legitimacy; and there was also the odd democratic weight of Sistani, who had come to see the ballot as his community's way out of fear and marginality. Under the banner of Sistani, with the old man keeping his distance from the rough-

and-tumble of politics, a big Shia electoral slate, the United Iraqi Alliance, was put forth. Ayad Allawi made his adjustment: he presented his own list to the electorate. It was known that the big Kurdish coalition—bringing together the two preeminent leaders, Jalal Talabani and Massoud Barzani—would claim the votes of Kurdistan. What remained to be decided was the balance between the Shia list and the forces arrayed around Ayad Allawi—the secular Shia, the old Baathists, the Sunni Arabs who dared defy the ban within their community on taking part in the elections. Ali Allawi writes, "Ayad Allawi was banking on the desire for order, security, Arab identity and material progress to push the Shi'a (and Sunni) voters in his direction. It was not a bad strategy, but it missed the zeitgeist."

Ayad Allawi's national security state—a variation on Hosni Mubarak's despotism, a state built on security services and crony capitalism—was overwhelmed in the elections. Bloodied by violence, hemmed in by scarcities and material needs, Iraqis had grown attached to their democratic process and were touchingly proud of it. It was what they had to show for the violence and the ruin all around them. In the end, Ayad Allawi's state fell to venality and corruption. His defense minister railed against Iran and the turbans, but a huge scam—"the largest robbery in the world," in the words of a decent judge, the head of the Integrity Commission—was perpetrated in his ministry, a theft of public funds somewhere between $1.3 billion and $2.3 billion. Finance is Ali Allawi's specialty—this would be the portfolio he would assume in the government that would replace the interim cabinet of Ayad Allawi. Those with a taste for this sort of detail can find in his pages an exacting description of the networks of corruption and patronage that reconstituted themselves under the CPA and the brief reign of Ayad

Allawi. And there is passion to spare in Ali Allawi's narrative of these scams: "Arab countries who shed crocodile tears about the plight of the Iraqi people did not bat an eyelid when a billion dollars plonked into secret accounts in their countries' banks."

This American war had called forth a genie that the Pax Americana did not like: a Shia-led Iraq. And so the Bush administration recoiled from the verdict of its own war. The Shia secularists, men of privilege and education, were equally surprised by what transpired in their country. "The fulcrum of Shi'a opinion moved decisively towards a religious and communal understanding of their identity," Allawi writes, "leaving other considerations—tribal, political, or regional—to play a distant and secondary role, at least for the time being. Most Shi'a secular politicians, together with the US and UK governments, were in deep denial about this fundamental shift in the persona of the Shi'a of Iraq." The Shia underclass had risen; the pain and the ceaseless terror inflicted on them by the jihadists and their Baathist allies led them straight into their ancient, and now very politicized, faith.

The important question now is whether the United States, under the pressure of a growing disaster, has finally accepted the Shia genie that it summoned. It was American power, direct and unapologetic, that pushed aside Prime Minister Ibrahim al-Jaafari in the spring of 2006. The United Iraqi Alliance put forth a man from Jaafari's political party and his social class, Nuri al-Maliki. A man of the hinterland with a strictly Arabic education, ill at ease with the Americans but eager to see his country through its torments, Maliki has entered into a marriage of convenience with the American occupation. When he signed Saddam Hussein's death warrant last December, he did it on his own and in defiance of the American regency. For

Maliki and his colleagues in the Dawaa Party, the execution of the tyrant was an act of fealty owed to "the first martyr," Ayatollah Muhammad Baqir al-Sadr, who had played a signal role in the birth of the Dawaa. It was hardly the only crime, or the greatest crime, for which Saddam deserved to be punished, but still justice was done.

I once observed about Ali Allawi that Turgenev would have loved such a man, the "liberal" caught in an illiberal world. Allawi feels genuine pity for the Shia underclass, but he is not of them. He had come into a hard country. He was elected to the National Assembly in the elections of January 30, 2005, but he stepped aside from the elections held a year later. There is a formality, a reticence, in Allawi's book, and it is very much in the man. The pronoun "I" hardly appears in his text. It does, though, in his preface. "The new Iraq was held together more by the numbing repetition of platitudes and quick-fix nostrums than by any vision," he writes. "When the Interim Government offered me the ambassadorship to the USA, I could not bring myself to accept it. I knew that I would faithfully have had to represent and reflect the views of a government with which I might be frequently in disagreement." But he did serve as his country's finance minister. Now he is in and out of his homeland, the disappointment leavened by the destruction of a despotism that would have otherwise lasted many more years.

It is true that the carpetbaggers and the profiteers have returned to Baghdad, and it is true that decent men and women have fled to neighboring lands, as waves of Iraqis once fled the terror of Saddam Hussein. It is certainly true that the sectarian violence in Iraq is excruciating and a threat to all prospects of decency. And yet it is not nightfall that has descended on Iraq, but a savage and uncertain dawn. Ali Allawi rates this war as one of America's "great strategic blunders." That may be, but all is not yet lost. The "neoconservatives"—a bête noire of Allawi—may have simplified Iraq's truth, and some of them may have given up on Iraqis and despaired of them and said of them the most uncharitable things; but at least they held out the promise of Arab liberty and broke with the notion that Arabs have tyranny in their DNA.

President Bush's Wilsonianism may have erred on the side of excessive optimism and may have come to him only after the hunt for weapons of mass destruction ran aground; but that is only the American side of this story. The Arab side is that modern-day Arabs had for decades been lamenting the cozy accommodation of American power to the forces of local autocracy. Lynndie England and Charles Graner were brutes and sadists at Abu Ghraib, but tens of thousands of American soldiers had for Iraqis nothing but tender mercies. The terrible errors of this war can never smother its honor, and Ali Allawi is schooled enough in the history and the sorrow of his land to know that. A new history was offering itself to the Iraqis, and in the tale of disappointment that Allawi brilliantly narrates, there was still the furtive shadow of hope, an echo of deliverance, an undisguised sense of fulfillment at the spectacle of men and women released from a terrible captivity.

"Under Saddam, we lived in a big prison; today we live in a kind of wilderness, I prefer the wilderness," an educated Iraqi woman, Dr. Lina Ziyad, observed in early 2004. This new liberty came with menace. To the Shia who had not ruled this country came newfound power. And the newly empowered who now disposed of the power of the state—the Ministry of Interior, to be exact—were no more immune to official cruelty and caprice than the old rulers. There was no built-in Shia resistance to the taste for dominion and privilege.

SOURCE NOTES:

This essay focuses in large part on the insightful book by Ali A. Allawi, *The Occupation of Iraq: Winning the War, Losing the Peace,* Yale University Press, 2007.

For an authorative portrait of Vietnam, read the late and much missed David Halberstam's book, *The Best and the Brightest,* twentieth anniversary edition (Ballantine Books, 1993).

For an intimate and compelling look into Iraq, see Dexter Filkins' *The Forever War* (Knopf, 2008).

Part III

Chapter 8

The Furrows of Algeria

REVIEW:

The German Mujahid, by Boualem Sansal; translated by
Frank Wynne

I.

From the terrible Algerian slaughter, and its terrible silence,
comes this small tale, told by an officer of the special forces who
broke with "Le Pouvoir" of his own country and sought asylum
in France. It is the autumn of 1994, deep into the season of
killing. An old and simple Algerian woman, accompanied by
two of her children, comes to the army barracks, to the very
building where the torturers did their grim work, in search of
her husband and her son. The two men were there; they had
already endured three days of torture. The woman was quite
certain where the men were being held. It was the same place,

This essay originally appeared in *The New Republic*, February 18, 2010,
and is republished here in slightly different form with the cooperation
and consent of the original publisher.

she told the astonished young Algerian officer, where the French held and tortured their prisoners during the "war of liberation" decades earlier. Her husband had been an old *mujahid* (a soldier in the holy war) and had known imprisonment under the French—and now again, during this most recent time of horror and sorrow. The old woman was never to see her husband and her son again. They perished in the ordeal of the new Algeria.

We shall never know, with precision, the number of Algerians who perished in the civil war that broke out in 1992. The Algerian rulers, not known for their fidelity to truth, and with so much to hide, owned up, in 1999, to a toll of 100,000 lives. More reliable estimates by Algeria's civic organizations put the toll at 200,000. The killing went on, a veritable hell, on the shores of the Mediterranean, some five hundred miles south of Marseilles. This was not the "African darkness" of Rwanda and Burundi; this was not the isolated jungle of Cambodia. The killing went on in the Mitidja plains, a stone's throw from Algiers. Meanwhile, in the Sahara, the work of the oil industry, and of natural gas, went on uninterrupted. An internal passport was needed for Algerians to gain access to the oil and gas fields. Expats and lucky Algerians lived here, behind high walls and checkpoints, guarded by the most sophisticated means of surveillance. The generals were unapologetic: this was *l'Algérie utile* (useful Algeria), sealed and off-limits to the terror. The generals and the men in the ruling party needed the money for their wives and their children, for the plunder and the structure of repression that they had put in place.

The war had begun, if a beginning can be assigned to it, in the fall of 1988. Riots swept the principal cities as the young took to the streets. Their grievances were bottomless: underemployment, a lack of basic consumer goods, rising food prices, the monopoly of the nomenklatura of the ruling National Liberation Front on power and privilege and opportunity. A quarter-century after the glory of independence, the Algerians tired of their own rulers. This was a ferocious revolt and a harbinger of much grief to come. Government buildings and state-owned properties were sacked, and several hundred demonstrators were gunned down by the forces of order. Chadli Bendjedid, a colorless, mediocre man at the apex of power, but in truth a front man for the brigade commanders and the security services, was cast in an impossible role: he was at once the cop and the would-be emancipator. And when the riots were put down, Bendjedid (the spitting image of Jeff Chandler, one of Hollywood's leading men in a bygone era) was repentant. He told his people that he understood the message of their revolt, conceded that many of those detained had been subjected to torture, and promised that the state would change its ways and open up the political system. Here was the Algerian Gorbachev. And as in the case of the Russian Gorbachev, the rot was deeper than he could comprehend. The bond between rulers and ruled had ruptured. The order had used up its myths. And there remained the fearsome officer corps: the state, Algeria in its entirety, had been their *ghanima* (war booty), seized from the French in the war in which a million *shuhada* (martyrs) had fallen.

The doors to power were suddenly ajar, and the Islamists rushed in to fill the void. The Algerians were keen to teach the nomenklatura a lesson, and so countless voters gulped down a beer or two before they cast their votes for an Islamist opposition, *Le Front Islamique du Salut* (the Islamic Salvation Front), also known as FIS. In June 1990, the FIS handed the ruling party an overwhelming defeat in the municipal elections and then trounced the ruling party again in the first round of legislative elections in December 1991. This was a broad, inchoate Islamist movement that had emerged from the deprivation and the anger. A philosophy professor was one of its leaders, but its rank and file were not philosophically inclined. They were merciless men keen to impose their reign of virtue and terror on an "ungodly population." They had no serious political rival. For the new men draping their desire for revenge and hegemony in Islamic colors, the time for retribution had come.

Before long, two armed camps would divide the country: Hezbollah (the Party of Allah) and Hizb França (the Party of France). Jeans were yielding to kamis in the urban alleyways, and the Islamists quickly imposed their writ on "liberated zones" they claimed as their own. Smoking was banned, as was the reading of magazines. The movement of women—to schools, to their places of employment—was severely restricted. The "Afghans" made their appearance in the land—the mujahideen who had done holy battle against the Soviet Union in Afghanistan. They were easily recognized by the paratrooper pants they wore, their long beards streaked with henna, the kohl around their eyes.

But meanwhile the generals were girding for battle, and in January 1992 they called off the scheduled national elections, sacked Bendjedid, dissolved the Islamic communes, and hauled off to prison the leaders of the FIS. In his book *La Sale Guerre* (*The Dirty War*), which appeared in 2001, Habib Souaïdia, with a military officer's knack for unadorned fact, captures the great tension and panic of this time. The lines were drawn, even in the ranks and the military academies: it was the *kaffirs* (the heretics) versus the traitors. The generals cast about for a titular figure, another front man, and they found him in Mohamed Boudiaf, one of the "historic leaders" of the war of liberation, a decent man who had been biding his time in a long exile in Morocco. He was brought in by the dominant cabal in the army, the Janviéristes, named for the coup they had mounted in January of the same year.

But Boudiaf still had the decency of his early break with the ruling party: he spoke openly of the "mafias" that controlled and plundered the economy. In June 1992, he was struck down by an officer of the presidential guard. The military cabal was done with the "historic leaders." No one believed the official story about how the assassin was an Islamist who had acted alone. In Habib Souaïdia's words, Boudiaf was caught between the hammer and the anvil. He was loathed by the Islamists for his unyielding secularism and detested by the "deciders" in the military for his campaign against the privileges of a ruling caste. Boudiaf disappeared as suddenly as he had appeared—a parenthesis, says Souaïdia, in the drama.

In the escalating war, the generals certainly proved their mettle: they killed without pity. They were also skilled in exploiting the fissures in the ranks of the Islamists and the travesties committed by the terrorists. In hindsight, we can grasp the cold-blooded and chilling efficiency of the Algerian military. The war to which they summoned their men was in truth a war against the population. There were standing orders for army units to stay in their barracks even as massacres were being committed nearby. The military said that it was important to terrorize the terrorists—which they did, and the Algerian population as a whole in the process. And there were also the "dirty tricks"—the killer squads of the army and the special forces and the *Département du Renseignement et de la Sécurité* (DRS) donning the attire of the Islamists, false beards and all, and taken by helicopter to targeted towns and villages to perpetrate frightful massacres. "Fear must change sides," the commanders exhorted their men. A killer colonel, surveying his command by helicopter, summed up the attitude of the cabal: "We are to spare no dog, no cat, no mules, no donkeys, and naturally, no Islamists. Each one of our soldiers is worth ten Islamists, be vigilant and merciless."

The corpses piled up, and no witnesses were to be left behind. There was a massacre strategy at work. The terror was pervasive, but targeted: the assailants knew their victims, sought them out, slaughtered entire families. Men and women were cut down by chainsaws. A boy who peddled cigarettes in the streets was killed in cold blood: an informer for the terrorists, it was said. Women suffered an ordeal all their own. The Islamists singled them out. Untold numbers of them were kidnapped, forced into *zawaj al motaa* (marriages of convenience) with the jihadists before they were murdered. The secret police had their own way with the young women: they had the *kabous et carta* (the gun and the professional badge), and so they blackmailed the women, forced them into sexual liaisons, and then turned them into informers.

Bodies turned up everywhere, even on treetops, dumped from the helicopters, and the grim practice of burning the cadavers developed. The other victims were buried, unrecognized, as *"l'Algérien X."* The forces of order and the Islamists were alike in their greed. They raided jewelry stores and extorted merchants; death came to those who paid and to those who did not. There were terrorists—the Tangos, they were called by the military—who posed as soldiers and soldiers who posed as terrorists. For the colonel who wanted to eradicate all the Islamists, along with the dogs and the cats and the mules, there was a prominent Islamist leader who told his men that the road to paradise was made easier, and a sure thing, if one beheaded a paratrooper. No need to bring back the bodies, one commander decreed, just the heads. The only bodies displayed atop military vehicles were the bodies of well-known Islamist leaders, to teach the population a lesson. Hooded men did what hooded men do in places where killers and their victims know each other. One young woman recognized her physics teacher hiding under his hood.

For all its radicalism and for the temperamental violence of Ali Belhadj, one of its preeminent leaders, the FIS still bore the mark of its early beginnings. It had hoped to win through the ballot box. It sought to endear itself to the population, with the usual mix of social services that are the familiar trademarks of the Muslim Brotherhood in the Arab East. But two or three years into the terror, the Algerian war was to hatch a true monster, the *Groupe Islamique Armé* (GIA). Indisputably, the GIA was a bastard child of the encounter between the Islamists and the security services of the regime. The mercy had drained out of the Islamists; they had lost faith in their ability to push the nomenklatura aside. For their part, the military commanders got the opposition they wanted—a nihilist breed that would scare the people and push them into the arms of the security forces. The terror and its dirty tricks had done their work: the ranks of the GIA included killers for hire, Islamists who had been turned around by both torture and inducement, and genuine fanatics making war against God's enemies.

Kill the adults to punish them, kill the children to save them: this was the code of the GIA. In the catacombs of this fight to the death, hell had found its enforcers. Many false emirs came out of the bowels of the security forces. The GIA could not win: this was a big country and a regime with means.

(The oil despotisms must always be seen as a case apart—they can kill as long as the revenues keep flowing in.) For the military establishment, that was the sweetness of the thing: it was not pretty, but it was deliverance nonetheless. It was hard to do the decent thing in this war. The scruples of Habib Souaïdia, and no doubt the scruples of so many good people caught between the two horrific camps, landed him, and them, in prison. Souaïdia had always wanted to be a soldier, but now he found himself in the company of assassins, brigands, and thieves. He arrested terrorists at great risk to himself and his men, only to see them released by his superiors. He grasped early on that for the army command, the soldiers and the police were cannon fodder. Clan wars made their way into the ranks, as the top commanders fought for privilege and turf. Reality mocked all custom and all tradition. The violence grew particularly intense during the holy month of Ramadan, when the Islamists upped the ante because "martyrdom" in the course of that month had great religious merit. And the army command obliged.

II.

It is no wonder that the Algerians needed a breathing spell before the silence could be breached and the truth told. A civil concord was declared in 1999, and an old retread from the ruling hierarchy, Abdelaziz Bouteflika—a foreign minister in the days when Algeria strutted on the world stage as a leader of the non-aligned movement who then spent a decade in exile—was thrust to the presidency of the republic. Algerians still could not be sure that their world had been brought back from the abyss. Bouteflika and the guardians of order were ready to be done with the violence, but there was to be no truth and rec-onciliation here. It was best, Algerians were told, not to look back. "Amnesty and amnesia" was the Algerian way out of the slaughter.

Yet some Algerians were to find their voice, and in the litera-ture of reckoning there is a special place of honor for the work of Boualem Sansal, particularly for his extraordinary novel *The German Mujahid*. Published by Gallimard in 2008, under the title *Le Village de l'Allemand, ou Le Journal des Frères Schiller (The Village of the German, or the Diary of the Schiller Brothers)*, this unsparing work of fiction is set—no, it is embedded—in that dirty war, which it renders with uncompromising honesty. Its author, we are told, was born in 1949. He studied engineer-ing and attained a doctorate in economics. By the arithmetic of it, he would have been thirteen years old when the French gave up and left in 1962 after the savage war of liberation. That is, he would have come into his own amid the high hopes of the Algerian revolution. Sansal served in the Ministry of Industry until 2003, when he was dismissed because of his writings. He continues to live in Algiers with his wife and two daughters. His first novel, *Le Serment des Barbares*, won a prestigious prize in France in 1999, and *The German Mujahid* is evidence of an honest man who is keen to bear witness to the horrors of his country's history.

As though Algerian reality did not provide Sansal with enough material, there also falls upon this great work the shadow of the Holocaust. Based on a true story, we are told by Sansal and his publishers, the larger inspiration for his novel comes from the work of Primo Levi. Somehow the Shoah had found its way into the remote Algerian countryside. Sansal's narrative tells the story of two brothers born in a small village to a German father and an Algerian mother and who were raised in France by an old friend of the father from the days of the war of liberation. Hans Schiller, the German father, had been in the Hitler Youth and served in the SS. Before this material, Sansal does not flinch. Arabs have had the hardest time dealing with the Holocaust—there has been denial and an insistence that the numbers, the six million, were a premeditated fabrication, and protest that the dark history was no affair of theirs, and an odd "resentment" that the Jews have this history of victimhood—but Sansal sails directly into the storm.

Nazi fugitives sought shelter, after all, in Cairo, Damascus, and Algiers. There were scientists among them, and propagandists, military officers, doctors of death, an Orientalist or two, and, of course, experts on "the Jewish question." They had been taken in by their Arab hosts and given the chance to bury their past. They were much-admired men, persecuted men on the run who had done battle against the Anglo-American world, and against the Jews who pulled the strings in the Western democracies.

And so a certain Hans Schiller—he is "the German mujahid"—had made his way to a remote village called Aïn Deb, "The Donkey's Well," in Algeria. He was in middle age, a man of forty-five, when he came to Aïn Deb, and he was never to leave the place again. He married the beautiful eighteen-year-old daughter of the local shaykh. And he fathered two sons: Rachid Helmut, nicknamed Rachel, the older of the two, and a wild younger son formed in the anarchy and violence of France's Muslim quarters, Malek Ulrich, known as Malrich. Rachel made a success of his life in France. He studied hard, married well, and worked for a big multinational company—aided, no doubt, by the Germanic looks he had inherited from his father.

The old Nazi horrors and the new Muslim terrors came together on the eight o'clock news in Paris on April 25, 1994. Aïn Deb, once "a bubble beyond time," was the lead story that day: armed men had stormed the village and cut the throats of thirty-eight of its inhabitants. The GIA had done it, Algerian officials said. Rachel scrambles to learn of the fate of his parents from the Algerian Embassy in Paris. At first he is told that there were no Aïcha and Hans Schiller on the list of the Islamists' victims. But the embassy man said that there were two names, Aïcha Madjali and a Hassan Hans, known as Si Mourad. This was Hans Schiller and the daughter of the local shaykh, the parents of the Schiller brothers.

Algeria had always hovered over the lives of the brothers as they negotiated their new world in France. It was the Algeria of the emigrants and of the imagination, the North Star of the emigrants' memory. The real Algeria, on the other side of the Mediterranean, had its own life—pillage and terror and rulers "actively preparing for the end of days." The talent that had taken Rachel into the mainstream of French corporate life, his meticulous attention to detail, now pushed him back into his past, and into his parents' world. He embarks on a quest that carries him all the way to Algeria, and then further back into his father's German world and the death camps of the Third Reich in Poland. This was his road to Damascus, he said.

Rachel conquers his fear of Algeria's ghosts and sets out to visit Aïn Deb and the graves of his parents. "Schiller, what is that . . . English . . . Jewish?" the man at the Algerian Consulate asks. No, it is Algerian, and they and dozens of their neighbors were massacred on April 25 in Aïn Deb. "Oh, yes, Aïn Deb. . . . You should have said." He is issued an Algerian passport after much waiting and pleading. "God, it must be degrading and dangerous to be Algerian full time." He pushes aside his wife's objections and arrives in an Algeria altered by the terror.

A journey deep into the countryside, a dark pilgrimage of three hundred kilometers from Algiers, takes him to the *bled*, his ancestral village. Sansal is exquisite in his rendering of the landscape; in his depiction of the connection between man and his physical setting, he puts one in mind of Cormac McCarthy. It is a solitary landscape, the world of Aïn Deb—"bare, rugged, silent wasteland ringed by infinite horizons. . . . In mathematical terms, I'd say that by some quantum shift we seem to have entered non-Euclidean space; there are no signs, no landmarks here that a human being can relate to, there is no sense of time, no possible human compassion, nothing but an insistent drone like the echo of some cataclysm from before the flood." The people who settled here were "clearly trying to hide from the world." Yet this was where Rachel was born and had played in childhood enchantment: he carried in his memory a more contented place. The villagers who survived the carnage remember him as Rachid, Shaykh Hassan's son, and they take him in. The little Arabic he learned in Paris proves useless, but still he tries, in an argot of French, English, German, and the "crumbs of Arabic and Berber" that he remembered.

Rachel returns from Algeria a different man, a man with terrible secrets. He keeps what he learned to himself and confides only to a diary, which he hides from his wife and his younger brother. What happened in Aïn Deb was that Rachel stumbled upon an old suitcase that contained his father's files, and his trail. There were three medals in the suitcase: the first had the symbols of the Hitler Youth; the second was a medal from the Wehrmacht; the third bore the insignia of the Waffen SS. There were photos of his father as a young man and then older in a black SS uniform. There were more recent photos from the time he was in the Algerian maquis, the war against the French. In one photo he is standing next to a "tall, bony guy with a haunted look wearing battle dress, smiling like his teeth hurt." Rachel recognized the bony guy. He was Houari Boumédiène, the leader of the Algerian maquis.

In the suitcase there were also newspaper clippings in French, English, and Italian, dispatches about the Nuremberg trials, about Martin Bormann, Hermann Göring, Rudolf Hess, and others captured later, Adolf Eichmann, Franz Stangl, Klaus Barbie. There were Algerian documents, one of them signed by Colonel Boumediène in 1957, appointing Si Mourad an adviser on logistics and weaponry. A battered little booklet in the suitcase gave Hans Schiller's history and military record: his birth in 1918 in Uelzen, his education and degree in chemical engineering, his regimental number. Schiller had risen to the rank of captain, and he was a hero, having been wounded "a bunch of times and decorated over and over."

So the man who had made his way to Aïn Deb, who was good at making things run, the man known as Si Mourad, had been in his earlier years a killer, and worked in places that meant nothing to his neighbors and his children: Dachau, Drancy, Auschwitz, Buchenwald, Majdanek. It would have been the better part of wisdom to leave this history alone, but Rachel peers into the shadows, and he cannot turn back. He goes to Uelzen, where he is jolted by the ordinariness of the place, so unlike the "grief and distress" he had expected. The terrible history he was looking for "had been erased, forgotten, swept under the carpet." He is on the verge of giving up, but a chance encounter on a park bench throws a floodlight onto the past: an old man remembers good old Hans, whom he last saw in

June 1941. But the old man has nothing else to offer, except to say that Hans was called to duty and did his duty. It is all ancient history, the old man says, he was the last of the Uelzen boys from the days of the war. "My family and your family and many other families had died in the bombings."

Rachel's diary captures the coming apart of a man's life under the weight of a terrible knowledge. The marriage to a local beauty, the comfortable house, the career in a multinational: all of it gave way. "My house has crumbled, grief has made me powerless, and I do not know why my father never told me." He learns at great cost to himself that trying to retrieve the truth about past wars is an infernal enterprise— there is "the silence, the selective amnesia, the half-truths, the carefully rehearsed lines, the pleas by devil's advocates, speech after speech, the worm-eaten papers." (Sansal knows whereof he speaks: this describes both the Third Reich and the war that consumed his country.) Rachel talks to his father across time, which was after all the purpose of the hectic travel. He tries to see his father in the "conscientious schoolboy, the fun-loving student, the decent, happy-go-lucky soldier." Surely he knew nothing of the Final Solution, which was a terrible state secret known only to the "Führer perched in his Eagle's Nest." He tries to absolve the young Hans: hadn't he fallen in with the Hitler Youth in the same way Rachel—or Rachid—had fallen in with the Youth of the FLN back in the village? It was nothing extreme, "just the crackpot rantings of rank amateurs."

Rachel has his father's papers and his own imagination. A vast underground network had aided the Nazi fugitives, and the son stays on the father's trail. He goes first to Turkey, technically neutral during the world war, but complicit, says the son, in the crimes of the Third Reich. And "they have a genocide of their own, one which is all the more terrible since they have the gall not to admit to it." But he is his father's son, and he cannot cast the first stone: there is guilt aplenty. After Turkey, he is off to Syria, and his final destination is Egypt. It is "a journey of thousands of miles underneath an ancient implacable sun."

Rachel knew Cairo on his own; he used to visit Egyptian clients on behalf of his corporate employers. But this new reckoning with Egypt was different. This was a journey to an Egypt haunted by his father—by Hans arriving there nearly five decades earlier, with his crimes in his suitcase. In Egypt, Hans became a new man. The secret services gave him a position, and the horrors of the death camps were set aside. This was a new land where a hookah and a glass of mint tea were easy to find, and a "belly dancer's navel is always at eye level." The Egypt of King Farouk and Nasser made a place for Hans Schiller. The years of the monarchy must have been particularly kind to Hans: he was an educated man, he spoke several languages, he was well-dressed. He charmed the ladies and their powerful patrons.

In Cairo, Rachel slips into his father's thoughts. But he wants an additional bond with Hans's horrific past, and he finds it in a picture of his father with some English ladies at the Great Pyramid. Rachel wants a similar picture of himself on the same site. Rachel borrows a pith helmet from a Dutch tourist, and some "old dears," English ladies on an outing, are happy to oblige, and he poses amid them. In five minutes he has a picture of himself in his father's pose on the same ground. And on the back of the new photograph, he writes an inscription: "Helmut Schiller, son of Hans Schiller, Giza, 11 April 1996." In this way he has become one with his lost father: "Half a century separates the two photographs, that and six million dead gone up in smoke." His quest has been fulfilled. Rachel returns to Paris, to his big house, and on the second anniversary of his parents' death he kills himself. When his neighbors find him dead in his garage, he looks as though he is asleep. He had been there all night, in the exhaust fumes. He was wearing these "creepy striped pajamas," his brother says, and his head was shaved like a convict.

III.

The diary, and the legacy, now pass on to the younger brother, to the young man from the *banlieue* (suburb), with a police record and without the learning of his older brother. But young Malrich has his own pertinent knowledge: he knows the hell of the new Islamists in France, the squalor and the cynicism of that world.

A self-appointed imam, a kind of capo of the neighborhood, with his guards and enforcers, offers Malrich a particular sort of solace. "When I heard that your parents had been savagely murdered, it grieved me truly," he tells him. "I immediately got in touch with our brothers in Algeria who are fighting for Allah, for His religion. . . . I need to tell you that your parents were murdered by the Algerian government, not by the holy warriors of Allah. It is their way, to kill people and put the blame on us." But Malrich, known also as Malek, needs no such comfort or encouragement. "Tell me, imam," he replies, "if you had power over the earth, where would you begin the genocide?"

The imam squirms and then tries to bully Malrich: a bunch of thugs is waiting outside, and Malrich had been body-searched and brought in for this talk "like a prisoner of war." But Malrich persists. He wants to know about the fate that would befall those who reject Allah's rule. The imam says that it is for Allah to decide: "He shall tell us what we should do and how we should do it." But Malrich is beyond religious intimidation: he already knows how the heretics and the infidels will be dealt with. "The way I see it, you round the kaffirs all up into camps surrounded by electric fences, you gas all the useless ones straight off, the rest of them, you divide into groups based on their skills and their gender, and you work them till they drop dead. Anyone who disobeys, you gas them. What do you think?" The imam of the *banlieue* tells Malrich that he is "dreaming" and asking for trouble; but the younger Schiller brother does not scare. "You don't get the point, imam, killing six million infidels isn't burning some girl like Nadia, or slitting the throats of forty villagers in Aïn Deb. Half-assed methods just won't work, it takes productivity. When you've worked it out, let me know, I'll drop by. Salam." Malrich was ready for anything the imam and the emir and their followers could throw at him. He was ready for battle with the imam and the emir and their followers, and he was ready to tell the jihadists about his father, and to lend them his brother's books.

In Sansal's unforgettable portrait of this malevolent figure, the totalitarianism of the first half of the twentieth century speaks to, and finds an echo in, a new totalitarianism. Its insistence upon this echo is one of the novel's most significant contributions to our understanding. After all, the Islamists did not descend from the sky. They were radical children of the faith, literalists in the way they read the scripture, angry men committed to forcing history's pace. They were convinced that the society around them had abandoned and betrayed the true faith. And in their attitude toward the Jews, in the way they dealt with the Zionist project in Palestine, and in the manner in which they came to read the Holocaust, the Islamists worked their will on older and "traditional" forms of prejudice, and forged a new and very lethal version of anti-Semitism.

As the Oxford scholar Ronald Nettler ably demonstrated years ago, it was Sayyid Qutb, the Lenin of the Islamists and their most relentless theorist, who made the intellectual breakthrough from the old biases and stereotypes of the Jews as a tolerated but vulnerable community in Islamic lands to the new view of the Jews as a deadly menace to God's people. Qutb accomplished this in a canonical document of the early 1950s called "Our Struggle with the Jews." No doubt he was aided in this ideological work by the panic, and the surprise, that had overwhelmed the Arabs after the defeat of their armies in the war of 1948. Military defeats were common in Arab history, but this one was different: it was at the hands of a people not exactly famous for their martial traditions. In truth, the Arabs did not know the Zionists who had prevailed in that test of arms; they knew only the Jews in their midst, the people of *harat al Yahud* (the Jewish Quarter) in Beirut and Fez and Baghdad and Damascus. Qutb was speaking to this panic; and he bequeathed this new malignancy to the Islamists who gloried in his teachings, and in his martyrdom at the hands of the secular autocracy of Nasser in 1966.

Qutb's "children" were to produce a worldview of the Jew cut to their own needs. The Jews became an apocalyptic myth and a vast threat to Allah's community. In Nettler's words, "All these ancient Islamic notions were here applied to the contemporary horror of Jewish statehood, in the context of Islam's general failings in the modern world. The result was a massive new literature of obloquy, pain and rage, completely derived from the most ancient Islamic sources, made modern by appropriate commentary, and supplemented by felicitous borrowing from such classical Western anti-Semitic philosophies as The Protocols of the Elders of Zion."

The jihadists who wrote off mainstream Muslims as apostates and strangers to Islam had no trouble formulating a virulent anti-Semitism. As they alternately winked at and denied the Nazi atrocities, they could partake of the Nazi inheritance—it was there for them, in Islamic lands, and also among the gangs of the *banlieue,* with their imams and emirs and storefront mosques. Young Malrich had drawn the essential distinction: the old totalitarianism had technology and industrial power at its disposal, whereas the new one had only the limited means of its adherents with which to keep the animus alive.

In this astonishing—and in contemporary Arab literature, perhaps unprecedented—mingling of old and new totalitarianisms, this skillfully drawn analogy between Islamic fascism and Nazi fascism, *The German Mujahid* is a genuinely brave book. It goes against the grain of the writer's own culture and tears down its taboos. And it is not the first evidence of Sansal's valiant dissent. Two years earlier, he had given his country the gift of a powerful polemic—a brief tract, a letter to his compatriots, called *Poste Restante: Alger.* More directly than his novel, this brief polemic explains why the matter of the Holocaust is taken up in so frontal a manner.

For Sansal, the matter of Algeria's identity is the essential point of departure. Arabs claimed Algeria in the 1950s when it erupted against French rule. I still recall, in the Beirut of my boyhood, in the *mashreq* (the Arab East), the agitation and the exhilaration that greeted Algeria's war of liberation. We did not know much about North Africa—France had effectively severed it from the culture of the Arab East—and the impressions of North Africa in my native Lebanon consisted in memories of the French colonial troops, Senegalese and Moroccans, who had carried out the orders of the French mandatory power and put down local rebellions. They left no goodwill behind them, the Moroccans: their Arabic was odd and incomprehensible, and they were obedient to their French masters. But Algeria was a case apart. On the eve of its eruption in 1954, the French settlers were one-tenth of the population, but France had implanted its vineyards, its language, and its customs on that North African soil. The anti-colonial war, as Sansal brilliantly remarks, was waged in French, and the proclamation of the great revolt against France was issued in language that the French Academy itself would have praised.

Algeria had been a long time in France's grip—one hundred and thirty-two years, to be exact. So it was willful for the Egyptians and the Syrians and the Lebanese to assert the Arabism of Algeria. It was a grand historical falsification, says Sansal, for the nomenklatura to proclaim that Arab identity. For Sansal, his "big and beautiful" country, at the heart of the world, cannot possibly be Arab. For a start, Berbers (Kabyle, Mozabites, Touareg, Chaoui) make up eighty percent of its population, and a bare sixteen percent to eighteen percent are Arabs, and there are also the small communities from Algeria's rich and mottled past—Jews, pieds-noirs, Turks, Africans. Sansal is unwilling to trade his country's true history for a fake Arab myth. A thousand peoples, he says, have lived in Algeria, bequeathing it a multiplicity of languages and loyalties. It has taken in the heritage of Judaism, Christianity, and Islam. The Numidians, the Jews, the Carthaginians, the Romans, the Byzantines, the Arabs, the Ottomans, the

French have all played their role in shaping the true character of the place.

Arabic may be the official language of Algeria, Sansal writes, but the Algerians do not know classical Arabic. The Arabic of the books, and the Arabic of official pronouncements, is alien to them—both reflecting and deepening the impasse between ruler and ruled. Modern Standard Arabic to the Algerians is what Latin was in the High Middle Ages in European life. Berbers speak and savor their own language, while ordinary Algerians speak the colloquial language of their daily life. And there is French—French is our war booty, as a celebrated Algerian adage poignantly said—the language of high administration and intellectual life. The self-appointed guardians of the temple, Sansal says, have offered up this myth of Arabism—but "the world is the world," and the myths of the rulers, the legend of the war of liberation, have all been shattered.

It is within its own frontiers, Sansal insists, and working with the true material of its history, that Algeria can dig its way out of the slaughter and the waste. It would be false and ridiculous for an Algerian to say "our ancestors, the Gauls," but no more false and ridiculous, Sansal declares, than speaking of "our ancestors, the Arabs." Algeria's history was not written by "free men," and it was time for Algerians to name and to honor their own world. A Nazi had made his way to the *bled*, the commanders and their death squads (who were known among the terrified population as the Ninjas) had plundered and raped, the emirs and their warriors of the faith had tortured and murdered: the whole unedifying truth must be acknowledged if it is to be exorcised. Amnesty and amnesia have their saving graces, but so does an honest rendition of the actual saga of Algeria.

When I read Sansal, I recall another Algerian writer. Long before the Ninjas and the Tangos and the slaughter, a native son of the Algerian soil looked into the future and, with remarkable prescience, foresaw its ordeal. "Tomorrow Algeria will be a land of ruins and corpses, that no force, no power in the world, will be able to restore in our century," Albert Camus wrote in 1955, when the war of liberation was one year old. "I am very anguished by the events in Algeria, a country that is stuck in my craw to the point where I can think of nothing else." By the evidence of things, and of *The First Man*, the heartbreaking autobiographical novel published posthumously, Algeria was Camus's North Star as well. He could not, or would not, say much about it— and the French left, as we know, had written him off as the "little white," the pied-noir who favored his mother's cause in Algeria over the abstract claim of justice. There was a "French fact" in Algeria, and Camus honored it, and there were the claims of the Algerians, and he honored those as well. He could hardly disown his own community. In *The First Man*, he gave stirring voice to his fidelity to his own: "Whole mobs had been coming here for more than a century, had plowed, dug furrows, deeper in some places, shakier and shakier in others, until the dusty earth covered them over and the place went back to its wild vegetation; and they had procreated and then disappeared. And so it was with their sons. And the sons and grandsons of these found themselves on this land, as he himself had, with no past, without ethics, without guidance, without religion, but glad to be so and to be in the light, fearful in the face of night and death."

In language that foreshadows Sansal, Camus observed that "men are abominable, especially under a ferocious sun." After two savage wars, the silence of Camus in the face of the first cycle of terrors has been justified and ennobled. More importantly for the legacy of this special son of Algiers, more and more Algerians now recognize Camus as one of their own, *ibn balad* (a son of the land). "Camus is an Algerian writer," Mohammed Dib, one of Algeria's best writers, said. Algerians honor him, he said, because they, too, "know the heartbreak that comes from living upside down." And across a long, tormented history, Camus would recognize his themes in Boualem Sansal, and their shared love of the land, and their panic and dread before its terrible beauty and its ferocious sun.

SOURCE NOTES:

Former military officer Habib Souaïdia's controversial and compelling book on the Algerian war, *La Sale Guerre* (The Dirty War) (France: La Découverte, 2001).

This essay focuses in large part on the remarkable book by the Algerian writer Boualem Sansal, *Le Village de l'Allamand, ou Le Journal des Freres Schiller* (The Village of the German, or The German Mujahid, or The Diary of the Schiller Brothers) (France: Gallimard, 2008).

Ronald Nettler captures the essence of Sayyid Qutb, the "Lenin of the Islamists," in his book *Past Trials and Present Tribulations: A Muslim Fundamentalist's View of the Jews*, Studies in Anti-Semitism Series (Pergamon, 1987).

One of the best twentieth-century novelists, a son of Algiers, Albert Camus, gave us the heartbreaking autobiographical novel *The First Man*, translated from the French by David Hapgood (Alfred A. Knopf, 1995).

Chapter 9

The Traveler's Luck

V. S. Naipaul's Misunderstanding of Islam

REVIEW:
Beyond Belief: Islamic Excursions
Among the Converted Peoples, by V. S. Naipaul

In *Finding the Centre*, a slender book that combined a fragment of an autobiography and a long travel chronicle, V. S. Naipaul wrote of the impulse that sent him on the road to remote places. Always, he said, there was "the blankness and anxiety of arrival," the risk of "not finding anything, not getting started on the chain of accidents and encounters." He was a looker, he said, and he would follow his luck: "To arrive at a place without knowing anyone there, and sometimes without an introduction; to learn how to move among strangers for the short time one could afford to be among them; to hold oneself in constant readiness for adventure or revelation." There was "glamour" in travel; more importantly, travel took him out of his "colonial shell," it became a substitute for the "mature social experience" that his background had denied him.

By now, after more than forty years of writing and twenty-two books, after stamping in his own inimitable prose the great

This essay originally appeared in *The New Republic*, July 13, 1998, and is republished here in slightly different form with the cooperation and consent of the original publisher.

themes of the postcolonial world, we recognize with ease the Naipaulian art and sensibility, the Naipaulian themes and settings. After his chronicles in the Caribbean and Argentina and Africa and India and the lands of Islam, after his chronicles of exiles who scrape their countries clean and flee to Western lands but take the life—and the panic—with them, the writer and his subjects have become inextricably linked: the "half-made societies" of the Third World, the "hustlers" of postcolonial politics, the Western sympathizers who go to revolutionary centers "with return air tickets," the promise of revolution making and unmaking those half-made societies.

And we know enough about the man himself, the writer moving among strangers, adding to his knowledge of the world, correcting for the limited world that was given him as a descendant of Indian migrants from the Gangetic plains born on a small island on the mouth of the great South American river, the Orinoco, conceiving for himself a literary ambition beyond Trinidad, away from its stress and its smallness, away from the black power that "undid" that restricted world, and away from his own Indian community and its immemorial customs and phobias. "We read," Naipaul once wrote in a memorable essay on his great exemplar Joseph Conrad, "to find out what we already know." We read Naipaul in that way, too. We come to Naipaulian material prepared—not to be startled or surprised, not for the novelty but for the delicacy, the wondrous reworking, the circling yet again of the rich old terrain.

But there came a time, in the mid-1980s, when Naipaul wearied of the politics and the obsessive nature of his themes. There was nothing left to debunk in the postcolonial societies; they had debunked themselves, and the hustlers and the jesters had been shown for what they were. There crept into Naipaul's work in this new phase of his life a spirit of acceptance, perhaps even a measure of atonement. To the extent that he could, he would arrive at some reconciliation with the "dark places" of the earth. This must have come with age, with the peace that he had made with himself and his life in England and his place in the literary world. Why else would he begin his new book with a defensive declaration? "This is a book about people. It is not a book of opinion."

This change of tone had been gathering pace. In *Finding the Centre*, the writer had made his way to the Ivory Coast, to its wet forests, and his chronicle of that journey, "The Crocodiles of Yamoussoukro," bespoke a new patience with the ways of distant lands. Gone was the old fury with pretense and make-believe. The ritual feeding of the crocodiles, in an artificial lake, on the grounds of President Félix Houphouët-Boigny's ancestral village, was presented on its own indigenous terms: the crocodiles as "totemic, emblematic creatures" representing the chief's magical authority. At Yamoussoukro, the writer caught a glimpse of an "African Africa," which has always been, in its own eyes, "complete, achieved, bursting with its own powers." A generation earlier, in a chronicle of Mobutu Sese Seko and Zaire, he had been scathing in his depiction of the cult of the ancestors and the "magical" authority of the ruler. He saw through the thing: the cult of the ancestors as a cover for dependence, the cult of the chief as a cover for authoritarianism and plunder. But this time around he would make no judgments. He was there for "the narrative."

There was a new peace also with India, his ancestral land. After his abrasive portraits of India in *An Area of Darkness* (1964) and *India: A Wounded Civilization* (1977), there appeared a third chronicle, *India: A Million Mutinies Now* (1990), a rambling account that spoke with some wonder of the emergence in India of a central will, of a vibrant, new society that was making its way past the old cruelties and the "nullity" of Indian history. Indeed, travel itself was becoming less necessary for the writer, less glamoured.

Thus the two major books of the past decade—*The Enigma of Arrival* (1987) and *A Way in the World* (1994)—were hybrid works of "imagined autobiography," and works of real literary genius. We can be strangers to ourselves, Naipaul said, and so these two books were meant to explore the mystery of his background and the "promptings" of his imagination. The fragments of his life, the inheritance that he was bequeathed, the peopling of the New World, the movement in the second half of this century of a whole class of people unsettled by the dissolution of empires: this was the stuff of these two books. There was a break with the political journalism of his earlier years. He had been captured by the controversies of the postcolonial world and non-Western nationalism, and these two books constituted a kind of reprieve. No more politics, no more wanderings, no more disputes.

Naipaul's new book is an uneasy mix of the two phases of his writerly life. He is traveling again—and again into contested matters. *Beyond Belief* is the retracing of an older journey that Naipaul had made in 1979 and early 1980 into four Islamic lands: Iran, Malaysia, Indonesia, Pakistan. The book that grew out of that earlier inquiry, *Among the Believers*, was not particularly subtle or learned. As he crudely put it, he traveled to these four countries to see "Islam in action." He journeyed into a great storm, his own panic about political Islam magnifying the panic that he found on the road. This knowledgeable man had left home unprepared. He had read little about these countries; instead he put his faith in his own inclinations. And also in the traveler's luck: it would bring him what it would bring him in chance encounters and conversations.

Naipaul's old unease with Islam persists, alas, into his new inquiry. True, the tone is slightly different. There is that opening disclaimer that this is a book about "people" and not "opinion." This time the work is informed by the traveler's desire to be fascinated but neutral, to be a "manager of narrative," to stay in the background. Yet the book's very reason for being, the theme of "conversion" which ties it together (these are "Islamic excursions among the converted peoples")—this is opinion through and through. And it is ill-considered opinion, too.

Consider this early passage, which states the book's central claim and weighs it down, to the point of sinking it.

> Islam is in its origins an Arab religion. Everyone not an Arab who is a Muslim is a convert. Islam is not simply a matter of conscience or private belief. It makes imperial demands. A convert's worldview alters. His holy places are in Arab lands; his sacred language is Arabic. His idea of history alters. He rejects his own; he becomes, whether he likes it or not, a part of the Arab story. The convert has to turn away from everything that is his. The disturbance for societies is immense, and even after a thousand years can remain unresolved; the turning away has to be done again and again. People develop fantasies about who and what they are; and in the Islam of converted countries there is an element of neurosis and nihilism. These countries can be easily set on the boil.

This is an odd, obtuse view of religion. Islam—like Christianity, its immediate predecessor—is a world religion. Its worldly and otherworldly ideals are universal. Strictly speaking, everyone outside the Hijaz—like everyone outside Galilee and Calvary—is a convert in these faiths. By this measure of conversion, Egypt is no less a converted land than Iran or Indonesia. Only four thousand horsemen came to Egypt from the Hijaz to subdue Egypt in the seventh century. Most likely Islam became a majority faith in Egypt as late as the fourteenth century. The Coptic faith endured, even as the Coptic language retreated to become the sacred language of liturgy; Egypt had imbued Islam with its own culture and temperament, with the rituals and the centralized rule of this unique people of the valley and the river.

No converted society, moreover, took the faith and left it as it was, unaltered. Conquered in 637 by Islam, Iran worked its will on the faith, stamped it with its own cosmology and symbolism and artistic flair and taste for philosophical argument. Iran did not surrender wholesale. Thus the period of "Arab ascendancy" in Islam was brief. The prestige of Arabian descent, the pride of the conquerors, soon dissipated; for the Arabs had given the conquered peoples an instrument of emancipation. That instrument was Islam itself.

After the Arab ascendancy, Islam made its great world-historical way. Hegemony passed from the Arabs to the Persians and then to the Turks. Traders, the movement of people and goods and ideas, took the faith from India to southeast Asia—Sumatra and Java and Borneo. Those "converts" had not known or met the Arabs. Indeed, only the most extreme of Arab nationalists (the ruling stratum in Iraq, for example, themselves descendants of "converts") would concur in the view of Islam put forth by Naipaul. His controlling notion of "conversion" represents a fundamental misunderstanding of what he rightly seeks to understand.

In search of authenticity, Naipaul has misconstrued it. No writer today would take his notebook to the Baltics, say, in search of "converted" Christians. Christianity came late to the west Slavs and the Balts; a whole arc of polytheism stretched from Saxony to the Arctic Circle. The chroniclers tell us that it was not until 1368 that the Lithuanian dynasty adopted Christianity in return for the Polish crown. Latin Christendom had made its way east of the Elbe with no small measure of difficulty. The first bishoprics were established in the tenth century; and there were violent pagan reactions in the lands of Eastern Europe before Christianity, and its bishoprics prevailed in the eleventh century. And for all the ideology of the *reconquista*, to give another example, the spread of Christianity in that most Catholic of domains in the Iberian Peninsula from its toeholds in Santiago and Catalonia was similarly a process of conquest and conversion. It was priests and monks from the French theological center in Cluny who did the work of conversion as the kingdoms in the north made their way southward. It was a similar process that played out centuries after the conversion of Persia to Islam; and this process was not in any way a qualification of the authenticity of the new Muslims. Quite the contrary. They were not a falling off, they were a fulfillment.

Five months in four countries, four vastly different societies brought together by the theme of "conversion." Naipaul can plead that his travels yield only fiction or narrative, but the truth is that his readers will come to him as they have always come to him, in search of authoritative judgments on political and civilizational matters. And Naipaul's "Islamic excursions" are of a piece, unfortunately, with the contemporary tendency to reduce the politics of Muslim societies to Islam, to religious categories. It is a shallow view.

In the year of this book's publication, we were treated to a great upheaval in Indonesia. The ruler has fallen; a perverted form of capitalism and plunder has imploded under the weight of debt and mismanagement and nepotism. Suharto, the man at the helm, at once a Javanese king and one of a handful of authoritarian rulers that anticommunism had thrown on the scene in the 1960s, had become a source of instability. An officer corps from which the ruler had risen stepped in to save the system by dispatching the ruler. This is an utterly secular tale. Its categories are political, profane. There is nothing Islamic about what transpired in Indonesia: the same script could have unfolded in a handful of Latin American dictatorships a decade or so ago.

Nor is there anything Islamic about the racial rage toward the Chinese minority in Indonesia. The rage toward, and the envy of, a minority skilled in the ways of the market, but marked by its own difference, is, alas, the common plot of our world. The clever trader, existing in the interstices, living off the fat of the land and the labor of the good sons of the soil, has been the classic stuff of anti-Semitism from the Iberian Peninsula in centuries past to Russia and Eastern Europe in more recent times. And this same kind of sentiment lies at the heart of Serbian historiography—the dread and the loathing of the merchants of Sarajevo and the worldliness of Sarajevo. Religion is hardly the only engine of injustice.

In a predominantly Muslim society, it would stand to reason that the language of obedience and the language of rebellion would be phrased in Islamic terms. The pious ruler begets the pious oppositionist. Yet the really remarkable thing about the unfolding struggle in Indonesia is the reticence of religion.

The students who laid siege to the Parliament spoke in familiar secular terms. This was not a reprise of Iran; it was a reprise of another place in the tropics, the Philippines and its "people power" that swept away Ferdinand Marcos and his cronies. The young had wearied of *Bapak* (Father) and wanted a new beginning. This is not Muslim; it is human.

The agitation in Jakarta included an association of "Muslim intellectuals," but it was domesticated and bought off. Its patron was none other than B.J. Habibie, Suharto's handpicked satrap and successor. Indeed, one of that association's leading figures, Imaduddin, offers a cautionary tale about the glib imputation of the actions of Muslims to Islam. Imaduddin appears in both of Naipaul's journeys, and he raises, for Naipaul, the risk of being taken in, the risk of looking for belief where there is only need and ambition. On that first passage, fifteen years earlier, Imaduddin was a lecturer in engineering at the Bandung Institute of Technology and a man on the fringe, a preacher and a rebel. A child of Sumatra (which is wilder and more zealous about the faith than Java), he had run afoul of the regime and had been imprisoned for fourteen months. Schooled in Iowa, the son of a man who, in his time, had gone to Al-Azhar University in Cairo for religious training, Imaduddin had struck Naipaul as a man of fire and brimstone. "For Imaduddin, as a Muslim and a Sumatran, Indonesia was a place to be cleansed," Naipaul wrote in *Among the Believers*.

But faith can be a pose. Fifteen years later, the same Imaduddin was a man of the regime. Thanks to Habibie's patronage, he had "shot up." He had a decent house in a decent neighborhood, a Mercedes-Benz, a driver, his own television program. He was now in "human resource development." He had become a promoter of Suharto and had given up on revolution, preaching a "doctrine of accelerated evolution." The faith was tethered to the career, made to serve it. Imaduddin told a visiting journalist this spring that Suharto was a "good Muslim," that the rebellious students had been misguided, that Suharto and Indonesia would ride out the time of troubles.

It is easy to be taken in by people and places we don't really know. On his earlier journey, one of Naipaul's Indonesian informants told him of the confusion—more precisely, the eclecticism—that lay at the heart of the culture and the religions of the place. Naipaul should have paid closer heed. "No one," his informant said, "could say precisely what he was. People said, 'I am a Muslim, but—.' Or 'I am a Christian, but—.'" It is this "but," this ambiguity, that is missing in a narrative of this sort. And so the faith must be invented, and it must be sharp if it is to serve the narrative.

The people of Indonesia lived long with cultural chaos. Islam had arrived here as a religion of India in the latter years of the fifteenth century, in Sumatra and Borneo and the harbors of trade in Java, before it penetrated the rice plains of the Javanese interior. The process of Islamization was slow and subtle. The princes of the trading harbors of Java's northern coast were the first to cross over to Islam. The tale has been masterfully told by Clifford Geertz in his brief, durable book, *Islam Observed*, which appeared in 1968. The princes and nobility of Majapahit, the last of the great Hindu-Buddhist states, had embraced the new faith and left Majapahit "a court without a country, an hieratic shell which soon collapsed entirely," as Geertz writes.

Geertz tells the extraordinary tale (mostly a legend, a metaphor, though it is about the life of a historical personage) of Indonesia's conversion to Islam through the life of a Javanese prince named Sunan Kalidjaga. It was Kalidjaga who brought Java from the shadow play world of *djaman Indu* (Hindu times) to *djaman Islam* (Islamic times). Born the son of a high court official of Majapahit, Kalidjaga's life mirrored the dislocations of his time, which was a time without order. He drifted from place to place; he was a drinker, a womanizer, and a gambler. Then, in Djapara, one of the harbor states, he happened upon Sunan Bonang, one of the great disciples of Islam.

Bonang had shown him the way to the faith, when the bandit-prince had tried to rob him of his jewelry. Bonang had turned a banyan tree to gold but was indifferent to worldly things. Bonang then left Kalidjaga on the banks of a river, perhaps for forty years, during which he survived floods and the comings and goings of crowds. He had seen the logic and power of the new faith. Kalidjaga converted to Islam, as Geertz pointedly observes, "without ever having read the Koran, entered a mosque, or heard a prayer." He was a transitional figure between the dying world of Majapahit and the great interior Muslim state of Mataram, which held sway until the Dutch shattered it in the eighteenth century.

It was folk Islam that had prevailed in Java and Borneo and Sumatra and the Celebes. The Indic tradition had been overthrown, but it had survived, Geertz writes, "stripped of the bulk of its ritual expression but not of its inward temper." Then Dutch dominion had settled in, and Islam had alternated between submission to colonial rule and rebellion. In this great historical seesaw, then, scriptural Islam was a latecomer. It arrived in the middle of the nineteenth century, with the steamships, and the pilgrimage to Mecca, and the elite education in Cairo's religious schools. Islam, scriptural Islam, had never had the place to itself. The "culture system" of Dutch colonialism had thrown it on the defensive. And the Indic tradition, misted over, had never been extinguished.

It would be hard to fit this kind of eclecticism into Naipaul's chronicle, hard to carry it along. Now and then he recognizes this complexity, and his informants give voice to it. But Naipaul's journey is in search of believers, people who could set countries "on the boil." But societies do not only boil; and in the age of the Iranian revolution it is odd to have forgotten that faith can also be an instrument of obedience, the prop of power.

Consider Abdul Rahman Wahid, whom Naipaul encountered on his trip. (Wahid would later serve as the country's president.) He was an influential leader of Indonesia's reformist Muslim movement, *Nahdlatul Ulama* (the renaissance of the religious scholars), which is said to have more than thirty million adherents. Wahid had followers and he had pedigree: his grandfather had made the pilgrimage to Mecca in the latter years of the nineteenth century and had come back to establish the *pesantren* (religious boarding schools), which served as the basis of Wahid's movement. Wahid's father had been schooled in religious subjects, but he had also acquired knowledge of Dutch and mathematics.

When Wahid inherited the leadership of the movement, he proceeded to take it out of politics. In the recent upheaval in Indonesia, Wahid was a man of caution. He had seen the mix of religion and politics in other Islamic lands and wished to spare his country that incendiary mix. "In our thought," he told Naipaul, "Islam is a moral force which works through ethics and morality." Not for this man were the furies and the simplifications of politicized religion. It was not easy to fit Wahid into Naipaul's narrative, and the writer's exasperation shows. Of

Wahid, he writes: "I wanted to get a picture, some conversation, a story. It wasn't easy."

The religion: it is not quite as total and as unworldly as Naipaul fears. It also carries the material world of men and women and their distress; it gives voice to their needs and their ways. It acts on the skills and the moral development and the material circumstances that are already there. It speaks calmly and confidently when a culture is ascendant and at peace, and it is made to wail when a people are trapped and feel betrayed. In unintended ways, Naipaul's two Islamic chronicles, read side by side, expose the profane forces that fill a religious faith, the ebb and the flow of human grievance expressed in the idiom of religion, the sharpening of the faith in times of distress, and the lapse into routine under more prosaic circumstances.

In the chronicle of 1981, Malaysia was a steamed place, where the Malay rage at the Chinese, the Malay sense that they had been disinherited by the Chinese, dominated the economy and created a combustible politics, a "general nervousness"— the odd sensation, in a land of steam and river and forest, of "the atmosphere of the ideological state." The fury of the Bumiputras, the sons of the soil, was everywhere: it was comprehensive, "the rage of pastoral people with limited, skills, limited money, and a limited grasp of the world."

But behold Malaysia in Naipaul's new chronicle. Prosperity had tamed the old rage. A young lawyer, a Malay, tells the writer that the Malays had become a "trading and manufacturing and innovative people. These are all words you would not have associated with Malays in the past." And there is Nasar. In the old chronicle, he was a *kampung* (village) boy in the Muslim Youth Movement, a young man of twenty-five. A generation later he is running a holding company that manages the affairs of eight corporations. "He remembered what he had been in 1979; he didn't put a gloss on it," Naipaul writes. The material world had altered. "The racial anxieties of sixteen years before had been swamped by the great new wealth, and new men had been created on both sides."

We may travel the world in search of a burning faith, but what we find instead are the great material facts that underpin the faith. Life had been easy for the pastoral people of Malaysia, one of Naipaul's Malay informants reflects. You could throw a seed and it would grow, you could put a bare hook in the water and you would catch fish. The Chinese who came from a "four-seasoned country" over the course of the nineteenth century had been more skilled. The Malays had to assimilate the skills of the modern world, so as to catch up. Of course, the material world may alter again in Malaysia, and the prosperity may crack. Back and forth, back and forth, men and women move between faith and the secular world, each a reflection of the other.

At least since the Iranian upheaval of 1979, it has been harder and harder to maintain the distinction between writing about Islam and writing about Muslims. It is a distinction with a great difference; but as a consequence of the eruption in Iran and the panic that its radicalism caused, a vast and varied world, societies of different temperaments and situations, has come to be arranged and analyzed under the gross rubric of politicized Islam. A whole industry has grown around this subject; it has given writers and journalists with precious little knowledge of distant societies an illusion of familiarity and mastery, a certain absolution from looking at Muslim lands soberly and unapocalyptically, with precision and detail. The subject is awash in intellectual complacency.

The politics must lie in the faith, the pundits and the visitors insist. Like all reductions, this one enjoys a certain economy: the ability to shrink distant and diverse societies into a core, a hot and glowing center, that is easy to identify and to explain. It is a useful trick, this trick of finding a faith, the same faith, in the casbah and alleyways of Algiers and among the pastoral, tropical people of the villages of the Malays. It is a curious and unremarked irony, this convergence of outlook between the radical activists of "political Islam," who simplify the world and insist on a single indivisible Islamic *umma* (nation), and the Western writers who chronicle this breed of religious radicals. For both, the world must be ordered and simplified and imputed a faith that has been "set on the boil."

This large assumption animated Naipaul's two Islamic inquiries. He gave voice to this sentiment in stark, unadorned terms in one of his meditations on contemporary culture, a talk called "Our Universal Civilization" which he gave at the Manhattan Institute in 1990, midway between his two trips. "Now traveling among non-Arab Muslims, I found myself among a colonized people who have been stripped by their faith of all that expanding intellectual life, all the varied life of the mind and senses, the expanding cultural and historical knowledge of the world, that I had been growing into on the other side of the world. I was among a people whose identity was more or less contained in the faith. I was among a people who wished to be pure. . . . No colonization could have been greater than this colonization by the faith." It is a strange thing to say about this most disabused of writers, but Naipaul's exploration of the Muslims turns out to be insufficiently secular.

"The faith abolished the past," Naipaul asserted in "Our Universal Civilization." "And when the past was abolished like this, more than an idea of history suffered. Human behavior, and ideals of good behavior could suffer." This was canonical to that Naipaulian journey: the "Mohammedan" faith—an odd designation of Islam for so worldly a man, for Muslims never refer to themselves as Mohammedans—abolished all that had existed before it. In truth, this was pure fantasy. Not even a faith as mighty, as "complete," as Naipaul took Islam to be, is capable of extirpating the past and the truths imposed by place and climate and rituals and transmitted ways. The Islamists would wish it to be otherwise, but the faith never had the world, and the believers, solely to itself. "In Malaysia, they were desperate to rid themselves of their past, desperate to cleanse their people of tribal or animist practices, all the subconscious life, freighted with the past, that links people to the earth on which they walk," Naipaul writes. But Naipaul knows that subconscious life, and the earth will win out.

"I had only my notes to go by," he writes in *Beyond Belief.* Yet in truth he had more than his notes to go by; he also had this large simplifying vision that he brought with him. And therein lie the limitations of the literary journey. The genre of travel writing, the form of the notes, is only what it is; the street yields only what the street yields. The foreign traveler is in a hurry. The language is strange to him, the interior spaces are forbidden to him. There are the guides and the interpreters—this industry of "minders" around the international hotels in the distressed locations on which foreign observers descend in search of the quick sound bite; and there are the English-language dailies, the *Tehran Times*, the *Jakarta Post*, the *Indonesian Times*; and there are the international hotels, gilded cages that provide shelter from the tumult and increase the traveler's loneliness.

A man of cultural marginality, it is easier for Naipaul to see the pain of other marginal people, even if he cannot extend a similar sympathy to the dominant faith. Of the Chinese of Malaysia, he writes: "I began to have some idea of how little the Chinese were protected in the last century and the early part of this, with a crumbling empire and civil war at home and rejection outside: spilling out, trying to find a footing wherever they could, always foreign, insulated by language and culture, surviving only through blind energy. Once self-awareness had begun to come, once blindness had begun to go, they would have needed philosophical or religions certainties as much as the Malays."

That is the Naipaulian way: the paragraph of intelligence and beauty, the insight that suddenly illuminates places and people that we have not quite known. Those notes that he kept are occasionally gorgeous, the traveler's luck joined to the writer's skill. Consider Naipaul's passage about Linus, a Catholic convert in Java, a poet lamenting the passing of old, simpler times: "Even the rice had changed. 'The old traditional rice was full of savor and taste.' He made a gesture, taking his fingers to his nose. 'The new Filipino rice—you can't eat it in the evening if you cook it in the morning.'" Or this passage about the rupture in his own and his family's soul, the distance in Trinidad from their sacred places in India: "My first eighteen years were spent two oceans away, on the other side of the globe, in the new world, in an island on the mouth of the one great South American river. The island had no sacred places; and it was nearly forty years after I had left the island that I identified the lack. I began to feel when I was quite young that there was an incompleteness, an emptiness, about the place, that the real world existed somewhere else. I used to feel that the climate had burned away history and possibility." And here is Naipaul writing with graceful penetration about the *Mohajirs*, the Muslim migrants from India, who came in great numbers to the feudal land of Sind:

> They had agitated more than anyone else for the separate Muslim state, and they came to Pakistan and Sind as to their own land. They found that it belonged to someone else; and the people to whom it belonged were not willing to let go. The mohajirs became the fifth nationality of Pakistan, after the Baluchis, the Pathans, the Punjabis, and the Sindhis. They were a nationality without territory. And that was where, a generation or two later, the war of Karachi began: with the mohajir wish for territory. They wished Karachi to be theirs; they were a majority in Karachi. Their passion, their sense of grievance, was like religion; it was a replay of the agitation by their fathers and grandfathers fifty years before for Pakistan.

It was Iran and its upheaval that prompted those Muslim inquiries of Naipaul; and his pages on Iran are the best of his new book. Here he is traveling into a great disappointment: by now the political faith, Islam in power, had behind it a generation of rule. The distress is everywhere; the faith has been dearly paid for. In a desert south of Tehran, by the vast mausoleum of Ayatollah Ruhollah Khomeini, there is the Martyrs' Cemetery. Naipaul goes there with his interpreter Mehrdad, a university student. "Below the pines and the elms everything was close together, the lines of headstones and picture-holders, the spindly shrubs that grew in the sand, and the flags, hemmed in by the shrubs and trees and not able to flutter, and like part of the vegetable growth." They had died by the tens of thousands, the children of the revolution, in the war with Iraq. The crowds were nearby, at Khomeini's shrine; but here there was hardly an attendant, and the desert dust "had ravaged the aluminum picture-holders. . . . Some of them were absolutely empty now; sometimes the photographs had decayed or collapsed within the frame." Reality had overwhelmed the revolution's poses: "We went to the blood fountain. It used to be famous. When it was set up early on during the war, it spouted purple-dyed water, and it was intended to stimulate ideas of blood and sacrifice and redemption. The fountain didn't play now; the basin was empty. There had been too much real blood."

He picks up another thread from his earlier journey, and the traveler's luck pays off: he seeks and finds Khomeini's hanging judge, the notorious Ayatollah Sadegh Khalkhali. He finds him in Qom. In the old revolutionary days, Khalkhali was a busy and important man. His revolutionary court in Tehran worked around the clock: it was high and bloody theater, and Khalkhali played it to the hilt, the revolution's justice and the revolution's spectacle. Hundreds were put to death by Khalkhali, and the hanging judge was a celebrity. In an audience that he gave Naipaul, he acted like his own jester: "I was a shepherd when I was a boy. Right now I know how to cut off a sheep's head." It was the way of a man who had come into great power; Khalkhali's bodyguards had rocked with laughter, and Khalkhali himself, warming to his own lines, had choked with laughter, "showing me his gums, his tongue, his gullet."

But a revolutionary ride is always bumpy, and often it is very dangerous. In the intervening years Khalkhali lost out. He is now a figure on the fringe. His court, his power, the bodyguards who laughed on cue are all gone. "He came in now," Naipaul relates. "And it was an entrance. He was barefooted, in simple white, like a penitent. . . . A short-sleeved white tunic, wet with perspiration down the middle of his chest, hung over a loose white lower garment. Step by dragging step he came in, very small, completely bald, baby-faced without his turban, head held down against his chest, looking up from below his forehead, eyes without mischief now and seemingly close to tears, as though he wished to dramatize his situation and needed pity."

Naipaul catches the pain of Iran, the terrible cruelty of its revolt, in a tale supplied to him by an old Iranian diplomat. The tale has the "quality of a folk myth," the sort of story perhaps "fabricated out of the general need, made up by no one but contributed to by everyone." A middle-aged woman in a chador is eager to have the eyesight of a young man restored; she takes him to a specialist; the specialist examines the boy and sees that he is mutilated beyond rehabilitation. He had lost his hands, his feet. The lady is not related to the boy, but she is always there for him; and the doctor grows curious about the young man and the woman in the chador. He learns from her that she had lost her own son, and that the mutilated boy, disfigured in Iran's war with Iraq, was her neighbor's son. "My own boy, my own son was executed because he belonged to an anti-revolutionary group. The person who reported him was this neighbor's son. I am happy my son is dead. He was executed, and that was all. I want to keep this piece of meat alive to take revenge. I want his mother to grieve for him every day."

No Javanese shadow play here. Here history is martyrdom and revenge. After the exertion, after the flamboyance, the new pain flowed into the country's painful history. "All that could be said was that the country had been given an almost universal knowledge of pain." The ground had burned in Iran; and we have no way of knowing what seeds will germinate in the smoldering earth, and neither does Naipaul.

A traveler can see only the exterior of things. He can render only what stories men and women in harsh places and times are willing to confide to strangers. Naipaul can take us to Qom; we can enter with him and his interpreter and his driver; we can see, through his eyes and his pen, the wonder of the place, of the town of high religious learning in the desert, a town of "an old idea of learning, with all its superseded emblems of color and dress." But this is as far as we, and he, can go; all that we, and he, can see.

He cannot report, for example, on the disputations that flourish in that world. We need more direct testimonies if we are to come to terms with that society and its inflammations. It is a feature of that Islamic civilization (in its Arab-Persian-Turkish zone, to be specific) that the truth of life is to be found beyond and behind the high walls and the drab exteriors, in the tiled courtyards and the private chambers that are meant to keep others out and to keep secrets in. Few hurried travelers, few *ghareebs* (strangers) are taken beyond the walls and the courtyard. It casts no aspersion on Naipaul's extraordinary talent as a writer to point out that he has no access to the inner precincts of that universe.

Traveling to Malaysia and Indonesia, Naipaul has gone where Joseph Conrad had been; and he is animated in no small measure by the calling to retrace Conrad's path. Conrad went to the Dutch East Indies in 1887 aboard the *Vidar*, a vessel owned by an Arab, which sailed under the Dutch flag and was commanded by an Englishman. He was thirty years old. His experience as a seaman nourished his art, and the archipelago and the waters of

Borneo served as the setting of *Almayer's Folly*, *Lord Jim*, *Youth*, and *An Outcast of the Islands*. It is in the Malay setting as well that "The Lagoon," the first short story of Conrad's that was read to Naipaul when he was a boy of ten, is situated.

What Conrad found in those harbors, what he bequeathed to us, was the tumult of that world: the clashing colonialisms in the fight over Borneo between the British and the Dutch; the piracy; the steamships beginning to carry the pilgrims to Mecca and Arabia; the mystery of "the East"; and the "thought of men of old, who centuries ago went that road in ships that sailed no better, to the land of palms, and spices, and yellow sands, and of brown nations ruled by kings more cruel than Nero the Roman, and more splendid than Solomon the Jew." In *Youth*, Conrad created what remains, for me, the most arresting image of the making of the modern world and the uprooting of people from traditional ways, the wrenching of the self that an ascendant culture forced on those who happened in its way:

And then, before I could open my lips, the East spoke to me, but it was in a Western voice. A torrent of words was poured into the enigmatical, the fateful silence; outlandish, angry words, mixed with words and even whole sentences of good English, less strange but even more surprising. The voice swore and cursed violently; it riddled the solemn peace of the bay by a volley of abuse. It began by calling me Pig, and from that went crescendo into unmentionable adjectives—in English. The man up there raged aloud in two languages, and with a sincerity in his fury that almost convinced me I had, in some way, sinned against the harmony of the universe.

"Whole sentences of good English," the world remade, the pain of a modernity to which men and women submit, against which men and women rebel: the whole wonder of that world. This is the Conradian standard of which Naipaul has fallen short. He does not capture the whole wonder. For it was not some simplified political and religious creed that Conrad sought and found in those harbors. He came with conceptions, but he made a voyage of discovery. And so he caught truths, deeper and more durable truths about himself and about us all.

SOURCE NOTES:

This essay is largely a reading of V. S. Naipaul's book *Finding the Centre* (Alfred P. Knopf, 1984) although it is premised on a review of his book, *Beyond Belief: Islamic Excursions Among the Converted Peoples* (Random House, 1998).

The foundation for Naipaul's *Finding the Centre* is from his book titled *Among the Believers* (Alfred P. Knopf, 1981).

The great cultural anthropologist Clifford Geertz wrote *Islam Observed: Religious Development in Morocco and Indonesia* (New Haven: Yale University Press, 1968).

Capturing the constraints of the modern world and the rebellion of men and women against these forces is the incomparable Joseph Conrad's novella, *Youth* (England: William Blackwood, 1902).

Chapter 10

The Humanist in the Alleys

Naguib Mahfouz, 1911–2006

I.

It was inevitable that the Pharaoh would give the great writer a military funeral. By the time of Naguib Mahfouz's death at the age of ninety-four, the novelist who had never had a tender thought for the military officers and their regime—who years earlier, when these officers were still young and full of perfect certitude, had written a novel in which a character standing for these men plunges to his death from a bridge over the Nile after disgrace had overwhelmed him—was to be claimed by the strongman of the military regime. Before the end came for Mahfouz, the gentle man with aquiline features became what he had never bargained for: national property, the Nobel laureate of the Arabs, called on by ministers of culture and hailed by the organs of the regime.

This essay originally appeared in *The New Republic*, September 25, 2006, and is republished here in slightly different form with the cooperation and consent of the original publisher.

Back in 1994, Mahfouz was stabbed in the neck by an apprentice electrician, a young Islamist who had never read a line of his work. He survived, but his writing hand was paralyzed. The regime assigned him a security detail, and the old (and safe) hedonism of his life, its erstwhile freedom, was now clearly behind him. Here, for a mediocre and philistine government that had smothered the cultural life of the land, was the perfect prop: the old, frail man with failing eyesight, hard of hearing, protected from further danger by the policemen and the undercover agents of the military autocracy.

The ordinary people of Cairo, who peopled and nourished this man's fiction, whose lives and guile he had depicted with such masterful simplicity for well over six decades, gave him their own funeral, far away from the mighty. "Farewell, Shakespeare of the Arabs" read a banner held aloft by a simple middle-aged man, an Egyptian Everyman. In a country with a darkening cultural landscape, in a place where *hanin* (yearning and nostalgia) for the past had come to express a despair over the country's present, Mahfouz was a link to all that Egyptians held dear about themselves—to an idea of *Misr*, Egypt, as a place of tolerance, as a land across continents that harmonized contending truths.

It wasn't just that the Nobel Prize had been given to one of their own. They were proud of it, to be sure, for they were by their own admission a people given to the "*khawaga* complex"— a feeling of inferiority before the foreigner, the white man. But more to the point was Mahfouz's fidelity to the simple, small bourgeois life of Cairo's alleyways. He was unspoiled; he was, in the way of his city, a creature of habits and routines. Until the boys of darkness struck in 1994, and he had to duck under armed guard into hotels secured by the police, he frequented the same coffeehouses, bought his papers from the same vendor, hung around with the same friends. No man was as free of affectation as this modest and decent man. There was a *shilla* of friends around him, a band, a gang. They called themselves the *harafish* (the rabble or the riffraff); but I can report that they flattered themselves, for when I spent some evenings with them, they proved to be a tame lot. They were writers and filmmakers and elderly actors. They were aging men who spoke sentimentally of the carousing and the ribaldry of some distant past. They remembered an orderly land; they talked of literary feuds now of no consequence to an Egypt choking on failure and need, physically overwhelmed in a metropolis bursting at the seams.

Mahfouz was born in 1911. His country had a population of eleven million then. He died in a country of some seventy-five million people. The Cairo of his birth was a graceful city of seven hundred thousand; today it is home to nearly twenty million people. No country could bequeath culture and learning to such numbers, or accommodate them in the world. The grace of the land, its old rhythm, has been routed, overwhelmed. And Mahfouz's characters wept for it all. In *The Day the Leader Was Killed*, a fictionalized account of Anwar el-Sadat's assassination, a middle-aged man, clearly standing in for Mahfouz himself, ponders his shrunken house amid the high-rise buildings and the sprawl of the ever more congested city, and weeps for his "pygmy of a house, by a river which itself had changed, which had lost its splendor and glory and is no longer capable of anger. Oh, how numerous are the cars, how large the fortunes, how bitter the poverty, and how many beloved ones had departed from the world."

This physical desolation, the crowded land pressed to the limit: they are a break with all that Egypt had known in the cozier bourgeois world of Mahfouz's youth. In *Echoes of an Autobiography*, a bewitching work of startling vignettes published in 1995, the writer's double, an aimless wanderer, happens upon a man alone playing a flute in homage to the beauty of the world. "It would be great if the people got to hear your melodies," the wanderer tells the flutist. But the flutist knows his people and knows what had become of Egypt. "They are busy quarreling and weeping," he answers.

A country that had hitherto prided itself on its protean identity—Europe beginning at Alexandria, the Arab-Islamic world at Cairo, Africa at Aswân—and had willingly jumbled faith and worldliness was overwhelmed by a single simple absolute. "The land, the land is full of bigotry," one of Mahfouz's older characters laments. And in the face of this purity, the wanderer—Abd Rabbo, or Servant of God, is the sly name given to him by the novelist—still insists on the oneness of faith and play, and on the meandering ways of the world. "I was walking along the road by the cemetery on my way back from the tavern," Abd Rabbo says. "A voice came to me from the grave and asked me, 'Why have you stopped visiting us and talking with us?'" He answers, "You only love talking of death and the dead and I have wearied of all that."

The shaykh of Al-Azhar and the mufti of the republic were certainly present at Mahfouz's funeral—the man's celebrity decreed it; but the writer had suffered his share of grief at the hands of the custodians of religion. It wasn't just the attempt on his life in 1994 by a religious fanatic. (The writ that declared his blood *halal* (permissible) was issued by the "blind shaykh" Omar Abdel Rahman, who would carry his bigotry from the oasis town of Fayoum, on the edge of the Western Desert, to Brooklyn and Jersey City, remarking that Salman Rushdie would never have dared to write *The Satanic Verses* had Mahfouz been killed for writing his great novel *Awlad Haretna*, a controversial work published in serial form in *Al Ahram* in 1959.) The official religious institution, Al-Azhar, had stopped well short of a call to murder, but its custodians nonetheless proscribed *Awlad Haretna*.

In this work (translated into English under the title *Children of Gebelawi*), Mahfouz played with fire. The angelic Mahfouz was no angel after all. He knowingly pushed into forbidden territory—both religious and political. The custodians of religious and political orthodoxies understood the allegory. In this immensely rich and subversive work, a godlike figure, Gebelawi, establishes a great dominion; the quarter where Gebelawi's writ runs is the world in miniature. Gebelawi has gardens and power and property; he rules, but he is not seen. No one in this cowed neighborhood contests his power. But then Gebelawi—in a clear allusion to the death of God in the modern world—dies, and his dominion is bequeathed to his son Adham, or Adam. Adham is the son of a slave woman, and his older siblings quarrel with Gebelawi's choice. Gebelawi has his way because Adham, he decrees, knows the names and the habits of the quarter and can whip it into submission.

In the rest of the story we read of Adham's betrayal and the heroic but doomed attempt of three prophets—stand-ins for Moses, Jesus, and Muhammad—to change the ways of men and to rescue the quarter from the rule of petty tyrants. The people pray and endure their fate—this is at once the strength of Mahfouz's characters and their paralyzing weakness—and wait for a deliverance that never comes. The surface tranquility of this quarter is a sham. Qassem, the Prophet Muhammad's double, had tried to dispense justice, Mahfouz wrote; he shared the war booty and the treasure. There was not much of it, but it was distributed with a measure of equity. Yet his heirs played havoc with the world and fought over his legacy, and the tyrants had their way with the *hara* (the quarter). Greed devoured everything, and in the coffeehouses poets and storytellers told of better days and dreamed of salvation. An old man bent by the years, a drunkard, agitates in a loud voice for a return to "the way things were under Qassem." One of the *futuwwa* (the bullies) beats the old man savagely.

The dreams of human improvement atrophy in this place; nothing remains of the great reformers. The three prophets become mere "names and songs sung by the poets of the coffeehouses under the gaze of people given to despair and surrender." Magic and drugs and superstitions take hold of the neighborhood. A redeemer turns up, a secular man with secular amulets and new tricks promising to give justice, but he is betrayed and buried alive by the overseer of the neighborhood and his policemen. So everything fails: the wisdom of the prophets, the secular talismans. This was 1959, and the Gamal Abdel Nasser regime read the work as an attack on the religious institutions and, of course, on the secular rulers, the military officers hoarding power for themselves. Mahfouz bent to the pressure; it was no use, he said, to offend Al-Azhar. He would refrain from publishing this piece of fiction in book form. Eight years later, it was published in Beirut, but the controversy swirling around it never disappeared.

II.

"Most Egyptians neither fear nor dislike thieves. But they do have an instinctive dislike for dogs," a man on the run from the police, a character by the name of Said Mahran, says in *The Thief and the Dogs*, which appeared in 1961. No one was fooled: Mahfouz's dogs stood for the forces of the autocracy of Nasser. Spare, dark, and unsentimental, *The Thief and the Dogs* gave voice to Mahfouz's disenchantment with the military class and with the opportunism of the functionaries of the regime who had broken the society and turned it into a dominion of their own.

In this novel, Said Mahran, a petty thief who had been betrayed by one of his men, is let out of prison on the anniversary of the revolution of the Free Officers. He is released into a world remade by that revolution. The man who betrayed him has become the head of Said's old gang; he is married to Said's wife, and he has custody of Said's beloved young daughter. No one is waiting for him; he is released with nothing but his blue suit and gym shoes. In prison, he had lived on the dream of revenge—against the man who had betrayed him, against his former wife. And he yearned for his daughter. But his daughter, an impressionable schoolgirl, spurns him, and his old nemesis, Ilish, has by now become a big man in the criminal world.

In his despair, he recalls an old friend he had known, one Rauf Ilwan, back then a "young peasant with shabby clothes, a big heart, and a direct and glittering style of writing." Rauf has risen in the world; he is one of the new men of this Nasserite revolution. He has become a celebrated and successful journalist; he lives in an elegant villa by the Nile. "How had Rauf managed it? And in such a short time! Not even thieves could dream of owning a thing like that. . . . You are indeed a mystery, Rauf Ilwan, and you must be made to reveal your secret."

In the old days Rauf had been a firebrand, and Said probes him across this new barrier of wealth and ease. "The news astounded us in prison. Who could have predicted such things. No class war now?" The man of this new order understands his old friend's mind. "Let there be a truce. Every struggle has its proper field of battle." Back when they were younger men, before the revolution had given him his new means, Rauf had preached a different doctrine: a revolver, he once told Said, is more important than a loaf of bread, "more important than the Sufi sessions you keep rushing off to the way your father did. What does a man need in this country, Said? He needs a gun and a book; the gun will take care of the past, the book is for the future. Therefore you must train and read." It had been legitimate to steal, to "relieve the exploiters of some of their guilt."

The encounter ends badly, and Said returns at night and breaks into Rauf's villa. But Rauf is waiting for him. He lets him go with a warning, and Said now has another account to settle with this man living in a "mansion of steel." Luck fails the ill-starred thief. He bungles an attempt on the life of the former underling who had taken from him his wife and his daughter; instead he shoots and kills an innocent tenant who had moved into his old nemesis's home. He finds shelter in the home, and in the arms, of Nur, a "lady of the night." He becomes something of a journalistic sensation as the papers write about his exploits. Rauf's paper is particularly relentless, for the journalist wants him out of the way, wants his own past buried and done with. But failure sticks to Said: he botches an attempt on Rauf's life. This was his one chance to make the world right, for a "world without morals is a universe without gravity." He had imagined himself telling the papers why he killed the journalist. Instead, he reads about Rauf explaining how he had known Said so many years back and how he had tried to help him build a new life. He learns that yet another innocent victim has fallen:

Rauf got away unscathed, but his *bawwab* (doorman) was killed. He is visited by the spirit of the doorman, and he hides in shame, but the spirit complains that "millions of people are killed by mistake and without due cause."

The world closes in on Said: after a night of torment he waits in vain for Nur to return at dawn. When she does not turn up, he suspects that perhaps she has succumbed to the reward offered by the police. He turns up at the home of Shaykh Ali al-Junaydi, a Sufi teacher of his father's, a kind and wise old man. He finds him leading his followers in prayer and chanting. "Memories came drifting by like clouds. He remembered his father, Amm Mahran, had swayed with the chanters, while he, then a young boy, had sat near the palm tree observing the scene wide-eyed. From the shadows emerged fancies about the immortal soul, living under the protection of the Most Compassionate." He thought also of his little daughter, in his arms, "speaking her first wonderful baby words." He felt his revolver, giving him the consolation that he might still find a way out and that perhaps for the first time "the thief would give chase to the dogs." He flees the shaykh's house and the neighborhood besieged by the police. He makes his way to the cemetery by the desert's edge, by Nur's flat. In the distance he hears the tracker dogs bark. "It was hopeless now to think of running away from the dark into the dark." The treacherous scoundrels had gotten away with it all. The dogs are closing in, and a triumphant voice calls on him to surrender. He chooses to fight. The shooting starts, he is surrounded. "Slowly the silence was spreading until the world seemed gripped in a strange stupefaction."

In truth, Mahfouz had never kindled to the revolution of Nasser and his fellow conspirators. "The Revolution has stolen the property of a few and the liberty of all," a man of the old order laments in *Miramar*, a rare work that the writer set in Alexandria, published on the eve of the Six Day War. The hooliganism of the revolution, the rise of men like Rauf Ilwan, the virulence of the new men against all the progress that came before their ascent to power—all this was deeply offensive to a man of Mahfouz's sensibility. He was forty in 1952, when the revolution had taken place. He was nearly a decade older than the coup-makers, and this had made all the difference. The true and first political love of this man was the bourgeois revolution of 1919, when Egypt erupted against British rule and Egyptian nationalism felt the stirrings of pride and dignity. This was in its way a springtime of nations—the collapse of empires, the claims of new nationalisms. Mahfouz fondly recalled, in deep old age, watching the demonstrations of 1919 from behind the window shutters in the old Cairo neighborhood of Jamaliyya, where he was born. He saw British soldiers gun down demonstrators; he recalled his illiterate mother attaching her thumbprint to a nationalist petition.

The Egyptians were not able to evict the British overlords, but they forced on them some major concessions. In early 1922, Britain renounced her protectorate over Egypt; then came the proclamation of Egypt's independence as a sovereign monarchy and the drafting of a constitution. The hero of this period—and no doubt the idol of Mahfouz—was the political leader Saad Zaghloul, the icon of Egyptian nationalism. "As a student in secondary school, I started buying newspapers to keep track of Saad's news, to read his speeches. I would read these speeches as though I was reading works of composition and art. When Saad Pasha Zaghloul died on August 23 in 1927, that was the worst day of my life. My whole being was taken by love for this leader." This devotion to Zaghloul—Mahfouz compares it to

the stirrings of first love—and to the revolution of 1919 suf-
fuses Mahfouz's work. His magnificent *Cairo Trilogy*, published
in 1956 but completed on the eve of the revolution of 1952,
pays tribute to the glorious hopes of 1919. Fahmi, a young
character who carries Mahfouz's own aspirations, says that the
stirrings of that time called up before his eyes "a new world, a
new home, a new people, all bursting with vitality and zeal."
Fahmi is willing to die for the homeland, for "faith is stronger
than death, and death more honorable than humiliation."

In *Amam al-Arsh* (*Before the Throne*), an inventive work of
fiction written in 1983, Mahfouz persists with his first love. In
this novel Egypt's rulers, from Mina to Sadat, turn up before
Osiris, the chief deity of Egyptian mythology. It is a courtroom
setting, and Egypt's rulers are here for history's verdict. Osiris is
flanked by Isis, acting as a counsel for the defense, and Horus,
as a court clerk. All the greats—Ramses II, Akhenaton and
Nefertiti, Muhammad Ali, Zaghloul, Nasser, and Sadat—are
here to tell of their accomplishments and to receive the judgment of history. They get to cross-examine one another, and
the lucky ones are invited to join the ranks of *al-khalidun*
(the immortals). There is no sentimentalism in Mahfouz, but
Zaghloul is treated with tenderness. Mahfouz has him entering
the court with great dignity. A man of attractive features, he
tells of his modest birth, his studies at Al-Azhar, his struggle
against the British, his exile by British authorities to the island
of Malta, his second exile to the Seychelles, his fidelity to home
and country. "You united the Egyptians as I have united their
kingdom. Thus you are my friend and my successor," Ramses II
says. Isis gives him her boundless enthusiasm: "Let the gods
bless this faithful, great son who proved that Egypt is a force that
is never conquered and never dies." Osiris gives him a fitting

judgment: "You are the first native Egyptian who ruled the land since the Pharaonic age. You came to power by the people's will. This is why I grant you the right to sit among the immortals of your forefathers."

A writer formed by the liberal currents of the interwar years was not destined to admire Nasser's revolt. Mahfouz dreaded the simplifications. The animus of the new military class toward the bourgeois revolution of 1919, toward the interlude that had formed Mahfouz and given him his most cherished memories, deeply offended him. He was a liberal and a pluralist in the best sense of those terms. He drew an essential distinction between his animus toward British rule in Egypt and his love of English letters and Western culture. He was a novelist, and his choice of craft told it all: the novel was a Western form, not an Arab one. Poetry was the beloved voice of the Arabs, and the great poets were the genuine immortals of Arab lore. It is said that the first successful attempt at an Arab novel was completed in 1911, the year of Mahfouz's birth, by Muhammad Husayn Haykal, a work titled *Zainab*. The Western canon in fiction was his inspiration; he had prepared for his calling as a student at the university. He was exceedingly well-read; he immersed himself in Western philosophy and literature. Mahfouz was not a mimic, nor did he concern himself with the paralyzing worry over authenticity. A man who spends decades at the same coffee-houses, with the same friends, has no reason to worry about authenticity. A Nobel laureate who sends his daughters to Stockholm to accept the prize for him is a man at ease with his own world.

After Mahfouz's death, the obituaries declared him the great Arab novelist. Fair enough, as far as it goes; but his identity as an Arab was idiosyncratic, to say the least. He visited another

Arab country only once, in 1963, when he spent three days in Yemen. That trip was made under duress, ordered by the chief of staff of the armed forces, Abdel Hakim Amer. Yemen was then a battleground between Egypt and Saudi Arabia, and an official delegation was sent to Yemen to show the flag. It did not take the writer long—just those three days—to recognize that the adventure in Yemen was doomed, that the Egyptians in Yemen were too far from home and would not prevail. And that was it: he never traveled to Arab lands again. He wished the Arabs well, but his fidelity was to Egypt.

There had been a strong intellectual current during Mahfouz's youth, known as pharaonism, which had ensnared some of Egypt's best minds. It stressed the unbroken connection between ancient and modern Egyptians. It drew a sharp distinction between Egypt and the neighboring lands. On some subliminal level, it no doubt closed the gap between Muslims and Copts. But Mahfouz did not worship at the shrine of the "Egypt of 5,000 years." He never visited the ancient temples in Luxor and Aswân. He had no urge to see the pharaonic monuments. Two or three of his earliest novels were set in ancient Egypt, but they were allegories. His canvas, his universe, his love, was Cairo, *al Qahira*, the City Victorious, founded in the latter years of the tenth century as a city of Islam, at first a Fatimid (Shia) city, then a city that carried the truth of Sunni Islam. But here things were harmonized: a Sunni city whose most beloved mosque is named after Imam Hussein, Shiism's iconic martyr, and whose most vibrant traditional neighborhood is named for Zainab, Hussein's faithful sister and the bearer of his cult, is a city that can blend conflicting truths. The great Cairene writer was not a provincial; he merely found a whole world in a single city. He never traveled to Upper Egypt:

in a country identified with the Nile delta and with the peas-
antry, he was unwilling to visit the countryside. Relatives had
taken him to Fayoum, not far from Cairo, when he was a boy,
but a week later, at his insistence, they were to bring him back
to the city he loved.

III.

Mahfouz neither gloated over the defeat of Nasserism in 1967
nor hid from its verdict. He had seen it coming. The rot of
Nasserism was the subtle theme of several of his novels. Yet
the military weakness of the regime genuinely shocked him.
He would speak of it again and again, and he would let his
characters give voice to it. After the defeat in the Six Day War,
there came a period of nihilism and despair. From *Mirrors*,
published in 1972: "When the thing happened on the 5th of
June 1967, he was shocked and overcome with confusion. He
would roam the coffeehouses and the salons as though it were
Judgment Day. 'Was our life a mirage, an illusion?' he asked.
. . . No one has gone mad, no one had committed suicide, no
one was overcome by a stroke or a heart attack. I must go mad
or commit suicide." A young man sees the only way out: emigration. This was new for a people who had hitherto dreaded
leaving the "valley" of Egypt for foreign lands. "Man is basi-
cally a traveling being, and the homeland is only the place that
guarantees you happiness and prosperity. That is why the elite
few dare travel, while the backward people stay behind." An
older relative rebukes him: "You want to travel toward civilization instead of nurturing it on your own land." The old man is
brushed aside.

Mahfouz's incomparable ear for his country's talk, his clear sense of his homeland's temptations, is best captured, I think, in the chatter of a Cairo coffeehouse in *Al-Karnak*, published in 1974 but clearly written before the October War of 1973. All that would play out in Egypt in the years to come is foreshadowed in this long passage:

There was but one dominant discussion at Al-Karnak: Day after day, week after week, month after month, year after year, we had no other topics to discuss. Exhausted by boredom one of us would say: let us choose another topic. We would show enthusiasm for that suggestion, raise some topic, deal with it with carelessness and then go back to our old topic, devouring it and devouring us, without interruption and with no end:

—"The war, there is no option but war."
—"No, it is the Fedayeen's struggle."
—"A peaceful settlement is also possible."
—"The only possible solution is that which is dictated by the great powers."
—"Negotiation means surrender."
—"Negotiations are a necessity. All the nations negotiate—even America and China and Russia and Pakistan and India."
—"Peace means that Israel would dominate the entire area."
—"Why should we fear peace? Were we swallowed up by the English and French?"
—"If the future proved that Israel is a 'good state' we would coexist with her and if it proved the reverse we

would eradicate her as we eradicated the crusaders' state before."

—"The future belongs to us. Look at our numbers and our wealth . . ."

—"Our real battle is a civilizational battle. Peace is more dangerous to us than war."

—"Let us then demobilize the army and rebuild ourselves."

—"Let us declare our neutrality and ask other states to recognize it."

—"What of the Fedayeen? You ignore the real catalyst in the situation."

—"We have been defeated and we must pay the price and leave the rest to the future."

—"The real enemy of the Arabs are the Arabs themselves."

—"Everything depends on the unity of the Arabs in the effort."

—"Half the Arabs . . . were victorious on the fifth of June [1967]."

—"Let's begin then with the internal situation. There is no escape."

—"Great. Religion, religion is everything."

It was no great surprise that Mahfouz was enthusiastic about Sadat's peace with Israel. He had seen its urgency and pined for it, even before Sadat made his way to that noble conclusion. Not out of love for Israel, to be sure: Mahfouz was an Egyptian, and he simply wanted deliverance for his homeland. His characters sought a break from the pan-Arab burden. It did not matter to him that he would be censured by the unions of Arab writers for his Arab deviationism, and that Arab intellectuals—

in Beirut and Ramallah and Algiers and London—would rebuke him. He had the verities of Cairo's alleys. He loved his neighbors, he knew them and pitied them, he wanted them spared ruinous wars. He owed his serenity to his Egyptian heart. It sustained him when "the street" and the unions of hack writers condemned him for his support of the peace. He paid no heed to those who said that the Nobel Prize had been granted to him not so much for his art but for his politics; that other luminaries of Arabic literature—the Syrian poet Adonis, the Egyptian playwright Yusuf Idris—deserved the prize more. He brushed all this aside. After all, the great award had come his way when he was in his late seventies. He had toiled as a civil servant—in the great bureaucratic society that Egypt has been since time immemorial—until the mandatory retirement age. He had his art and his friends and his coffeehouses, and in this world he was truly at peace.

It was no mystery to Mahfouz that this new peace with Israel would be unloved. To make this peace, Sadat had to glorify the October War of 1973 and claim it as his and Egypt's great victory, so as to move away from the shadow of the legendary Nasser. But glories and victories were not the material of Egyptian history. So the cunning land would take the peace and reject the peacemaker. Mahfouz circled this riddle of his country's capriciousness in *The Day the Leader Was Killed*, a short work of fiction published in 1985 and built around Sadat's assassination four years earlier. In that work, a shrewd Mahfouzian character, Alwan Mohtashami, notes the cruel irony that Nasser in his defeat was more beloved than Sadat. His own grandfather once told him, Alwan narrates, that theirs was a people who felt "more comfortable with defeat than with victory. We have been so used to defeat that its rhythm has taken hold of us. That is why we loved the sad songs and heroes who are martyrs. . . . Gamal was the martyr of the fifth of June. But this vain, victorious man has strayed from the normal course of things. He brought us new feelings we were not ready for. He asked us to change the melody we have been used to for generations. He thus aroused our wrath and resentment. He then claimed the victory for himself, exaggerated it, leaving for the rest of us poverty and corruption." Mahfouz called on Sadat's widow in the aftermath of this book and explained that he had never meant the work as an indictment of Sadat or a justification of his assassination. It was art, he said, the writer's license, literature made out of what was said in the land of Egypt.

IV.

It is dark in Mahfouz's world. This is the Mahfouzian paradox: the juxtaposition of the joy and lightness of the man himself with the utter hopelessness of his fiction. In the fiction, all the bourgeois verities come tumbling down. Men and women are trapped, and Mahfouz offers no way out for them save forgetfulness, perhaps, and old age. The women betray the men, and the men are scoundrels. The men betray what they proclaim to cherish. Young countrywomen come to the city and lose their way, surrendering to lust or to sweet promises. It is a bitter and veritably Sisyphean existence, with failure playing out under watchful eyes.

Consider Zohra, in *Miramar*, a lovely young *fellaha* (peasant) who turns up at an Alexandria pension called Miramar, having fled her native village in search of freedom. Mariana, an old

Greek innkeeper shipwrecked in this town—the first revolution of 1919 had killed her husband, and the revolution of 1952 had driven out her people—offers Zohra work and a new home. She gives her the opportunity to learn to read and write. In this world of fixed hierarchies, she spoils her by giving her dreams beyond her station. But Miramar is a boardinghouse, and there turns up on the premises one Sarhan el-Beheiry, a young man of the new order. He is taken by Zohra and offers to marry her the way the early Muslims used to marry, without a contract and without witnesses, for "God is our witness." Lust for Zohra, though, would yield to this man's love of advancement. He takes "her heart and her honor" and proposes marriage to Zohra's middle-class teacher. Sarhan el-Beheiry loved the workers at the mill. He lusted for the lovely peasant woman but wanted the easy life. He spoke well of the revolution as the best of a bad lot: "Some people don't like the Revolution. But look at it this way: what other system could we have in its place? If you think clearly, you will realize that it has to be either the communists or the Muslim Brotherhood. Which of these lots would you prefer to the Revolution?" Greed tempts this man and then destroys him: a scam for some easy money goes wrong, he commits suicide, and the peace of Mariana's pension is shattered as the boarders go separate ways and Zohra leaves, sure that she will find a better place.

But the most memorable of Mahfouz's women is surely Hamida, the doomed heroine of his novel *Midaq Alley*, from 1947. The pretty girl of the alley, she strays, seduced by the lure of a life without "household drudgery, pregnancy, children and filth." A pimp offers her the promise of a life like that of "the film stars." She crosses from the alley to New Street. "She heard him call a taxi and suddenly he opened the door for her to enter. She raised a foot to step in and that one movement marked the dividing point between her two lives." A life of prostitution awaits her. Abbas, a good simple boy of the alley who had loved her, tracks her down. She wishes to use him to avenge herself against her seducer. But Abbas falters; he plunges into a group of British soldiers at a bar, where he comes upon Hamida in their midst. As a childhood friend who had come with him freezes in terror, he is beaten to death. The tale ends with the alley's strength, the alley's curse: "This crisis too, like all the others, finally subsided and the alley returned to its usual state of indifference and forgetfulness. It continued, as was its custom, to weep in the morning when there was material for tears, and resound with laughter in the evening. And in the time between, doors and windows would creak as they were opened and then creak again as they were closed."

If there is truth in the conventional notion of Mahfouz as holding up a mirror to his country, the image in the mirror was decidedly not pretty. This son of Egypt was unillusioned about his country. He saw it for what it was: a hemmed-in land, suffocated by poverty, its bourgeoisie brittle and uncertain, and close to the abyss. Mahfouz's is a ruthlessly material world— stark and pitiless, driven by need and desire. God visits this world, but not convincingly, as men and women think of Him and His mercy mostly when they falter, when they are undone by calamity or by their own greed, or when they are led astray by the force of their own desires. God forgives, but His creatures suspect that they are on their own, subject to the writ of the rulers and the moneymen and the bullies. Men stalk and prey on women, and the women return the favor. It is harsh in

Mahfouz's alleys. Men and women survive; there is even grace and gossip in the evening, on the rooftops and in the coffeehouses; there are hilarious storytellers and charming rogues— but the pimp is never far from the comely girl, and he has a way of knowing when she is ready to sink. There is order in this universe, but it hangs by a slender thread.

Mahfouz offered his country no consolation. He was not a nationalist disguising his country's blemishes or addling it with false escape. He never worried about how he would be read in distant lands. Egypt was the canvas on which this man of sublime talents drew his unforgettable portraits of impossible lives. Readers came to him looking for Egypt and its political condition, its mind, and its moods. For this reason, he has been read also as a social historian of his country. (For this I, too, must plead guilty, having for three decades used his fiction in that way.) But there runs through his output—well over fifty works of fiction—a different, and more universal, concern. He gave voice to it in paying tribute to an Israeli scholar, Sasson Somekh, who had done a huge amount of work on Mahfouz and who understood—this is what Mahfouz appreciated so much—that at the heart of his fiction lay not Egypt's modern history, but something even grander: man's battle with time.

On the day of Mahfouz's death, a young Iranian-American author and journalist, Afshin Molavi, left a message of condolence on my answering machine in New York. I was a little startled. I was not a friend of the great Cairene, only his devoted fan and bewitched reader, who picked up his novels when I was a boy in Beirut and have recalled, for so many years, his unforgettable characters. I had been privileged to spend some time in his company. But the message was, in a humble way, not at all inappropriate. It reminded me of an essay, a eulogy for the great Isaiah Berlin, written by Leon Wieseltier in *The New Republic* in 1997. "'When a sage dies,' says the Talmud, 'all are his kin,'" Wieseltier wrote, and this was to be the unifying theme of his essay. Even those who did not know the sage directly, who did not study under him, were under obligation to mourn him, to rend their garments for the departed. In Cairo, but also far beyond it, there should be mourning for Naguib Mahfouz. We were, many of us, his kin. And he was the last of a breed. Now there is only the barren soil of the autocratic land; there is Pharaoh, and his court, and his military funerals.

SOURCE NOTES:

The Day the Leader Was Killed (American University of Cairo Press in 1997), by Naguib Mahfouz, is a fictionalized account of the assassination of Anwar el-Sadat

Mahfouz's controversial novel, *Awlad Haretna* (*Children of Gebelawi*), English translation, was published by Three Continents Press in 1988.

Mahfouz writes in vignettes in *Echoes of an Autobiography*, English translation (Doubleday, 1997).

Mahfouz captures his country's voice in the chatter of the coffeehouses in *Karnak Café (Al-Karnak)*, English translation (Tara Press, 2008).

The heartbreaking story of Zohra, a boarder at a pension escaping an old life in search of a new and better one, is told by Naguib Mahfouz in *Miramar*, English translation (Anchor, 1992).

One cannot read Naguib Mahfouz's *Midaq Alley*, English translation (Anchor, 1991), without weeping for the tragic figure of Hamida as she struggles to survive.

In tribute to Isaiah Berlin is Leon Wieseltier's "When a Sage Dies, All Are His Kin: Isaiah Berlin, 1909–1997," *The New Republic*, December 1, 1997.

Part IV

Chapter 11

The Making of Strangers

Muslims, Jews, and the Other 1492

A s a child of the Arab world, I was given a touched-up version of the history of al-Andalus, a fabled time of Muslim splendor in the Iberian Peninsula. A brilliant Arab-Judeo culture had flowered there, Arab history taught. A poet of our time, the Syrian-born Nizar Qabbani who had written Arabic poetry's most moving verse, had once remarked that while on a visit to Granada he had roamed its streets while searching his pockets for the keys to its houses. A hill overlooking that enchanting city had summed up the Muslim grief over its loss: *El Ultimo Sospiro del Moro* (The Moor's Last Sigh). On that ridge, the storytellers say, Boabdil, the last king of Granada, had paused to catch a final glimpse of his lost realm. Boabdil's unsentimental mother is said to have taunted him during his moment of grief. "You should weep like a woman for the land you could not defend like a man." The fall of the city had taken place on January 2, 1492.

This essay originally appeared in *TriQuarterly* in a special thematic issue on "The Other," December 22, 2007; it is republished here in slightly different form with the knowledge of the original publisher (all rights reverted back to author after the original publication).

It was not in Granada, but farther north, in Madrid, in late 1991, that the cult of al-Andalus came back to me, a good many years after quitting Beirut, the city of my boyhood. I had come to Madrid with a television network to witness and comment on a grand diplomatic spectacle that American diplomacy had assembled in the aftermath of the first American-led campaign against Saddam Hussein. The occasion was scripted, and few things were left to chance. This was taking place amid the retrospectives, and the celebration and the rampant revisionism of the quincentennial of Christopher Columbus's voyage of discovery. It was a good "venue," the innocent said of Madrid, the right place for Muslims and Jews to come together. They had built a world of tolerance, it was said, and they had shared a similar fate—banishment and expulsion in the very same year, the year Columbus set sail for the New World. This history had its complications: a portrait of Charles V slaughtering the Moors was hurriedly removed from Madrid's Royal Palace, the conference's site. Then Yitzhak Shamir, the prime minister of Israel, a man with no eagerness to please, allowed himself a remembrance of what had happened in Spain: "In its two thousand years of wandering, the Jewish people paused here for several hundred years until they were expelled five hundred years ago. It was in Spain that the great Jewish poet and philosopher Yehuda Halevi expressed the yearning for Zion of all Jews, in the words, 'My heart is in the East while I am in the uttermost West.'"

This was an evocation of "the other 1492," which ran parallel to Columbus's voyage to the New World. If Granada had fallen on January 2, the "Edict of Expulsion" of Spain's Jews was issued on March 31. It gave the Jews a grace period of four months: they were ordered to quit their land by the end of July. By a twist of fate, and due to the pleas of one of Iberian Jewry's most influential courtiers of Ferdinand and Isabella, Don Isaac Abravanel, they were given a reprieve of two days. Don Isaac had pleaded for his people's right to stay, but it was to no avail. The ships bearing them to exile left Spanish waters on the second of August. This "fleet of woe and misery," the historian Samuel Eliot Morison has written, was to sail parallel to a "fleet of high promise." Columbus's fleet was ready for sea on the second of August. The men received their communion at the Church of St. George in Palos on that day. The *Captain General* set sail in the dawn hours of the next day.

Three destinies were being forged: the expulsion of the Jews and the Muslims and Spain's high adventure in the New World. Those in Madrid, in 1991, had they known the history, could have heard both the Moor's Last Sigh and the pleading by Don Isaac to Ferdinand of Aragon and to Isabella of Castile, which fell on deaf ears. For those in the know, these two tales of banishment had been linked, seen as a bond between Muslims and Jews. It was in that vein that Yasir Arafat, four years after Madrid, in 1995, and then in the middle of a brief reconciliation with Israel, would evoke that history. "I understand that before the British Mandate, Arabs and Jews used to live together in peace. Remember, we were both expelled from Spain in the thirteenth century." The crafty chieftain had the wrong century of course, but he had fallen back on that fabled history. Men make of the past what they wish. What follows is another attempt to tell what was shared—and what wasn't—in an Iberian Peninsula that once was a venue where Christians, Jews, and Muslims together made a tangled history.

History is kind and generous to Abravanel; he had been a faithful courtier of the "most Catholic sovereigns." He had given

Ferdinand and Isabella eight years of distinguished service: he had organized the chaotic finances of Castile and Aragon; he had been helpful in the final push against the Muslims of Granada. The work of the *Reconquista* against Muslim Spain completed, Don Isaac was suddenly thrown into the supreme challenge of his life.

Don Isaac (1437–1508) hailed from the apex of Iberian Jewry. Born in Portugal, he had risen in the life of its court; he was treasurer and confidant of Portugal's ruler, Alfonso V, and a leader of the Jewish community of Lisbon. But fate, court intrigue, and the death of Alfonso in 1481, a conspiracy that earned Abravanel the enmity of the new Portuguese king, drove Abravanel across the border to Castile. The Holy Office of the Inquisition was busy at work grinding down its victims when Don Isaac had found his way into the court of the Spanish sovereigns. But the obsession of the Inquisition was with the *Conversos* (also known as the *Marranos*, or Jewish converts to Christianity). Jews like Don Isaac thought they were beyond the fire's reach.

Fragments survive of Abravanel's futile pleas to the Spanish sovereigns. There is the narrative by Don Isaac himself recorded in exile: "Thrice on my knees I besought the King. 'Regard us, King, use not thy subjects so cruelly.' But as the adder closes its ear with dust against the voice of the charmer, so the King hardened his heart against entreaties of his supplicants." Don Isaac and his fellow Jewish notables appealed to Ferdinand's greed, offered him vast sums of gold. The drawn-out war against Granada had run down the treasury. Ferdinand was sure to show some interest in the offer. But he brushed it aside at a later meeting. The Jews would give it one final desperate try: They would beseech Isabella. But there, too, they would fail. Where

Ferdinand had hinted to his courtiers that Isabella's religious piety had forced his hand, she was to shift the burden from herself. "Do you believe that this comes upon you from us? The Lord has put this thing into the heart of the King."

Ferdinand and Isabella offered Don Isaac and other Jewish notables in their service the chance to stay in Spain with their wealth and position intact. In return, they would of course have to undergo baptism and conversion. Abravanel chose dispossession and exile; the edict had prohibited the Jews from taking any gold, coins, or silver with them. The proud Jew had lived in the shadow of one forced conversion: his grandfather, Don Samuel Abravanel, had, under duress, converted to Christianity late in the preceding century during a terrible time for Castilian Jews. Some years later the grandfather had slipped across the border to Portugal and returned to Judaism.

The tale of the grandfather had only steeled the will of Don Isaac: he would leave the "land of persecution" behind him. There were lands where the life of the faith could be lived—the Italian city-states, the Netherlands, the Muslim domains of the Ottoman sultan, the Barbary states of Tunis, Algiers, and Tripoli—and there was a haven in Egypt. Don Isaac chose the city of Naples.

Boabdil would not fare so well with the Muslim historians: he had lost a kingdom. But in truth, there was not much that Boabdil could have done. Granada was living on borrowed time. The impetus behind the *Reconquista* was too tenacious for Granada to withstand. The Moorish chieftain cut the best possible deal: an estate for himself, a pledge of safety for the people of his city, safe passage for those who could not bear to live under Christian rule. The victors made yet another promise: Muslims who stayed behind were not to be molested; their religious rights were to be honored. That pledge would be violated. The *Mudejares* (the remaining Muslims under Christian rule) would face, a decade hence, the same choice offered the Jews: conversion or exile. A century later the *Moriscos* (Moorish converts to Christianity) were expelled.

Spain was for the Spaniards: there was a mission of discovery at sea, and there was a mission of zeal at home. The bridges to Islam and to the Jews would be burned. Spain was awakening to a new sense of power. As Fernand Braudel put it in his great work, *The Mediterranean and the Mediterranean World in the Age of Philip II*, Spain, an outpost of Christendom and an underdog in Europe's affairs, was recasting itself as the quintessential "Church Militant." The "two unwanted religions," Islam and Judaism, would be "pruned" like some excess growth. *Limpieza de sangre* (purity of blood): this was to be Spain's way of integrating itself with Europe. What had been a land of fluid and mixed identities, a Christian-Muslim-Judaic setting, now sought the comfort of purity.

The Pyrenees had been more of a barrier than the Strait of Gibraltar: North Africa had had a more formative influence on the Iberian Peninsula than did the societies of Europe to the north. The only way out of this cultural confusion, it seemed, was a violent extirpation of the cultural patterns of what had passed in the peninsula since its conquest by Islam early in the eighth century. Set the Jews aside and consider the Christian-Muslim relationship: cultural hybrids of every kind emerged in that tangled relationship. They are recounted for us by the historian Américo Castro in his celebrated book, *The Structure of Spanish History*. There were the *Mozarabs*, bilingual Christians who lived under Muslim rule; the *Mudejares*, Muslims who lived under the Christians; and the *Moriscos*, the Muslims who had converted to Christianity. Then there were *Muladies*, Christians who turned Islamic, and the *Tornadizos*, Moors who turned Christian. To all these were added a special breed, the *Enaciados*, men and women who roved back and forth between the two religions and went wherever fear, ambition, or fate took them. When Fernando III of Castile declared himself, in 1236, "King of the Three Religions," he expressed the cultural diversity of a land at the crossroads. There came a time when Spain wanted to "resolve" all this cultural confusion, put an end to it. The way out was provided by militant Catholicism, a state religion, which brooked a relentless doctrine of blood purity and no compromise. That purity was, of course, delusional, as the sober among the Spaniards knew. Half a century after the establishment of the Inquisition, a luminary of the Spanish realm made the observation that speaking evil of the *Converso* "touches the majority of the Spanish nobility." But the drive for purity would be rendered more deadly and more neurotic by this kind of inheritance.

In the legend of Moorish Spain, the Jews of Toledo opened the gates of the city to the Muslim conquerors. They were eager to welcome the Muslim armies, which had overrun the Visigothic kingdom early in the eighth century. The legend is groundless. In the war between the Goths and the Muslim armies, the Jews were, for the most part, quiet spectators. To be sure, they were glad to see the defeat of the Goths. The same must have been true of the Ibero-Roman natives of the peninsula. The Goths had been severe rulers. They had not allowed the Jews to sing their psalms, to celebrate Passover, to testify in court against Christians, or to observe their dietary laws. Forced baptism of Jews was a recurring phenomenon under Visigothic rule. Centuries later Montesquieu was to observe that all the laws of the Inquisition had been part of the "Visigothic code" that regulated the conduct of the Jews in seventh-century Spain.

It was a polyglot world that the Muslims came to rule in the Iberian Peninsula. There were Arabs, Berbers, Jews, and blacks, Muslims of native Spanish stock and native Christians. Islam was overextended in Spain; it thus made its accommodation with its habitat. The world of the Jews, turned on itself under the Visigoths, grew larger with the coming of Muslim rule. The peninsula had been opened up to the international order of Islam, to the culture of the Mediterranean basin and the commerce and the traffic. Islam stayed long in the peninsula: eight centuries separate the conquest from the fall of Granada. The Jews were there for all the changes of fortune. The romanticism about that golden age of Iberian Jewry under Islam should be kept in check. There were seasons of bliss, and there were calamitous times. The golden age was brief: several generations of Muslims, Jews, and *Mozarabs* (Arabized Christians) were its beneficiaries from the early years of the tenth century to the mid-eleventh century. At its zenith, Iberian Islam built an urban order of tranquility and brilliance. The cities thrived. Córdoba, on the banks of the Guadilquivir, then the seat of Muslim rule, with a self-styled caliph (successor to the Prophet) at its helm, had a population of a quarter-million people. It was unmatched by any European city at the time; its only rivals were Baghdad and Constantinople. It is principally from Córdoba's great moment that the romance of al-Andalus is drawn.

Romance aside, Jews did well by the onset of Muslim rule. They were favored by the rulers: they were loyal and useful subjects. The politics of the peninsula were a whirlwind: Berbers from North Africa versus Arabs, tribal Arabs who came with or after the conquest versus "neo-Arabs" keen to claim their share of the spoils of the new dominion, Slavs who were soldiers and mercenaries striking when the occasion presented itself, and Christians with some ties of faith to their coreligionists in the lands to the north. The Jews were unique in this politics of factions. They needed the protection of central authority, and they paid it in the coin of loyalty. "They tied their destiny to Moslem dominion and stood by it in all areas of life as loyal aides," Eliyahu Ashtor tells us in his work, *The Jews of Moslem Spain*. Christians under Muslim rule had been defeated, but there were always monks and priests ready to fling themselves against the dominant faith. The proximity of Christian states to the north, Navarre and Castile, and the states in the Asturias and Galicia, provided the Christians with hope that revenge may yet be had against the Moors. The Jews wanted nothing to do with the past. The Muslim order was not fully theirs, but it afforded them protection. It was not long before the lands of Andalusia, now lands of immigration, attracted a Jewish migration from North Africa and from the eastern domains of Islam.

The economy of Muslim Spain, tied as it was to the larger economy of the Muslim world, boomed and provided the Jews with the material bases for a cultural awakening. Virtually all sectors of the Andalusian economy were open to the Jews. They were active in agriculture and tilled their own lands. They were fully present in the textile works of Andalusian cities, in the international commerce carried out between the lands of Islam and those of Christendom. The grandees of Jewish society, the men with wealth, emulated their Muslim counterparts: they subsidized poets and men of letters and nurtured a lively environment. Literacy spread. Jewish academies opened in Córdoba, Granada, Toledo, and Barcelona. A rich body of Judeo-Arabic philosophy was to become the distinctive gift of this age. By the tenth century the Jews of the Iberian Peninsula who had looked to the Babylonian academies and the Talmudists of Iraq for guidance felt confident enough to stand on their own. Those old academies in the east had fallen on hard times, because the political center of the Islamic caliphate in Baghdad had eroded. Stability had done wonders for the Jews of Muslim Spain. Abdurrahman III, an enlightened ruler in Córdoba who had reigned for an incredibly long period of time (from 912 until his death in 962), had given the Jews, and his own people, a reprieve from political disorder, and they had made the most of it.

This was the age of the great Jewish courtiers, men who rose by their talents in the courts of Andalusia. For a good deal of his reign, Abdurrahman in Córdoba relied on Hasdai Ibn Shaprut, a learned and subtle Jew who had made his way on a familiar track from medicine to court life and politics and diplomacy. A patron of the arts, Shaprut sponsored studies of the Torah, acquired rare manuscripts of religious texts, and used the weight and the access he had as one of Córdoba's leading diplomats and emissaries to protect his own community and uphold its interests at court.

A secular political culture prevailed in Andalusia: the Muslim *ulama* and theologians railed against this attribute of court life, this nearly cavalier way toward the faith. This was what had enabled the Jews to succeed at court. "No office, except that of the ruler, seemed to be out of the reach of a talented and ambitious Jew," Norman Stillman has written of Andalusia in his historical survey, *The Jews of Arab Lands*. Success at court was not without its hazards, though. It called forth its steady companion—the wrath of the crowd. Courtiers rose, but the wise ones among them understood the fickle ways of fate. The life of Shmuel Ben Naghrela (993–1056), a figure of great accomplishment in the Andalusian world as a poet and a courtier, spanned the possibilities and the hazards of Jewish life in that world: the author Hillel Halkin had described this poet and courtier of renown as the first "postancient Jew" in both the realms of politics and letters. At the apex of his fame and power, Naghrela had risen to the rank of chief minister of the court of Granada; he had become the first *nagid*, or governor of the Jews of the realm. This courtier had been born in the cosmopolitan world of Córdoba to a family of means and learning. He had been tutored by great Talmudists and had prospered in the spice trade. He was a "learned merchant," the backbone of Andalusian life. He had made his way to Granada after the fall of Córdoba to Berber forces in 1013. From tax collector he had risen to the peak of court life under two Berber kings of Granada, Habus ibn Maksan (ruled 1019–38) and his son Badis. Naghrela commanded the troops of Granada for nearly two decades.

The full irony of Naghrela's life, the precariousness of the journey that he had made, and the hazards of Jewish existence in Andalusia are given away by the fate of his son Joseph. Ten years after Naghrela's death, his son, the inheritor of his position as Nagid, was crucified by a mob on the city's main gate in an anti-Jewish riot. Joseph had taken success for granted. Where the father had lived in the Jewish quarter, the son had his residence built on a high hill in Granada where the Muslim nobility lived. Joseph was, says one chronicle, "proud to his own hurt and the Berber princes were jealous of him." This riot was the first massacre of Jews in Muslim Spain. The date was December 30, 1066. About fifteen hundred families perished in that riot.

More troubles were yet to come. The political unity of the Andalusian world had cracked. The authority of Córdoba had slipped away. By the mid-eleventh century, it was the age of *muluk al-tawa 'if* (the Party Kings), the warlords and pretenders who carved up Muslim Spain into petty and warring turfs. The Party Kings were "men thrown up by the road." They were adventurers and mercenaries, Berbers from North Africa, soldiers of fortune who had overthrown their masters. There must have been about thirty ministates in Andalusia at the height of its fragmentation. Six of them were the leading states: Zaragoza in the north; Badajoz, Toledo, and Valencia in the center of the peninsula; Seville and Granada in the south. The fall of Toledo in 1085 to the armies of Alfonso VI of León-Castile put on cruel display the weakness of the Party Kings. Toledo had been the ecclesiastical seat of the old Visigothic kingdom: its return to Christian sovereignty was seen as evidence of divine favor. This was certainly the way Alfonso billed it as he claimed the city and sponsored the establishment there of Spain's largest archdiocese: "By the hidden judgment of God," a charter of his read, "this city was for 376 years in the hands of the Moors, blasphemers of the Christian faith. . . . Inspired by God's grace I moved an army against this city, where my ancestors once reigned in power and wealth."

Chastened by Toledo's fall, the Party Kings sought deliverance and help from the Muslims of North Africa. They appealed to *Almoravids*, Berber camel nomads who had subdued Morocco. The Party Kings knew the risks of bringing the *Almoravids*, a violent lot, into their midst. But they chanced it. The ruler of Granada justified the gamble by saying that he would rather end up as a camel driver in Morocco than a swineherd in Castile. The North Africans checked the Christians, but only temporarily. The Berbers could not arrest the chaos: they brought a fair measure of it with them, as they set out to extract from the population what they believed was their due. Another Berber invasion, one of a wholly different nature, that of *Almohads*, a more religiously zealous and fanatic lot, was to take place nearly a century later. The men of this expedition (the Taliban of their time) were a tyrannical lot, intolerant of Jews and Christians and of the "free souls" within the Muslim population. No sooner had they swept into Spain than they began a ruthless assault against its old ways. Andalusia had fallen on hard times, but it was still light years ahead of the wilderness of Morocco. A ruler of this band of puritans found the relative freedom of the Jews difficult to countenance. He decreed that they were to wear distinctive dress, "because they had become so bold as to wear Muslim clothing and in their dress looked like the noblest among them, mingling with the Muslims in external affairs, without being distinguished from the servants of God." More important still, the North African zealots sought the conversion of the Christians and the Jews of their conquered realm.

The Jews scattered in every direction. Vast numbers of them migrated north into Christian lands. Some fled into the eastern provinces of Islam. Moses ben Maimon, better known as Maimonides (1131–1204), quit his native Córdoba for Morocco and then finally found a haven in Cairo, where he became a physician to the great Muslim ruler Saladin. The golden age of the Jews of Muslim Spain had drawn to a close.

No measure of zeal could keep the Andalusian world intact. In 1212 *Almohads* sustained a major military defeat against Christian forces; soon they quit the Iberian Peninsula and returned to North Africa. The Muslim states were defenseless. Córdoba fell in 1236, Valencia was conquered by the armies of Aragon in 1238, and Seville's turn came ten years later. By 1264, all that remained of Islam's rule was the kingdom of Granada and its surroundings.

Luck and geography worked in Granada's favor. Historian L. P. Harvey's book *Islamic Spain: 1250–1500* sums up the reasons for Granada's longevity: "a mountainous situation facilitating defense, distance from centers of Christian population, and a long sea coast, through which could pass military aid from North Africa." Granada stayed the hand of fate for more than two centuries. It looked away as other Muslim strongholds fell to Castile. It may have participated—on the side of the Castilians—in the demise of Muslim rule in rival principalities. Granada's rulers stood idly by at a crucial time in 1264 when Muslim rebellions erupted in Lower Andalusia and in Murcia against Christian rule. The defeat of those rebellions left Granada as the sole stronghold of Andalusian Islam. The jurists rendered opinions that worked in Granada's favor. Muslims living under Christian rule were encouraged to migrate to Granada where the life of the faith could be lived. This proved to be a mixed blessing. Granada had the soldiers to withstand the warfare of siege and attrition. But hers was a divided and turbulent population. Once Christian Spain finally had a singular royal will at work as it did after 1474, the Granadan stronghold was marked for extinction.

Nor was Granada helped by what had transpired in 1453 in the great fight between Christendom and Islam, the loss of Constantinople to the Turks. There came to the societies of Europe a new politics of religious passion, a desire for revenge, and for a measure of absolution for what had not been done for Constantinople. (The loss of Constantinople was no small factor in the zeal and eschatological excitement with which the project of Christopher Columbus's came to be viewed; new lands of the faith, new conquests had to replace what was lost to the Turks.) Constantinople, a doomed and dying city, had fought and fallen alone. Western Christendom had not cared much about the fate of Byzantium. The Venetian galleys that were supposed to come to the rescue of Constantinople never turned up. Venice had hedged her bets; her commerce with the domains of the Grand Turk was of greater importance than the struggle for Constantinople. A small contingent of Genoese quit the fight as the final push for the city was unfolding. France was recovering from the ravages of the Hundred Years' Wars; England was run down by her French wars, and, besides, Constantinople was a distant world.

Aragon was close to the fire, but her monarch, Alfonso V, was busy with his campaigns in Italy. The papacy had tried to rouse Europe to the defense of Constantinople. But it was too little and too late, for the papacy itself had waged a long campaign of its own against the schismatics of Byzantium. Men being what they are, Constantinople was ennobled by its fall and loss. Four decades later, the fall of Constantinople would be avenged in the fight for Granada—a doomed Muslim outpost in the West for a doomed Christian outpost lost to the Muslims.

The pressure on Granada had subsided prior to 1453. Castile, whose brash energy was to drive the politics of the peninsula and to fashion the new history of Spain, was to launch six minor expeditions against Granada between 1455 and 1457. A sly Castilian monarch undertook these expeditions, because they were genuinely popular and they were a good way of raising revenue, doing God's work under papal auspices. Nothing durable was to come of these expeditions. The final push against Granada would come later, after the union of the crowns of

Castile and Aragon: Granada now mattered. It stood in the way of a great cause. Its conquest would provide a heroic enterprise worthy of this new Spain and its sovereigns.

The *Reconquista* was above all, though, a true embodiment and reflection of Castile—of both its ideology and its material reality. J. H. Elliott's book, *Imperial Spain*, has given us a definitive portrait of Castilian society. A pastoral, nomadic society, Castile was aristocratic and religious and, by the end of the fifteenth century, overpopulated. Sheep farming was a mainstay of the Castilian economy. The push southward, into the agricultural Muslim lands of Andalusia, was the pushing outward of a religious and an economic frontier. *Reconquista* gave the *hidalgos* (the minor nobility of Castile) and its priests a calling and a project and an escape from the limitations of their harsh, barren soil. The "*Reconquista*," Elliott writes, "was not one but many things. It was at once a crusade against the infidel, a succession of military expeditions in search of plunder, and a popular migration." All three aspects of the *Reconquista* stamped themselves forcefully on the forms of Castilian life.

The Castilian advantages over Granada had become overwhelming by the end of the fifteenth century. There was, to begin with, a great demographic disparity. The figures for those years of the fifteenth century are admittedly unreliable, but they do give us a sense of scale: the population of Castile could have approximated five million then, Aragon around a million inhabitants, and Granada a mere 300,000 people. In the end, though, Granada was doomed because her agricultural hinterland had fallen to the Castilians. The land onto which the Granadans had been pushed back was of poor soil and could not produce the grain and foodstuffs they needed. True enough, there was treason in Granada and there were divisions: a bitter feud between Boabdil and his father, for all intents and purposes a civil war, sapped the unity and the confidence of the Granadans. But the harsh balance of forces, those facts of demography and economy, had rendered the judgment that mattered. There were hopes in Granada (those echo the idle hopes of the defenders of Constantinople four decades earlier) that outside help would come to the rescue. But Granada stood alone. Its surrender came in a public ceremony, with Boabdil handing over the keys to the city to the Spanish monarchs. In his logbook, Columbus, who was there for the final permission to embark on his endeavor, recorded the scene:

> On January 2 in the year 1492, when your Highnesses had concluded their war with the Moors who reigned in Europe, I saw your Highnesses banners victoriously raised on the towers of the Alhambra, the citadel of that city, and the Moorish king come out of the city gates and kiss the hands of your Highnesses, and the prince, my Lord. And later in that same month . . . your Highnesses decided to send me, Christopher Columbus, to see those parts of India and the princes and peoples of these lands, and consider the best means for their conversion . . . I departed from the city of Granada on Saturday May 12 and went to the port of Palos, where I prepared three ships.

Hope had deluded the Jews in the domains of Ferdinand and Isabella. Faithful to the crown, they had done what they could for the final push of the *Reconquista*. While the military effort against the Moors went on, the public animus toward the Jews in Christian Spain seemed to subside. But this was deceptive. Spain no longer needed her Jews. The crown, traditionally the protector of the Jews against the church and the townsmen, would be more audacious and independent now. The Jews would be dispossessed and fed to the mob in the service of royal absolutism. The great calamity of Spanish Jewry, the destruction of the Sephardic world, was unfolding like some play.

There was nothing the Jews could do to avert the wrath of those who sought their destruction. Pick up the trail a good century before the Inquisition and the "Edict of Expulsion": over the course of that pivotal century, the place of the Jews in Spain had become untenable. The Jews farmed the taxes of the state; they were the ideal scapegoat for all the disgruntled. The priests who led the mob in intermittent outbursts against the Jews saw a Jewish conspiracy behind every cruel turn of fate. Jewish physicians were carrying poison under their fingernails, Jewish sorcerers were everywhere, a Jewish cabal was out to undo Christianity. When the great plague, the black death, swept Europe in 1348–49, a rumor swept Spain and the lands beyond that a Jew from Toledo was the principal culprit: with the help of a rabbi from France the culprit had put together a deadly concoction of dried snakes, frogs, and scorpions, mixed with a consecrated host and the heart and liver of a slain Christian. The Holy See proclaimed the falsity of the charge, but it was to no avail: 15,000 Jews were killed by the mob in Toledo.

The Jewish world was hit with great ferocity in a wave of massacres that took place in 1391. The trouble began in Seville and spread to Córdoba, Valencia, and Barcelona. The economic life of the peninsula had stagnated, and the oppression of the nobility had impoverished the land. A fiery preacher, one Fernando Martinez, worked with this deadly material. Before the great terror subsided, some twenty-five thousand may have been killed. The crowd and its preachers offered the Jews of Spain the choice of baptism or death. More than half of the Jews of Castile may have chosen conversion. A new legislation of great severity was passed in 1412: the so-called Ordinance on the Enclosure of the Jews and Moors at Valladolid. The Jews were now to wear a distinctive yellow garment; Jews and Moors were banned from serving as spice dealers, tax farmers, money-lenders, physicians, or surgeons; they were to live in separate enclosures locked and guarded at night. A massive wave of conversions was to take place from 1412 to 1415.

Baptism bought time for those who chose it. But the cruel century separating the great terror of 1391 and the "Edict of Expulsion" posed a new crisis for the Jews at every turn. Where they had been a people apart, the sin of the Jews was separation. Now it was their assimilation that agitated their enemies. The basic alliance at work against the Jews had been a coming together of the church and the burgher-class townsmen. Most of the clerical establishment had accepted the conversion of the majority of Spain's Jewry as the final word on the matter. But the burgher class had felt cheated by the willingness of the Jews to come into the fold. The enemy was now within.

The grand inquisitor doing his work in the 1480s would claim that he was hunting down crypto-Jews among the *Conversos*. We know better now, thanks to the massive research done by the Israeli historian Benzion Netanyahu. (Benjamin, a son of this historian, would become prime minister of Israel.) His huge book, published in 1995, *The Origins of the Inquisition*, turns that great story inside out. In the drama laid out for us by Netanyahu, conversion to Christianity had worked. It had depleted the Jewish world and increased the self-confidence of the *Conversos*. They were no longer a minority that had gone astray; they now outnumbered the Jews of the realm. Moreover, forced conversions had given way to voluntary ones. "The attachment to Judaism was weakening; the trend toward Christianity was intensified. The migration from Spain, which at first was not inconsiderable, was, after a few years, reduced to insignificant proportions," Netanyahu writes. Here and there the grand inquisitor may have found a *Converso* who did not eat pork,who ate meat during Lent, or who observed the Sabbath; but the trend toward assimilation was unmistakable. And the Jews soon wrote off the *Conversos*; they were lost to Judaism, "Christianized beyond recovery."

Conversos now flocked into professions from which they had been excluded—the law, the army, the universities, the clerical establishment. By 1480, half the important offices in the court of Aragon were occupied by *Conversos* or their children. Spanish life now yielded a new breed: the *Conversos* bent on undoing the world of their erstwhile faith and kinsmen. The case of Solomon Halevi, once a chief rabbi of the city of Burgos who was christened Don Pablo de Santa Maria and rose to the rank of bishop of his city, and the more celebrated case of the Talmudist Joshua Halorqi, who became one of the great, merciless defenders of his new faith, illuminate this terrible force at work.

Halevi had gone over to Christianity during the great terror of 1391. His learning, talent, and ambition took him to the heights of power in his new faith: he served as an adviser and a tutor to two Castilian monarchs, and he was papal nuncio of Benedict XIII in the court of Castile. In his new incarnation, as Don Pablo de Santa Maria, this *Converso* was seized with a deadly animus toward the Jews. Writing in his old age, in 1434, in a document titled *Scrutinium Scripturarum*, he described the Jews as people of "diabolical persuasion . . . who had risen to high stations in the royal palaces and the palaces of the grandees," a people who posed a deadly menace to the souls of the Christians. He went as far as praising the massacres of 1391 as deeds stirred up by God. "The rabbi-bishop," the Spanish historian Américo Castro has observed, "was conjuring up, as he wrote, the ghosts of his own life—shouting down the voice of his own conscience."

Halorqi, christened as Jeronimo de Santa Fe, was to serve as the church's principal spokesman in a disputation convened by Benedict XIII in the city of Tortosa in 1413 between the church and the rabbinic establishment. The former Talmudist was unrelenting in his attitude toward the Jews. He, too, at the end of his career published a notoriously anti-Jewish work, *Hebraeomastix* (*the Scourge of the Hebrews*). A wicked sentiment had been unleashed: the politics of purity. A reign of terror, of informers preying on others in the hope that they themselves would be spared, had descended on the Jews and the *Conversos* alike. The Jews had been quick to understand the enmity of the *Conversos*. They were to dispense with the cherished notion that the *Conversos* were *anusim* (forced converts) who were destined to return to the faith.

The eagerness of the *Conversos* to belong to the new faith and to assimilate would bring them no relief. Their success backfired. Since the *Conversos* had been beneficiaries of monarchic power, they were caught in the unending struggle between the rulers and the cities of the realm attempting to defend their prerogatives and autonomy. The leaders of the cities, Netanyahu writes, had gotten rid of the Jews in high office only to see their descendants "in the very offices from which the Jews had been ousted, and in many others which they had never held. To the patricians of the cities it appeared as if history had played a cruel joke upon them."

Kings could pledge and provide protection when their power and interests dictated and made possible such protection, and the well-intentioned authorities of the church could welcome the new converts. Yet, the patricians of the cities and the urban mob, the little people (*populo menudo*), would not be reconciled to the gains made by the *Conversos*.

There was no way that this animus could be appeased. It drew on the old stereotypes of the Jew—worked them over to serve new socioeconomic and psychological resentments and extended them to the *Conversos*. Where the church had blessed the intermarriage of old and new Christians, the enemies of the *Conversos* saw this phenomenon as an evil sure to contaminate Spain and bring about its ruin. The racist agitators who grew increasingly shrill in the decades that led to the Inquisition convinced broad segments of the population that the *Conversos* had worked their guile and evil ways on nobility and court alike. If the Jews had slipped through the gates as converts, they had to be banished and destroyed. The line had to be redrawn.

This great new force of hatred for the *Conversos* was fully understood by the Catholic sovereigns when they set up the Holy Office of the Inquisition in 1481. It is said that Ferdinand of Aragon, the cold and unsentimental ruler who drove and manipulated the Inquisition, was the model on whom Niccolò Machiavelli fashioned his own ideal prince. Ferdinand was crafty, shrewd, and unwavering. For him, the Inquisition was an instrument of royal power: The wealth of the condemned would be his, and there would be renown and moral credit thrown into the bargain. The persecution of the *Conversos* was one sure way the commoners of the realm would be won over, convinced that they and their rulers were engaged in a common enterprise. Hitherto, sheltered by royal power, the *Conversos* would now become its helpless victims. The *Conversos* and those who remained true to the Jewish faith may have taken two separate paths. In one swift, terrible decade, they would be brought together: the Inquisition in 1481 against the *Conversos* and the "Edict of Expulsion" of the Jews in 1492. The campaign to root out heresy among the Jewish converts led to the banishment of an entire people.

Don Isaac Abravanel was shrewd and wise enough to know that the animus and the spirit that seized the Iberian Peninsula would know no rest. He didn't think that those who opted for conversion could ever convince the old Christians that they were of them. In one of his commentaries on the *Conversos*, he wrote: "The indigenous people of the land will always call them 'Jews,' and they shall be designated 'Israel' against their will, and they would be accused of Judaizing secretly, and they will be burnt at the stake."

Spain had prevailed: She had cast out her Jews and subdued the Muslims. But she would remain brittle and insecure. The fear (partly real, partly a phantom called up by the state's functionaries and the diehards among the clergy) persisted of a Muslim invasion from North Africa or Turkey. Those generous terms offered the Muslims during Granada's capitulations ran counter to the spirit of the age. The first archbishop of Granada, Hernando de Talavera, a man of great civility and tolerance, did his best to preserve the dignity of the Moors, to reconcile them to the new order; he refrained from a policy of forced conversion to Christianity. But Talavera was overruled and pushed aside by Francisco Ximenez de Cisneros, the archbishop of Toledo, who came to Granada in 1499 bent on eradicating Islam from the newly conquered realm. The harshness of Cisneros's policy triggered a rebellion in Alpujarras, the slopes of the Sierra Nevada, in 1499. The rebellion was put down, and the Moors were given the choice that had been offered the Jews in 1492: conversion or exile. The Granadans had converted en masse, and the new policy of forced conversion was extended throughout Castile.

The *Moriscos*, the new Christians, as they came to be called, clung to their labor, their agricultural work, and their crafts in the aftermath of their conversion. "They were diligent in the cultivation of gardens," one Spanish chronicler, Friar Alonso Fernandez, said. "They all paid their taxes and assessments willingly, and were moderate in their food and dress." They were a humble lot, he added, and lived apart from the society of old Christians, "preferring that their own life not be the object of gazing." The silk industry in Granada provided them with a decent living. In Valencia, where they formed a tight community, they were perhaps the mainstay of the economy and the feudal estates of the Christian landowners. The latter had a vested interest in protecting the *Moriscos*, in keeping religious and racial zeal in check. But there would be no easy way of staying the furies. The Holy Office of the Inquisition was anxious to do its work, to root out heresy from the land. And the rank and file among the old Christians resented the *Moriscos* for "spending too little, working too hard, breeding too fast." The *Moriscos* had submitted but had retained their customs, attire, and ancestral language. The Christianization had been skin-deep. It was an uneasy coexistence with the "new Christians" keeping to themselves. No Christian victory, though, could take from the *Moriscos* the memory of what had been theirs—the splendor and the power. Victor and vanquished knew that old history, were caught in its grip. Andalusian communities in the cities of North Africa dreamed of the restoration of their world. Spain was never sure that its Moorish nemesis had been slain once and for all.

The peace between Spain and its *Morisco* communities broke down between 1566 and 1567. The balance had ruptured at a time of great difficulty for Spain. The Turks were on the move in the eastern Mediterranean and North Africa; Protestant rebellions and agitations had hit the Netherlands and Flanders. Fear gripped Spain of a double encirclement: the Muslims from the South, the Protestants from the North. Keen to demonstrate its zeal in defending the faith, the court issued an edict prohibiting the use of Arabic, banning Moorish attire, and forcing *Morisco* women to unveil in public. At a ceremony in Granada, all artificial baths, those symbols of Moorish culture and "decadence," were destroyed. The bullying came during a troubled time for the silk industry. The result was a great rebellion, again in Alpujarras, in 1568. The rising was put down with great difficulty.

Troops had to be brought home from campaigns in Italy and Flanders in order to subdue the rebellion. For one fleeting moment, it seemed, the phantom that had stalked Spain since its victory over Granada came to life. "Don't you know that we are in Spain, and that we have owned this land for 900 years?" said the rebel *Morisco* leader Don Fernando de Valor (Ibn Humeja) as he summoned his followers. "We are no band of thieves, but a kingdom; nor is Spain less abandoned to vices than was Rome." The rebels had given it all but could not win. Spain would take no chances in the aftermath of this second uprising. The *Moriscos* were to be dispersed throughout the kingdom. The *Moriscos* of Granada were to be "thinned out," and thousands were dispatched to Castile to fend for themselves in hostile, new surroundings. The Turks were to be denied a "fifth column" in so vital and so exposed a location in the peninsula.

The experiment in assimilation had proven a failure. In 1590, the cardinal of Toledo described the *Moriscos* as "true Mohammedans like those of Algiers." Spain was done with assimilation. She had won renown in the Christian world by her expulsion of the Jews, Braudel tells us. There was no price to be paid for her cruelty to the Moors. The fate of the *Conversos* was a preview of what would befall the *Moriscos*. In the years between 1609 and 1614, radical new legislation during the reign of Philip III would sweep the *Moriscos*, a community of some three hundred thousand people, out of the country. They were herded to the frontiers and shipped to North Africa.

No welcome mat was rolled out for the *Moriscos* in the cities of North Africa. Ahmed Ibn Mohammed al-Makkari, a North African historian who wrote an exhaustive and poignant history of Islam in Spain, described the cruel fate that awaited the evicted on the other shore: "Many thousands of the unfortunate emigrants went to Fez, thousands to Telemsan, from Oran; the greater part took to the road to Tunis. Few, however, reached the place of their destination for they were assailed on the road . . . and they were plundered and ill-treated, especially on the road to Fez and Telemsan. Those who directed their course to Tunis were more fortunate; they, for the most part, reached that place in safety, and peopled the desert towns and districts of the country. God, indeed, is the master of all lands and dominions, and gives them to whomsoever He pleases."

Spain now wanted to be done with everything Moorish: customs, architecture, attire, and public baths. All these were banned, along with Arabic, the language of the "proscribed race." J. H. Elliott illuminates in authoritative detail the context that nurtured this radical new spirit. Spain was a deeply troubled country by the beginning of the seventeenth century. The court needed a sideshow and a scapegoat, and the expulsion of the *Moriscos* provided it. The Spanish war against the forces of international Protestantism, the Dutch and the English, had ended in stalemate and frustration. The defeat of the armada had been a blow to the nation's sense of itself. The Castilian economy, hitherto heated by the influx of gold and silver bullion from the New World, had run aground. The *hidalgos* were restless and embittered. The windfall society and its inflationary spiral had unsettled Castile; its confidence had cracked. The empire had been heady, extravagant, and costly, but its benefits were not easy to see. The world of the merchant families and beneficiaries of the Atlantic trade had grown larger with the new wealth: appetites had been whetted among the merchants for the ways and lifestyle of the nobility. Then that world had closed up again.

It was these second thoughts about empire and the new wealth from the Indies, which Miguel de Cervantes had immortalized in *Don Quixote*, the great literary work of this period of Castilian history. "Is it not better to stay peacefully at home instead of roaming the world in search of better bread than is made of wheat, not to mention that many who go for wool come home shorn?" Don Quixote's exasperated niece asked her uncle, the knight-errant and fantasist. A pastoral society had wandered far and now felt betrayed. Castile had come out of a cruel past, and after so much striving felt itself shortchanged and trapped: "Happy times and fortunate ages," said Don Quixote as he sat amid a group of goatherds, "were those that our ancestors called golden, not because gold (so prized in this our Iron Age) was gotten in that era without any labors, but because those who lived in it knew not those two words *thine* and *mine*. In that holy age all things were in common." Spain had begun to wail for itself. There was a sense that divine providence had been withdrawn. The assault on the *Moriscos* was good royal theater and, perhaps, a bow to the heavens and to the true church, a hope that the favor of divine providence would return.

Banished and cast out, the *Morisco* would now become a benign ghost: Cervantes gives the *Morisco*, once Hispanic through and through, a fleeting and furtive return to his old land. Ricote, an old *Morisco*, turns up in his ancestral land amid a band of German travelers. This Ricote, speaking pure Castilian, is a man who had found within himself some acceptance of the great banishment: it was not safe, he is made to say, "for Spain to nurse the serpent in its bosom." In exile he still retained the memory of home: "Wherever in the world we are, we weep for Spain, for after all, there we were born and it is our fatherland. Nowhere can we find the compassion that our misfortunes crave; in the Barbary and other parts of Africa, where we expected to be welcomed and cherished, it is there where they treat us with the greatest inhumanity. We did not know our happiness until we had lost it."

A tale of dubious authenticity has the Ottoman Sultan Bayezid II (ruled 1481–1512) wondering about Ferdinand and the folly of his expulsion of the Jews: "Do they call this Ferdinand a wise Prince who impoverishes his kingdom and thereby enriches mine?" The tale aside, the lands of Islam provided safe havens for the Jews. The gates of many Muslim realms were opened before the Sephardim. They were a skilled people, and the new lands were eager to accommodate them. They brought with them new skills in the making of weaponry and gunpowder, in printing and medicine. They knew the languages of Europe. In the great struggle of the age between Islam and Christendom, the Jews found a reprieve. For the rulers of the Ottoman Empire the Jews were ideal subjects.

By the standards of Europe in the High Middle Ages, the world of Islam was, on the whole, a tolerant world. It was not an "interfaith utopia" (to borrow the words of the distinguished historian of Islam, Bernard Lewis). The life the Jews led was circumscribed. It was a life without illusions. There was a clear division of labor; political power, careers in the bureaucracy and the military were off-limits. There was a body of discriminatory law: houses of worship could not be built higher than mosques; Jews and Christians were often required to wear distinctive garb. They could not bear arms or ride horses. They had to pay higher taxes than those paid by Muslims. And some Muslim realms were harder than others. Morocco stood out in the degradation it heaped upon the Jews. Here Islam was frontier Islam, embittered by wars against Portugal and Spain. The Jews were the only non-Muslim community in Morocco. The limits imposed upon them, enclosed ghettos, which functioned like the *juderias* of Aragon and Castile, recalled the degradations of Europe. The Jews of Morocco lived at the mercy of the elements; it was feast or famine. Merciful sultans alternated with cruel ones. What the sultans gave, the preachers and the mob frequently took away. The protection the rulers offered in this wild and anarchic realm could never withstand what one historian described as the three miseries of Morocco: plague, famine, and civil war.

It was easier in other Muslim lands. The private domain Islamic rule conceded the freedom from forced conversions must have seemed particularly generous when compared to what prevailed in Medieval Europe. A Jew writing to his coreligionists in Europe described Turkey as a land where "every man may dwell at peace under his own vine and fig tree." The Jews were a people on the run. The tolerance in the new surroundings seemed wondrous. A *Converso* who made a new life in Turkey and returned to the faith spoke of Turkey in nearly messianic terms, describing it as "a broad expansive sea which our Lord has opened with the rod of his mercy. Here the gates of liberty are wide open for you that you may fully practice your Judaism."

Jewish centers of learning and commerce sprouted throughout the Muslim world. Salonika, conquered by the Turks early in the 1400s, was to become, for all practical purposes, a Jewish city. Jews became the city's overwhelming majority and dominated its public life until its loss to the Greeks in 1912. A substantial Jewish colony put down roots in Istanbul. The town of Safed, in Palestine, attracted Jewish textile makers and scholars and became a famous center of learning. Close by there was a protected niche for the Jews in the life of Egypt. Baghdad's Jewry was perhaps in a league by itself. It had its academies, a vigorous mercantile elite with far-flung commercial operations.

Then the world of the Jews of Islam closed up. It happened over a long period of time. The civilization of Islam itself went into eclipse; its Ottoman standard-bearers were overtaken by Europe in the seventeenth century. The Jews who had done well by a civilization in the midst of a surge were to suffer its demise. Increasingly the Christian European powers set the terms of the traffic with Islamic lands. For intermediaries these European powers preferred the local Christian communities— Greeks, Armenians, Arabs. And these local Christians were sworn enemies of the Jews, bent on cutting them out of international commerce and diplomacy. The knowledge of foreign languages, science, and medicine that Jews had brought with them from Europe had receded and been rendered obsolete. European missions were busy at work shoring up the skills and the privileges of the Christians of the east. On the defensive, the Islamic order itself was growing increasingly xenophobic and intolerant. The submission to Europe had to be hidden under displays of chauvinism. The Jews of Islam headed into a long night. The center of the Jewish world had long shifted westward. Historian Bernard Lewis sums up the closing up of that Jewish world in the east in his book *The Jews of Islam*:

"The growing segregation, the dwindling tolerance, the diminished participation, the worsening poverty, both material and intellectual, of the Jewish communities under Muslim rule."

From this long slumber the Jews of the east were awakened by a movement fashioned by their kinsmen in the west: modern Zionism. It came calling on them and summoned them to a new undertaking. The Jews of Islam had been spared both the gift of modern European history (the enlightenment, the bourgeois age, the emancipation) and then the horrors visited on European Jewry. Zionism had been spun with European thread. But the Jews of the east took to it. To be sure, there were many who had wanted to sit out the fight between Arab and Jew in Palestine and to avert their gaze. Some of the leading figures of Egyptian Jewry—the Chief Rabbi Haim Nahum, the head of the community; a banker by the name of Joseph Aslan de Cattaoui Pasha, whose family had presided over the community since the mid-nineteenth century—were men devoted to "King and country" and had wanted nothing to do with Zionism. But the ground burned in Egypt. Fascist doctrines of nationalism and a new Islamic militancy were sweeping through the place. Palestine and the struggle between Arab and Jew were too close: The world of Egyptian Jewry couldn't withstand all of this.

It was now past living those circumscribed lives. Modern nationalism—in its Arab and Jewish variants—blew away the world of the Arab Jews. The braver and younger souls among the Jews of Arab lands didn't care to live the quiet and worried lives of their elders. When the first Arab-Israeli war of 1948 broke out, there were some eight hundred thousand Jews in the Arab world, some six percent of world Jewry. A decade or so later, *harat al-Yahud* (the Jewish quarter) in Muslim cities belonged to memory. The large Jewish communities in Morocco, Algeria, Egypt, and Iraq were banished. There was a new and altered geography of Jewish life. The center of gravity had shifted again, toward two poles: the New World and Israel.

Setting sail to the New World, Columbus had had little to say about that parallel "fleet of woe and misery" that carried the Jews out of Spain. He was careful to note, though, that he wanted the Jews excluded from the lands he would discover and claim for Spain. History outwitted him.

Chroniclers are forever writing the present into the past, working their will, and their needs, on it. Benzion Netanyahu wrote his big history of the *Conversos* as a cautionary tale against the follies of assimilation. Within the Zionist world, he belonged to the revisionist current of Vladimir Jabotinsky. You can see the *conversos* and their destruction as a statement by Netanyahu on those within Israel who would think that there was a "normal" world for Israel beyond the siege that has marked its history. For my part, I have told my small (derivative) history against the background of the passing of the world of Arab Jewry and of the rise, within Europe, of a militant Islamism. The world of the Arab Jews is familiar to me. I saw it in its twilight. There was a Jewish quarter in Beirut, Wadi Abu Jamil; there were synagogues and Jewish banks and schools. They were part of the city of my boyhood. Today the Jews are gone and Wadi Abu Jamil is a Hezbollah stronghold. The "return" of Islam to Europe is an altogether different matter. Madrid, London, Glasgow, and Amsterdam have had their encounters with this new politicized religion. This is not Eurabia and never will be. A new history of Islam in Europe is in the making. The story of Iberian Islam twists and turns. It can be irony or precedent, it can be read as a tale of civilizations in conflict, or of neighbors who once knew the normalcy of quotidian life.

On March 11, 2004, there would befall Madrid a shattering event that overwhelmed all that had been said about Islam in the Iberian Peninsula. In the morning rush hour, ten bombs tore through four commuter trains, killing more than two hundred people, wounding some fifteen hundred, in the deadliest terror attack in Europe since the Second World War. The initial suspicion that this was a deed of Basque terrorists immediately gave way to the real verdict: this was the work of terrorists drawn from the ranks of Al Qaeda. "This is part of settling old accounts with Spain, the Crusader, and American ally in its war against Islam," read a letter sent to a London-based Arabic daily. Islam had returned to Spain, brought forth by young men from Arab and North African lands—drifters, jihadists on the run from their governments, desperate men driven by economic need. This was not an Islamic *reconquista*, though there were true believers given to such thoughts. It was the pressure of overpopulated lands with a "youth bulge."—shades of Castile, in earlier centuries, pushing southward into the Muslim principalities of the peninsula. Across the Strait of Gibraltar from Spain, the despair was deep. In Algeria there were young people who were called the *harragga*, those who burn their documents, figuratively burying the past to cross the strait into Spain and European destinations beyond. A circle was closed: in the history given Arab and Muslim children, there is a place of honor for the commander Tariq bin Ziyad, who led his Berber troops into the peninsula in the year 711. The history insists that he had burned his ships after he landed on the coast and exhorted his men, saying that they had no choice but to fight for they had the sea to their back and the enemy to their front. (He would give his name to the place of his disembarkation, *Jabal Tariq*, the Mountain of Tariq or Gibraltar.) The strait, simultaneously dividing and beckoning people, had seen whole histories pass to and fro.

SOURCE NOTES:

The departure of the Jews from Spain and the role of Don Isaac Abravanel in the final futile pleas are the subjects of large body of writings. Jacob Minkin's *Abarbanel and the Expulsion of the Jews from Spain* (Behrman's Jewish Book House, 1938) is a storyteller's account. Benzion Netanyahu's *Don Isaac Abravanel: Statesman and Philosopher* (The Jewish Publication Society of America, 1953) is a more formidable scholarly treatment. J. B. Trend's edited book, *Isaac Abravanel: Six Lectures*, covers the scholarship and writings of Abravanel. Eliyahu Ashtor's three-volume *The Jews of Moslem Spain* (The Jewish Publication Society of America, 1992) is a reliable account of that subject. It is from Ashtor's book that the discussion of the Jewish courtiers is drawn.

Samuel Eliot Morison's *The Great Explorers* (Oxford University Press, 1978) juxtaposes the two departures from Spain: that of Christopher Columbus and the Jews.

For a historical perspective of the Jews in the Muslim world, see Norman Stillman's *The Jews of Arab Lands* (The Jewish Publication Society of America, 1979).

Fernand Braudel's great work, *The Mediterranean and the Mediterranean World in the Age of Phillip II* (Harper & Row,

1966), tells us of the rise of the power of Spain in the world of Christendom.

The life of Shmuel Ben Naghrela is the subject of Peter Cole's *Selected Poems of Shmuel HaNagid* (Princeton University Press, 1996). The essayist Hillel Halkin takes up Naghrela's life in "First Post-Ancient Jew," *Commentary*, September, 1993.

Peter Cole's magnificent book, *The Dream of the Poem: Hebrew Poetry from Muslim and Christian Spain 950–1492* (Princeton University Press, 2007), provides by far the most authoritative treatment of the Judeo-Arabic literary tradition in the Iberian Peninsula that I have seen.

The age of the "Party Kings" of Muslim Spain is covered by L. P. Harvey, *Islamic Spain* (University of Chicago Press, 1990), and by Thomas Glick, *Islamic and Christian Spain in the Early Middle Ages* (Princeton University Press, 1979). The North African historian Ahmed Ibn Mohammed al-Makkari's traditional chronicle, *Nafhu-t-Tib Nim Ghosni-L-Andalusi-R-Rattib*, written in 1629, is available, abbreviated, in English under the title *The History of the Mohammedan Dynasties in Spain*, translated in 1840 by the Spanish scholar Pascual De Gayangos (Johnson Reprint Corporation, 1964).

The account of Alfonso VI's conquest of Toledo and the establishment there of a bishopric is from Robert Bartlett's *The Making of Europe* (Princeton University Press, 1993).

J. H. Elliott's *Imperial Spain: 1469–1716* (London: Penguin Books, 1990) provides both narrative and interpretation of Castilian history. It also touches on the resentment of the old Christians toward the *Moriscos* spending too little.

Benzion Netanyahu's *The Marranos of Spain* (American Academy for Jewish Research, 1966) is a revisionist account of the

Jewish converts to Christianity. It is superseded by Netanyahu's more recent work, *The Origins of the Inquisition* (Random House, 1995). The more conventional assessment that the *Conversos* or the *Marranos* were crypto-Jews is that of Cecil Roth's *History of the Marranos* (Hermon Press, 1974). Netanyahu's is by far the more profound and the more disturbing exploration.

On the *Conversos* at war with their old faith, and so much else of Spanish history, few if any books can rival that of Spanish historian Américo Castro's *The Structure of Spanish History*, English translation (Princeton University Press, 1954). It is from Castro's superb work that the tales of Solomon Halevi and Joshua Halorqi are drawn. Castro's work is also the source of the *Morisco* leader's remarks in summoning his followers to rebellion.

Don Isaac Abravanel's bleak prophesy about the difficulties of assimilation is from Jose Faur, *In the Shadow of History* (State University of New York Press, 1992).

Two accounts of the Jews in Turkey and the Muslim domains stand out: Norman Stillman's *The Jews of Arab Lands* (The Jewish Publication Society, 1979) and Bernard Lewis's *The Jews of Islam* (Princeton University Press, 1984).

Miguel de Cervantes' classic tale, *Don Quixote,* reprint edition (Signet Classics, 2011).

The Jews of Morocco are the subject of Jane S. Gerber's very good scholarly book, *Jewish Society in Fez: 1450–1700* (Brill, 1980).

Perhaps the best and most accessible single volume on the culture of medieval Spain is Maria Rosa Menocal's *The Ornament of the World* (Little, Brown, 2002).

Fouad Ajami was born in 1945 in Arnoun, Lebanon. He was the Herbert and Jane Dwight Senior Fellow at the Hoover Institution and the cochair of its Working Group on Islamism and the International Order. From 1980 to 2011 he was professor and director of Middle East Studies at The Johns Hopkins School of Advanced International Studies. He authored several books: *The Arab Predicament, The Vanished Imam: Musa al Sadr and the Shia of Lebanon, Beirut: City of Regrets, The Dream Palace of the Arabs, The Foreigner's Gift: The Americans, the Arabs, and the Iraqis in Iraq, The Syrian Rebellion* (Hoover Institution Press, 2012), and, most recently, a monograph, *The Struggle for Mastery in the Fertile Crescent* (Hoover Institution Press, 2014). He was a widely published essayist whose writings, reviews, and columns of opinion appeared in *Foreign Affairs, The New Republic, The Wall Street Journal, The New York Times Book Review, Foreign Policy, The New York Times Magazine,* and other forums in the United States and abroad.

Ajami was the recipient of the five-year MacArthur Prize Fellowship, which he was awarded in 1982. In 2006, he was granted the Bradley Prize for Outstanding Achievement. In November 2006, he was awarded the National Humanities Medal by the President of the United States. In June 2011, he was awarded The Eric Breindel Prize for Excellence in Opinion

Journalism. In November 2011, he received the seventh annual Benjamin Franklin Public Service Award from the Foreign Policy Research Institute in Philadelphia. His writings charted the road to 9/11, the Iraq war, and the US presence in the Arab-Islamic world. Fouad Ajami died on June 22, 2014.

HERBERT AND JANE DWIGHT
WORKING GROUP ON
ISLAMISM AND THE
INTERNATIONAL ORDER

THE HERBERT AND JANE DWIGHT WORKING GROUP ON ISLAMISM AND THE INTERNATIONAL ORDER seeks to engage in the task of reversing Islamic radicalism through reforming and strengthening the legitimate role of the state across the entire Muslim world. Efforts will draw on the intellectual resources of an array of scholars and practitioners from within the United States and abroad, to foster the pursuit of modernity, human flourishing, and the rule of law and reason in Islamic lands—developments that are critical to the very order of the international system.

Founded by Fouad Ajami, the Working Group is chaired by Hoover fellow Charles Hill. Current membership includes Zeyno Baran, Russell A. Berman, Marius Deeb, Reuel Marc Gerecht, Ziad Haider, R. John Hughes, Nibras Kazimi, Bernard Lewis, Habib C. Malik, Abbas Milani, Camille Pecastaing, Itamar Rabinovich, Colonel Joel Rayburn, Lee Smith, Samuel Tadros, Joshua Teitelbaum, and Tunku Varadarajan.

INDEX